Lecture Notes in Computer Science 11285

Commenced Publication in 1973
Founding and Former Series Editors:
Gerhard Goos, Juris Hartmanis, and Jan van Leeuwen

More information about this series at http://www.springer.com/series/7407

Josep Silva (Ed.)

Functional and Constraint Logic Programming

26th International Workshop, WFLP 2018
Frankfurt/Main, Germany, September 6, 2018
Revised Selected Papers

 Springer

Editor
Josep Silva
Universitat Politècnica de València
Valencia, Spain

ISSN 0302-9743 ISSN 1611-3349 (electronic)
Lecture Notes in Computer Science
ISBN 978-3-030-16201-6 ISBN 978-3-030-16202-3 (eBook)
https://doi.org/10.1007/978-3-030-16202-3

Library of Congress Control Number: 2019934957

LNCS Sublibrary: SL1 – Theoretical Computer Science and General Issues

This Springer imprint is published by the registered company Springer Nature Switzerland AG
The registered company address is: Gewerbestrasse 11, 6330 Cham, Switzerland

Preface

This volume contains the proceedings of the 26th International Workshop on Functional and (Constraint) Logic Programming (WFLP 2018), held in Frankfurt am Main, Germany, September 6, 2018.

WFLP aims at bringing together researchers, students, and practitioners interested in functional programming, logic programming, and their integration. WFLP has a reputation for being a lively and friendly forum, and it is open for presenting and discussing work in progress, technical contributions, experience reports, experiments, reviews, and system descriptions.

WFLP 2018 put particular stress on the connections between theory and practice. This stress was reflected in the composition of the Program Committee (PC) and, ultimately, in the program of the workshop. The call for papers attracted 19 submissions, of which the PC, after careful and thorough discussions, accepted 12 for presentation at the workshop. After the workshop, there was a second independent review to publish the best papers in Springer's *Lecture Notes in Computer Science*. Each paper was reviewed by at least four PC members using a single-blind reviewing process. The PC selected ten papers for publication, those contained in this volume.

The accepted papers cover different programming areas of functional and logic programming, including code generation, verification, and debugging. The invited speaker was Laure Gonnord, who presented a talk about experiences in designing scalable static analyses. All the talks motivated interesting and live scientific discussions.

Putting together WFLP 2018 was a team effort. First of all, I would like to thank the authors of the submitted papers and the presenter of the invited talk. Without the PC we would have had no program either, and I am very grateful to the PC members for their hard work. Supporting the PC were a number of additional reviewers, and I would like to acknowledge their contribution. In general, the reviews were very detailed and helpful, and they produced constructive criticism.

I am greatly indebted to Michael Hanus for his help and advice with the organization, encouragement, and support throughout the process. The general chair, David Sabel, did a great job in the coordination and organization of the event. A special thanks to him and to the Computer Science Institute of the Goethe University Frankfurt am Main for hosting the event. Finally, I also want to acknowledge the cooperation of the other two co-events: the 20th International Symposium on Principles and Practice of Declarative Programming (PPDP 2018), whose chair was Peter Thiemann; and the 28th International Symposium on Logic-based Program Synthesis and Transformation (LOPSTR 2018), whose chairs were Fred Mesnard and Peter Stuckey.

February 2019   Josep Silva

Organization

Program Chair

Josep Silva   Universitat Politècnica de València, Spain

Program Committee

Slim Abdennadher   German University in Cairo, Egypt
Maria Alpuente   Universitat Politècnica de València, Spain
Sergio Antoy   Portland State University, USA
Olaf Chitil   University of Kent, UK
Maria del Mar Gallardo   Universidad de Málaga, Spain
Michael Hanus   University of Kiel, Germany
Herbert Kuchen   University of Münster, Germany
Kostis Sagonas   Uppsala University, Sweden
Tom Schrijvers   KU Leuven, Belgium
Sibylle Schwarz   HTWK Leipzig, Germany
Martina Seidl   Johannes Kepler University Linz, Austria
Dietmar Seipel   University of Würzburg, Germany
Salvador Tamarit   Universidad Politécnica de Madrid, Spain
Janis Voigtländer   University of Duisburg-Essen, Germany
Johannes Waldmann   HTWK Leipzig, Germany

Organizing Committee Chair

David Sabel   Goethe-University Frankfurt am Main, Germany

Additional Reviewers

Joachim Breitner   Sergio Pérez
Jan Christoph Dageförde   Nada Sharaf
Vincent von Hof   Wouter Swierstra
Georgios Karachalias   Jan Rasmus Tikovsky
Fernando Martínez-Plumed   Alexander Vandenbroucke
Falco Nogatz   Clara Waldmann
Adrian Palacios   Matthew Weaver

Contents

Compilers and Code Generation

Transpiling Programming Computable Functions to Answer Set Programs

Ingmar Dasseville[✉] and Marc Denecker

Department of Computer Science, KU Leuven, 3001 Leuven, Belgium
{ingmar.dasseville,marc.denecker}@cs.kuleuven.be

Abstract. Programming Computable Functions (PCF) is a simplified programming language which provides the theoretical basis of modern functional programming languages. Answer set programming (ASP) is a programming paradigm focused on solving search problems. In this paper we provide a translation from PCF to ASP. Using this translation it becomes possible to specify search problems using PCF.

1 Introduction

A lot of research aims to put more abstraction layers into modelling languages for search problems. One common approach is to add templates or macros to a language to enable the reuse of a concept [6,7,11]. Some languages such as HiLog [3] introduce higher order language constructs with first order semantics to mimic this kind of features. While the lambda calculus is generally not considered a regular modelling language, one of its strengths is the ability to easily define abstractions. We aim to shrink this gap by showing how the lambda calculus can be translated into existing paradigms. Our end goal is to leverage existing search technology for logic programming languages to serve as a search engine for problems specified in functional languages.

In this paper we introduce a transpiling algorithm between Programming Computable Functions, a programming language based on the lambda calculus and Answer Set Programming, a logic-based modelling language. This transpilation is a source-to-source translation of programs. We show how this can be the basis for a functional modelling language which combines the advantages of easy abstractions and reasoning over non-defined symbols. Transpiling Programmable Computable Functions to other languages like C [10], or a theorem prover like Coq [5] has been done before. But as far as the authors are aware, no approaches to translate it into logic programs have been done before.

In Sect. 2 we introduce the source language of our transpiler: Programming Computable Functions. In Sect. 3 we introduce the target language of our transpiler: Answer Set Programming. In Sect. 4 we describe the translation algorithm. Finally, in Sect. 5 we motivate why this kind of translation can be useful in practice. An implementation of the translator is made available online (https://dtai. cs.kuleuven.be/krr/pcf2asp), where it can be tested with your own examples.

© Springer Nature Switzerland AG 2019
J. Silva (Ed.): WFLP 2018, LNCS 11285, pp. 3–17, 2019.
https://doi.org/10.1007/978-3-030-16202-3_1

2 Programming Computable Functions

Programming Computable Functions [8,15] (PCF) is a programming language
based on the lambda calculus. It is not used as an end-user language; instead it
provides a strong theoretical basis for more elaborate languages, such as Lisp,
Caml or Haskell. There are many small variations of PCF, some extend it with
booleans, tuples or arithmetic operators. One such variation is known as Mini-
ML [4]. The particular flavor is irrelevant for the principles in this paper.

2.1 Syntax

The syntax of PCF relies heavily on the standard lambda calculus, extended
with natural numbers, a selection construct and a fixpoint operator. We identify
the following language constructs:

- function application e_1e_2, which is left associative,
- a lambda abstraction λx.e, abstracting the variable x out of the expression
  e,
- for each numeral $n \in \mathbb{N}$, a constant n,
- constants succ, representing the successor function over $\mathbb{N}$, pred representing
  the predecessor function over $\mathbb{N}$,
- a constant fix, representing the fixpoint operator, also known as the Y-
  combinator, and
- a ternary language construct ifz e_z then e_t else e_e, representing an if
  zero-then-else.

Suppose that $\mathbb{I}$ is an infinite supply of identifiers. The syntax of PCF can be
inductively defined as:

e = x ($\in \mathbb{I}$) | e e | λx.e
  | n ($\in \mathbb{N}$) | succ | pred | fix | ifz e then e else e

Example 1. (λx. succ (succ x)) (succ 0) is a complicated way to write the
number 3.

The expression fix allows us to write functions which would require recursive
definitions in most programming languages. It takes a function f as argument
and returns the fixpoint x of that function so that $f(x) = x$. From this it follows
that fix satisfies the equation fix f = f (fix f).

Example 2. A traditional recursive definition for the double of a number x could
be:
    double x = ifz x then 0 else 1 + 1 + double (x-1)
It is possible to rewrite this using fix, by abstracting both double and x, and
using pred and succ for the increments and decrements:

    fix (λdouble. λx. ifz x then 0 else succ (succ (double (pred x)))

The informal meaning of this expression is the doubling function.

Example 3. `fix (λplus. λa. λb. ifz a then b else plus (pred a) (succ b))` it a PCF term that can be informally read as the binary sum function over integers.

2.2 Operational Semantics

When considering expressions, we traditionally consider only those without free variables. However, when considering the operational semantics, we will generalise this to situations where free variables can occur. For this reason we introduce environments and closures through a mutually inductive definition.

Definition 1. *An* environment E *is a mapping from identifiers to closures. A* closure *(E,e) consists of an environment E and an expression e, where the environment must interpret at least all the free variables in e.*

We say an environment interprets an identifier x if it contains a mapping for x. The closure to which E maps an interpreted variable x is written as E[x].

Example 4. `({a ↦ ({},succ 0)},succ a)` is a valid closure which will evaluate to the number 2.

Evaluation Context. The evaluation relation $\Downarrow$ is a relation between closures and values, which we will write as follows:

$$E, e \Downarrow V.$$

(E,e) is the closure that is being evaluated. When considering the evaluation of an expression without an explicit environment, we assume it has no free variables and we interpret this is as the closure with the empty environment.
V is the value that corresponds to the expression, this can either be a natural number or a closure. A natural number can be implicitly used as a closure with the empty environment.

Notation. We will describe both the semantics of PCF and the translation algorithm using a set of inference rules. These are rules of the form

$$\frac{\text{Premise}_1 \quad \dots \quad \text{Premise}_n}{\text{Conclusion}}$$

An algorithmic interpretation of these rules will lead to a program which can evaluate/translate PCF. Most often, the easiest way to read this kind of rules is bottom up.

Evaluation Rules. The following inference rules determine the operational semantics for PCF through the evaluation relation $\Downarrow$.

$$\frac{E[\mathsf{x}]=(E_2,e) \qquad E_2, e \Downarrow V}{E, \mathsf{x} \ \Downarrow \ V}$$

$$\frac{E, e_1 \Downarrow (E_2, \lambda\mathsf{x}.e_3) \qquad E, e_2 \Downarrow V \qquad E_2 \cup \{\mathsf{x} \mapsto V\}, e_3 \ \Downarrow V_{ap}}{E, e_1 e_2 \ \Downarrow V_{ap}}$$

$$\frac{}{E, \lambda\mathsf{x}.f \ \Downarrow (E, \lambda\mathsf{x}.f)}$$

$$\frac{}{E, n(\in \mathbb{N}) \ \Downarrow \ n}$$

$$\frac{E, e \ \Downarrow n}{E, \mathsf{succ}\ e \ \Downarrow n+1}$$

$$\frac{E, e \ \Downarrow n+1}{E, \mathsf{pred}\ e \ \Downarrow n}$$

$$\frac{E, e_z \Downarrow 0 \qquad E, e_t \Downarrow V}{E, \mathsf{ifz}\ e_z\ \mathsf{then}\ e_t\ \mathsf{else}\ e_e \ \Downarrow \ V}$$

$$\frac{E, e_z \Downarrow n \qquad n > 0 \qquad E, e_e \Downarrow V}{E, \mathsf{ifz}\ e_z\ \mathsf{then}\ e_t\ \mathsf{else}\ e_e \ \Downarrow \ V}$$

$$\frac{E \cup \{\mathsf{x} \mapsto (E, \mathsf{fix}\ (\lambda\mathsf{x}.e))\}, e \ \Downarrow V}{E, \mathsf{fix}\ (\lambda\mathsf{x}.e) \ \Downarrow V}$$

These rules form an inductive definition of the evaluation relation $\Downarrow$. Note that this is a call-by-value semantics. This can be seen in the rule of applications, as the subexpression e_2 is evaluated before adding it to the environment. A call-by-name semantics would just add the closure containing e_2 instead of the evaluation of e_2.

Example 5. In the below tree you can follow the semantics of an expression using multiple inference rules. Every horizontal line represents the application of one evaluation rule.

$$\frac{\dfrac{\{(\mathsf{f} \mapsto (\emptyset, \mathsf{fix}\ (\lambda\mathsf{f}.\ 4))\}, 4 \Downarrow 4}{\emptyset, (\mathsf{fix}\ (\lambda\mathsf{f}.\ 4)) \Downarrow 4} \quad 4 > 0 \quad \dfrac{\emptyset, 2 \Downarrow 2 \quad \dfrac{\{\mathsf{x} \mapsto 2\}, \mathsf{x} \Downarrow 2}{\{\mathsf{x} \mapsto 2\}, \mathsf{pred}\ \mathsf{x} \Downarrow 1}}{\emptyset, (\lambda\mathsf{x}.\ \mathsf{pred}\ \mathsf{x})\ 2 \Downarrow 1}}{\emptyset, \mathsf{ifz}\ (\mathsf{fix}\ (\lambda\mathsf{f}.\ 4))\ \mathsf{then}\ 3\ \mathsf{else}\ (\lambda\mathsf{x}.\ \mathsf{pred}\ \mathsf{x})\ 2 \Downarrow 1}$$

Listing 1. An example ASP program and its solutions

(a) An ASP Program	(b) The Answer Sets
1 p(1). p(2). p(3). p(4).	Answer Set 1:
2 1 {q(X) : p(X) } 2.	p(1) p(2) p(3) p(4)
3 r(X + Y) :- q(X), q(Y).	q(1) q(4) r(2) r(5) r(8)
4 :- not r(5).	Answer Set 2:
	p(1) p(2) p(3) p(4)
	q(2) q(3) r(4) r(5) r(6)

3 Answer Set Programming

Answer Set Programming [1] (ASP) is a modelling language with a strong basis in logic programming. It is mainly used as a language to specify NP-hard search problems [14]. There are a lot of different systems supporting a unified ASP standard [2]. An ASP program is essentially a logic program with some extra syntactic restrictions. An ASP solver computes the answer sets of the program under the stable semantics. An answer set consists of a set of atoms which together represent the solution of a problem. One program may have zero, one or multiple answer sets.

3.1 Language

An ASP program is a set of rules of the form:

head :- body$_1$,...,body$_n$,not body$_{n+1}$,...,not body$_m$

The first n body atoms are positive, the others are negative. The head and body atoms of the rules are of the form id(term$_1$,...,term$_n$). Body atoms can also be comparisons $(<, >, =, \neq)$ between terms. Terms can be either constants, variables, or arithmetic expressions over terms. Constants are numbers or named constants (strings starting with a lowercase character). Variables are represented as strings starting with an uppercase character. An ASP program is considered *safe* if all rules are safe. A rule is considered safe if all variables occurring in the rule, occur at least once in a positive body. If the head is omitted, the rule is considered a constraint. In this case no instantiations of the body of the rule should exist such that all the bodies are true.

Choice rules are a common syntactic extension for ASP. These allow heads of the form c_l {a(X) : b(X) } c_u, where $c_l, c_u \in \mathbb{N}$ and $c_l \leq c_u$. This head is considered true if between c_l and c_u instances of a(X) are true, given b(X). They allow to easily introduce symbols that are not uniquely defined. We can for instance declare p to be a singleton containing a number between 1 and 10 with the choice rule: 1 {p(X) : X = 1..10 } 1. The ASP program containing only this line has 10 answer sets, one for each possible singleton.

Example 6. In Listing 1 you can see an example ASP program together with its answer sets. The first line of the program defines the predicate p as the numbers between 1 and 4. The second line is a choice rule with no bodies. It states that q is a subset of p and contains 1 or 2 elements. The third line says that r is the sum of any two elements (possibly the same one) from q. The fourth line asserts that r should contain 5.

3.2   Grounding (and Solving)

To understand the details of the translation mechanism, basic knowledge of how an ASP system constructs an answer set is needed. Constructing answer sets happens in two phases: grounding and solving [12]. The grounding process transforms the ASP program to an equivalent propositional program. The solver then constructs the actual answer sets from this propositional format. The translation from PCF described in this paper will produce a fully positive, monotone theory without choice rules or constraints, i.e. there are no negations present in the program. ASP grounders produce the actual (unique) answer set for this kind of programs. Note that not all ASP systems use the same algorithms, but the information presented here is common to most systems.

The grounding process uses a bottom-up induction of the program. At any point in time, the grounder contains a set of atoms which are possibly part of an answer set. This set starts empty, and by the end of the process this set contains an overapproximation of all answer sets. The grounder tries to instantiate rules using this set of atoms. Whenever a rule is instantiated, the instantiated head is added to this set, and the ground instantiation of the rule is added to the grounding of the program. ASP grounders require that all variables occur in a positive body atom, this is the so-called safety requirement on rules. Safe rules have the property that only the positive part of the program is essential for finding all rule instantiations and current grounding approaches heavily rely on this property.

Example 7. Consider the rule `d(X-1) :- d(X), X > 0` and the current set of grounded atoms is just the singleton $\{d(1)\}$. The grounder can now instantiate the body atom `d(X)` with X$=$ 1. The other body atom $1 > 0$ can be statically evaluated to be true. This leads to the newly ground rule `d(0) :- d(1)` and `d(0)` is added to the set of grounded atoms. The grounder can now try to instantiate the rule with X$=$ 0, but the comparison $0 > 0$ prevents the rule to be added to the ground program.

After the grounding phase, an ASP solver can produce the actual answer sets based on the grounding. An ASP solver typically uses a SAT solver extended with some ASP specific propagators. The inner workings of these programs are not needed to understand the contents of this paper.

4   Translation

In this section we explain the core of the translation mechanism. Section 4.1 defines the relation between the translation and the PCF semantics. Section 4.2

introduces some conventions which explain the structure of the resulting program. Finally, Sect. 4.3 explains the static part of the translation. Section 4.4 defines the translation relation between PCF expressions and the dynamic part of the translation.

4.1   Characterisation of the Translation

Translation Relation. The translation is characterised using a relation $\rightsquigarrow$ which we will write as follows:

$$(E, S_1),\ e\ \rightsquigarrow\ A,\ (t, S_2).$$

E is a mapping from PCF-variables to ASP-terms for at least the free variables in e. This works analogously to the environment of the PCF semantics, which was the mapping from PCF-variables to closures.

$\mathbf{S_1}$ is a set of ASP atoms ensuring the ASP-terms in E are safe and constraints enforcing the ifzero-semantics.

e is the PCF expression that is translated.

A is the ASP program consisting of a set of safe ASP rules, this is the program that contains all the helper rules to translate e.

t is the ASP term which represents the translation of e.

$\mathbf{S_2}$ is the set of ASP atoms ensuring that t is safe.

It can be unintuitive that there are ASP-terms occuring on both sides of the translation relation. The explanation for this lies in the handling of free variables. The translation relation will be defined structurally, this means that for the translation of a composite term, the translation of its subterms are needed. This implies that when translating the expression $(\lambda x.\ x))$, the subterm x needs to be translated as well. The translation needs some context to interpret this x and the context of a translation environment will be some information about the parts which are already translated.

A PCF expression corresponds to a single value, but a logic program corresponds to an answer set with a lot of atoms. We need a way to indicate the actual value that is meant with the logic program. The *result*-predicate is used to indicate the resulting value of the program.

Definition 2. *The ASP translation of a PCF expression e determined by $\rightsquigarrow$ is the ASP program A such that $(\emptyset, \emptyset), e \rightsquigarrow A', (t, S)$ and $A = A' \cup \{result(t) : -S\}$.*

Soundness of the Translation. PCF inherently works on expressions which evaluate to a particular value, ASP programs define relations. A certain equivalence criterion is needed to validate the translation. For this we use the *result*-predicate. For ease of defining the correspondence the soundness criterion is restricted to programs with a numeric evaluation.

Definition 3. *A sound translator for PCF to ASP maps every PCF expression e to an ASP program A with a unique answer set. This answer set contains at most one atom for the result-predicate. If $\emptyset, e \Downarrow n \in \mathbb{N}$, then $result(n)$ must be an element of the answer set of A.*

Claim. The translation of PCF expressions determined by $\rightsquigarrow$ is a sound translator.

In this paper we will not prove this claim. We state it here to give the reader an intuition about the correspondence between a program and its translation.

4.2 Conventions

In the translation, all PCF expressions e correspond to a tuple (t, S) where t is an ASP term and S is a set of ASP bodies. Natural numbers have constants in both PCF and ASP which have a natural correspondence. PCF functions are identified by an ASP term t_f, so that for every ASP term t_x, the tuple $(Y, \{inter(t_f, t_x), Y)\})$ denotes the image of the function t_f applied to t_x. All functions have infinite domains, and thus the full function cannot be represented in a finite answer set. The *domain* predicate serves the purpose of making a finite estimate of the relevant parts of the function. If at some point in the evaluation of e, the function t_f is applied to the value t_x, $domain(t_f, t_x)$ should be true. The *inter*-predicate only needs to be defined for the domain of the function, resulting in a finite answer set containing the relevant parts of the interpretation of the function.

Remember that *result* predicate is used as the predicate determining the final result of the program. So the translation of a PCF expression is an ASP program, defining only 3 predicates:

1. *inter*: determines the interpretation of functions
2. *domain*: determines the (relevant) domain of functions
3. *result*: determines the end result

Magic Set Transformation. In these conventions a link with the magic set transformations [13] of logic programs appears. The magic set transformation allows us to transform a query, which is traditionally executed top-down, to a program, which can be executed bottom-up. It uses the *magic* predicates to indicate which subqueries needs to be performed. As explained in Sect. 3.2, ASP uses a bottom-up grounding process. So, the translation from PCF to ASP also converts a top-down query (the evaluation of PCF) to a bottom-up process (the ASP grounding). The *domain*-predicate has a function similar to the *magic* predicates: it indicates for which arguments a function needs to be calculated.

4.3 Static Preamble

The translation of any PCF expression consists of a dynamic part and a static part. The static part ensures that the interpetation of the succ, pred and fix

Listing 2. Static preamble of the ASP translation

```
1  inter((pred,X),X-1)  :- domain(pred,X), X > 0.
2  inter((succ,X),X+1)  :- domain(succ,X).
3  inter((fix,F),Y)     :- domain(fix,F), inter((F,f(F)),Y).
4  inter((f(F),X),Y)    :- domain(f(F),X), inter((F,f(F)),FIX),
5                          inter((FIX,X),Y).
6  domain(F,f(F))       :- domain(fix,F).
7  domain(FIX,X)        :- domain(f(F),X), inter((F,f(F)),FIX).
```

builtins is taken care of. The dynamic part is produced by the translation algorithm and takes care of the actual PCF expression. The static part is the same for every translation and can be seen in Listing 2. The first two lines of the static part ensure the right translation of the pred and succ terms. E.g. the PCF-term succ correctly corresponds to the ASP tuple $(succ, \{\})$ according to the conventions defined in Sect. 4.2. For instance, if somewhere the PCF-term succ 0 needs to be evaluated. The term will translate to $(Y, \{inter((succ, 0), Y)\})$ which will result in Y being equal to 1 in the answer set.

Just like pred and succ, the PCF- and ASP-term of fix are the same. But the required rules in the preamble are more complex. A naive translation could look like this:

```
inter((fix,F),Z) :- inter((fix,F),Y), inter((F,Y),Z).
```

This rule most closely represents fix $f = f$ (fix f), but in the stable semantics this equation is not correctly represented by the above rule. Instead, an intermediate term f(F) is introduced to symbolically represent the fixpoint of F in ASP. Now we are able to write the fixpoint as the function F applied to the symbolic function f(F) as can be seen on line 3. If the fixpoint is a function, we need to be able to apply it to arguments. Line 4 serves this purpose: to apply X to a fixpoint of a function, you can apply F to this fixpoint (to ensure we do not have the symbolic representation) and then apply X to the result. Finally, lines 6 and 7 ensure that the function applications performed in lines 3 and 4 are all well-defined through the domain predicates.

4.4 Translation Algorithm

In this section we present the translation algorithm as a definition for the translation relation $\leadsto$ using inference rules. Sometimes new ASP constants or variables are needed in the translation. We suppose there is some global supply of those. We use the notation $head \leftarrow B$ for the ASP rule where $head$ is the head atom and B is the set of body atoms.

Scoping. When translating an expression, the free variables in this expression need to be filled in. As we translate nested expressions level per level, we need to pass these values along the expression tree. For this reason, we do not just associate an identifier with a function but a tuple containing an identifier and the current scope. The current scope is a tupling of the full codomain of the translation environment E. We will refer to it as $scope_E$.

Builtins (numbers, Pred, Succ, Fix)

$$\overline{(E,S),\, b \,\rightsquigarrow\, \emptyset,\, (b,S)}$$

Builtins are relatively easy to translate. The hard work is taken care of by the static preamble described in Sect. 4.3. A builtin produces no new ASP rules and is translated by itself. Safety is however taken into account, not for the scoping of variables, but for the handling of the if-zero constraints.

Variable

$$\overline{(E,S),\, x \,\rightsquigarrow\, \emptyset,\, (E[x],S)}$$

The algorithm carries around a mapping that represents how variables should be translated. This makes translating it a simple variable easy: just look it up in the mapping and combine it with the required safety.

Application

$$\frac{(E,S),\, e_1 \,\rightsquigarrow\, A_1,\, (t_1, B_1) \qquad (E,S),\, e_2 \,\rightsquigarrow\, A_2,\, (t_2, B_2)}{(E,S),\, e_1 e_2 \,\rightsquigarrow\, A_1 \cup A_2 \cup rule_{domain},\, (X, body_{inter} \cup B_1 \cup B_2)}$$

$$X = a\ new\ ASP\ variable$$
$$rule_{domain} = \{domain(t_1, t_2) \leftarrow B_1 \cup B_2\}$$
$$body_{inter} = \{inter((t_1, t_2), X)\}$$

Applications are translated by independently translating the two subexpressions. The produced ASP programs need to be combined, with the additional rule that t_2 should be added to the domain of the function t_1. To obtain the resulting value, we use the *inter*-predicate according to the conventions explained in Sect. 4.2.

Example 8. The rule below shows how the application rule can be used to translate the successor of 1. The static part of the translation ensures that the inter-relation for succ is interpreted correctly so that in any solution. The X gets evaluated to 2.

$$\frac{(\emptyset,\emptyset),\, \textsf{succ} \,\rightsquigarrow\, \emptyset,\, (\textsf{succ}, \emptyset) \qquad (\emptyset,\emptyset),\, 1 \,\rightsquigarrow\, \emptyset,\, (1, \emptyset)}{(\emptyset,\emptyset),\, \textsf{succ 1} \,\rightsquigarrow\, \{domain(succ, 1)\},\, (X, inter((succ, 1), X))}$$

Lambda

$$\frac{(E \cup (\mathsf{x}, X), S \cup body_{domain}), e \rightsquigarrow A, (t, B)}{(E,S), \lambda \mathsf{x}.\ e \rightsquigarrow A \cup rule_{inter}, ((l, scope_E), S)}$$

$$X = a\ new\ ASP\ variable$$
$$l = a\ new\ ASP\ constant$$
$$rule_{inter} = \{inter(((l, scope_E), X), t) \leftarrow B\}$$
$$body_{domain} = \{domain((l, scope_E), X)\}$$

Lambda expressions bring a new variable into scope, so they modify the (E, S)-environment before recursively translating the body of the expression. The freshly scoped variable needs to be put into the scoping function E, for this we assign it a new ASP variable (X in the rule). This variable should have a finite range, so we invent a new name for our function (l in the rule) and we use the *domain* predicate to restrict X to the domain of the function. The resulting translation (t, B) represents the image of the function, so the rule $rule_{inter}$ is added to couple the representation of the function to its interpretation.

Example 9. $(\emptyset, \emptyset)(\lambda \mathsf{x}.2) \rightsquigarrow \{inter(((l, ()), X), 2)\ \leftarrow\ domain((l, ()), X)\}$, $((l, ()), \emptyset)$ This can be read as follows: The translation of the constant function to 2 in an empty environment is represented by the constant $(l, ())$. The interpretation of $(l, ())$ when applied to any term X in the domain of $(l, ())$ is 2.

If Zero-then-else

$$\frac{\begin{array}{c}(E,S),\ e_{\mathsf{ifz}} \rightsquigarrow A_{\mathsf{ifz}},\ (t_{\mathsf{ifz}}, B_{\mathsf{ifz}}) \\ (E, B_{\mathsf{ifz}} \cup \{t_{\mathsf{ifz}} = 0\}),\ e_{\mathsf{then}} \rightsquigarrow A_{\mathsf{then}},\ (t_{\mathsf{then}}, B_{\mathsf{then}}) \\ (E, B_{\mathsf{ifz}} \cup \{t_{\mathsf{ifz}} \neq 0\}),\ e_{\mathsf{else}} \rightsquigarrow A_{\mathsf{else}},\ (t_{\mathsf{else}}, B_{\mathsf{else}})\end{array}}{(E,S),\ \mathsf{if}\ e_{\mathsf{ifz}}\ \mathsf{then}\ e_{\mathsf{then}}\ \mathsf{else}\ e_{\mathsf{else}} \rightsquigarrow A_{\mathsf{ite}} \cup rule_{\mathsf{ite}}, (X, S \cup body_{\mathsf{ite}})}$$

$$X = a\ new\ ASP\ variable$$
$$ite = a\ new\ ASP\ constant$$
$$rule_{ite} = \{inter((ite, scope_E), t_{\mathsf{then}}) \leftarrow B_{\mathsf{then}},$$
$$inter((ite, scope_E), t_{\mathsf{else}}) \leftarrow B_{\mathsf{else}}\}$$
$$body_{ite} = \{inter((ite, scope_E), X)\}$$
$$A_{\mathsf{ite}} = A_{\mathsf{ifz}} \cup A_{\mathsf{then}} \cup A_{\mathsf{else}}$$

If zero expressions are translated using the translations of its three subexpressions. But we need to alter the safety to ensure that the "then"-part is only evaluated if the"if"-part is 0 (and the analog for the "else" part). To construct

Listing 3. Translation of (λx. ifz x then succ else pred) 2 4

```
1  inter(((ite1,(X0)),succ):-domain((l0,()),X0),X0=0.
2  inter(((ite1,(X0)),pred):-domain((l0,()),X0),X0<>0.
3  inter((((l0,()),X0),X1):-domain((l0,()),X0),inter(((ite1,(X0)),X1).
4  domain((l0,()),2).
5  domain(X2,4):-inter((((l0,()),2),X2).
6  result(X3):-inter((((l0,()),2),X2),inter((X2,4),X3).
7  % omitted static part visible in Listing 1
```

the value of the full expression we define an intermediate symbol (*ite* in the rule) to represent the union of the "then" and the "else" part. Because the extra safety (= 0, ≠ 0) is mutually exclusive, only one of those terms will have a denotation, so the interpretation of *ite* will be unique.

Example 10. The translation of (λx. ifz x then succ else pred) 2 4 is visible in Listing 3. The static part is omitted. Lines 1 and 2 are result of the if zero-then-else translation. Line 3 is the result of the lambda translation. Lines 4 and 5 are the result of the application. And in line 6 the end result can be seen. This rule can be read as follows: Let X2 be the application of the function to 2. Let X3 be application of X2 to 4. The final result is X3.

4.5 Optimisations

The translation algorithm which is given in the previous section is not an optimal translation. A lot of optimisations are possible, for instance, not all variables in scope need to be present in $scope_E$, only the ones which are actually used in the subexpression. Applying such optimisations can significantly reduce the size of the grounding of the ASP program. The possibilities here are very interesting research topics, but are considered out of scope for this paper.

4.6 Implementation

An implementation was made in Kotlin. The runtime uses Clingo [9] to run the resulting ASP files, but the resulting specifications could be used with any ASP-Core-2 [2] compliant system. On https://dtai.cs.kuleuven.be/krr/pcf2asp you can find a tool on which you can try out the translation. A few example PCF formulas are provided, but you can ask for translations of arbitrary PCF formulas and see their corresponding answer set.

5 Applications

5.1 Multiple Interpretations for One Variable

Directly translating PCF gives us little more than a traditional interpreter of PCF would do, but based on this translation we can provide extra functionality, leveraging the existing ASP solvers. Traditional PCF does not support the

Listing 4. $a + b = c$ in PCF

```
1   (λeq. λplus.
2         eq (plus a b) c)
3
4   (fix (λeq.λx.λy. ifz x then (ifz y then 0 else 1)
5                          else (ifz y then 1 else eq (pred x) (pred y))))
6   (fix (λplus.λx.λy. ifz y then x else plus (succ x) (pred y)))
```

Listing 5. $a + b = c$ in ASP

```
1   1{a(X)}1 :- X=1..10.
2   1{b(X)}1 :- X=1..10.
3   1{c(X)}1 :- X=1..10.
4   :- not result(0).
5   ...
6   domain(X1,A):-domain((l0,()),X0),domain((l1,(X0)),X1),a(A).
7   ...
```

possibility that the interpretation of a term is not uniquely defined, but we can extend PCF so we can declare the variable a as a number between 1 and 10 without defining its specific value. In that case we can get (at most) 10 different evaluations of our program, one for each interpretation of a. It is easy to extend the translation to encode this in ASP.

Traditional interpreters solve the question: "What is the evaluation of this program?". But using these variables another question can be interesting: what value(s) for a should I choose so that the program evaluates to 0. We can leverage the strengths of ASP solvers to find the solutions. Expressing that the evaluation should be zero can be done through a simple ASP constraint:

```
:- not result(0).
```

When this constraint is added, the resulting answer sets will now all have the same interpretation (0) for the *result* predicate, but we are interested in the interpretation for a.

Example 11. In Listing 4 you can see a PCF expression representing that $a + b = c$. If we now use choice rules in ASP to translate these variables to the domain of natural numbers between 0 and 10, we can use ASP to find multiple solutions of this equation. An example of how this would look in ASP an be seen in Listing 5.

The problem in Example 11 can easily be generalised to arbitrarily complex polynomials to model mixed integer problems. A graph coloring problem can be represented by using a new constant for each node that needs to be colored and writing down an expression that evaluated to 0 if the graph is colored correctly.

An important thing to note here is that ASP does not naively calculate the result for all possible values of the choice rules. It uses a CDCL-based solving algorithm to explore the search space in an intelligent way.

5.2 Towards a More Expressive Language

PCF is not intended to be an end-user language, but it serves as a basis for many real world programming languages. Analogously, we are developing a more expressive language based on the principles of PCF. This language includes more complex data types for representations which are more elegant than possible in PCF. Together with the multiple-model semantics of ASP this leads to an interesting modelling language. Using these ideas the new Functional Modelling System (FMS) is being developed. On the website https://dtai.cs.kuleuven.be/krr/fms a demonstration of this new system can be found. This system is an extension of PCF with some more practical language constructs and uses the translation principles described in this paper to use ASP as a solver engine for this new language. However as indicated in Sect. 4.5, a lot of optimisations are needed to be competitive with native ASP encodings. The efficiency of these translators have not been formally investigated yet.

6 Conclusion

We presented a translation from PCF to ASP programs. A basic translation is easily implemented, and many optimisations are possible. With only small changes, we can exploit the search power of ASP to solve problems expressed in PCF. This translation can serve as a basis to use functional programming techniques in modelling languages for search problems, or even tighter integrations between functional and logical languages. FMS is under development now and uses the techniques described in this paper as a basis for its language.

References

1. Brewka, G., Eiter, T., Truszczynski, M.: Answer set programming at a glance. Commun. ACM **54**(12), 92–103 (2011)
2. Calimeri, F., et al.: ASP-Core-2 input language format. Technical report, ASP Standardization Working Group (2013)
3. Chen, W., Kifer, M., Warren, D.S.: HiLog: a foundation for higher-order logic programming. J. Log. Program. **15**(3), 187–230 (1993)
4. Clément, D., Despeyroux, J., Despeyroux, T., Kahn, G.: A simple applicative language: mini-ML. In: LISP and Functional Programming, pp. 13–27 (1986)
5. Dargaye, Z., Leroy, X.: Mechanized verification of CPS transformations. In: Dershowitz, N., Voronkov, A. (eds.) LPAR 2007. LNCS (LNAI), vol. 4790, pp. 211–225. Springer, Heidelberg (2007). https://doi.org/10.1007/978-3-540-75560-9_17
6. Dasseville, I., van der Hallen, M., Bogaerts, B., Janssens, G., Denecker, M.: A compositional typed higher-order logic with definitions. In: Carro, M., King, A., De Vos, M., Saeedloei, N. (eds.) ICLP 2016. OASIcs, vol. 52, pp. 14.1–14.14. Schloss Dagstuhl, November 2016

7. Dasseville, I., van der Hallen, M., Janssens, G., Denecker, M.: Semantics of templates in a compositional framework for building logics. TPLP **15**(4–5), 681–695 (2015)
8. Dowek, G., Lévy, J.-J.: Introduction to the Theory of Programming Languages. Undergraduate Topics in Computer Science. Springer, Heidelberg (2011). https://doi.org/10.1007/978-0-85729-076-2
9. Gebser, M., Kaminski, R., Kaufmann, B., Schaub, T.: Clingo = ASP + control: preliminary report. CoRR, abs/1405.3694 (2014)
10. Gratzer, D.: A tiny compiler for a typed higher order language (2015)
11. Ianni, G., Ielpa, G., Pietramala, A., Santoro, M.C., Calimeri, F.: Enhancing answer set programming with templates. In: Delgrande, J.P., Schaub, T. (eds.) Proceedings of the 10th International Workshop on Non-Monotonic Reasoning (NMR 2004), Whistler, Canada, 6–8 June 2004, pp. 233–239 (2004)
12. Kaufmann, B., Leone, N., Perri, S., Schaub, T.: Grounding and solving in answer set programming. AI Mag. **37**(3), 25–32 (2016)
13. Mumick, I.S., Finkelstein, S.J., Pirahesh, H., Ramakrishnan, R.: Magic is relevant. In: Garcia-Molina, H., Jagadish, H.V. (eds.) Proceedings of the 1990 ACM SIGMOD International Conference on Management of Data, Atlantic City, NJ, 23–25 May 1990, pp. 247–258. ACM Press (1990)
14. Niemelä, I.: Answer set programming: a declarative approach to solving search problems. In: Fisher, M., van der Hoek, W., Konev, B., Lisitsa, A. (eds.) JELIA 2006. LNCS (LNAI), vol. 4160, pp. 15–18. Springer, Heidelberg (2006). https://doi.org/10.1007/11853886_2
15. Plotkin, G.D.: LCF considered as a programming language. Theor. Comput. Sci. **5**(3), 223–255 (1977)

Code Generation for Higher Inductive Types

A Study in Agda Metaprogramming

Paventhan Vivekanandan[(✉)] [ID]

Indiana University, Bloomington, IN, USA
pvivekan@umail.iu.edu

Abstract. Higher inductive types are inductive types that include non-trivial higher-dimensional structure, represented as identifications that are not reflexivity. While work proceeds on type theories with a computational interpretation of univalence and higher inductive types, it is convenient to encode these structures in more traditional type theories with mature implementations. However, these encodings involve a great deal of error-prone additional syntax. We present a library that uses Agda's metaprogramming facilities to automate this process, allowing higher inductive types to be specified with minimal additional syntax.

Keywords: Higher inductive type · Elaboration · Elimination rules · Computation rules

1 Introduction

Type theory unites programming and mathematics in a delightful synthesis, in which we can write programs and proofs in the same language. Work on higher-dimensional type theory has revealed a beautiful higher-dimensional structure, lurking just beyond reach. In particular, higher inductive types provide a natural encoding of many otherwise-difficult mathematical concepts, and univalence lets us work in our type theory the way we do on paper: up to isomorphism. Homotopy type theory, however, is not yet done. We do not yet have a mature theory or a mature implementation.

While work proceeds on prototype implementations of higher-dimensional type theories [5,15], much work remains before they will be as convenient for experimentation with new ideas as Coq, Agda, or Idris is today. In the meantime, it is useful to be able to experiment with ideas from higher-dimensional type theory in our existing systems. If one is willing to put up with some boilerplate code, it is possible to encode higher inductive types and univalence using postulated identities.

Boilerplate postulates, however, are not just inconvenient, they are also an opportunity to make mistakes. Luckily, this boilerplate code can be mechanically generated using Agda's recent support for *elaborator reflection* [12], a paradigm

© Springer Nature Switzerland AG 2019
J. Silva (Ed.): WFLP 2018, LNCS 11285, pp. 18–35, 2019.
https://doi.org/10.1007/978-3-030-16202-3_2

for metaprogramming in an implementation of type theory. An elaborator is the part of the implementation that translates a convenient language designed for humans into a much simpler, more explicit, verbose language designed to be easy for a machine to process. Elaborator reflection directly exposes the primitive components of the elaborator to metaprograms written in the language being elaborated, allowing them to put these components to new uses.

Homotopy type theory has thus far primarily been applied to the encoding of mathematics, rather than to programming. Nevertheless, there are a few applications of homotopy type theory to programming. Applications such as homotopical patch theory [6] discuss a model of the core of the Darcs [27] version control system using patch theory [23] encoded as a higher inductive type (HIT). Containers in homotopy type theory [2,3] implement data structures such as multisets and cycles. Automating the HIT boilerplate code allows more programmers to begin experimenting with programming using HITs.

Using Agda's elaborator reflection, we automatically generate the support code for many useful higher inductive types, specifically those that include additional paths between constructors, but not paths between paths, which is sufficient for treating various interesting examples on the programming side [6,7,30]. We automate the production of the recursion principles, induction principles, and their computational behavior. Angiuli et al.'s encoding of patch theory as a higher inductive type [6] requires approximately 1500 lines of code when represented using rewriting [8,13], a new feature of Agda which allows the addition of new reduction rules. Using our library, the encoding can be expressed in just 70 lines.

This paper makes the following contributions:

- We describe the design and implementation of a metaprogram that automates an encoding of higher inductive types with one dimensional paths using Agda's elaborator reflection.
- We demonstrate applications of this metaprogram to examples from the literature, including vector and circle as well as larger systems, including both patch theory and specifying cryptographic schemes.
- This metaprogram serves as an example of the additional power available in Agda's elaborator reflection relative to earlier metaprogramming APIs.

In Agda, we don't have built-in primitives to support the definition of higher inductive types. In this paper, we use rewriting to define higher inductive types. Unlike [8], we use basic modules, without parameters, to encode higher inductive types. This is because Agda's reflection library does not have primitives to support introducing parameterized modules.

2 Background

2.1 Higher Inductive Types

Homotopy type theory [29] is a research program that aims to develop univalent, higher-dimensional type theories. A universe is *univalent* when equivalences

```
data Circle : Set where
  base : Circle
  loop : base ≡ base
```

Fig. 1. A specification of a higher inductive type

between types are considered equivalent to identifications between types. A type theory is univalent when every universe in the type theory is univalent; it is *higher-dimensional* when we allow non-trivial identifications that every structure in the theory must nevertheless respect. Identifications between elements of a type are considered to be at the lowest dimension, while identifications between identifications at dimension n are at dimension $n+1$. Voevodsky added univalence to type theories as an axiom [25], asserting new identifications without providing a means to compute with them. While more recent work arranges the computational mechanisms of the type theory such that univalence can be derived, as is done in cubical type theories [5,15], we are concerned with modeling concepts from homotopy type theory in existing, mature implementations of type theory, so we follow Univalent Foundations Program [29] in modeling paths using Martin-Löf's identity type. Higher-dimensional structure can arise from univalence, but it can also be introduced by defining new type formers that introduce not only introduction and elimination principles, but also new non-trivial identifications.

In homotopy type theories, one tends to think of types not as collections of distinct elements, but rather through the metaphor of topological spaces. The individual elements of the type correspond with points in the topological space, and identifications correspond to paths in this space.

While work proceeds on the general schematic characterization of higher inductive types [7,9,17], it is convenient to syntactically represent the higher inductive types that we know are acceptable using a syntax similar to a traditional inductive type by providing its constructors (*i.e.* its points); we additionally specify the higher-dimensional structure by providing additional constructors for paths. For example, Fig. 1 describes `Circle` [6], which is a higher inductive type with one point constructor `base` and one non-trivial path constructor `loop`.

Figure 2 represents the implementation of `Circle` in Agda. Inside module `Circle`, the type S and the constructors `base` and `loop` and the recursion and induction principles are declared as postulates. `recS` ignores the path argument and simply computes to the appropriate answer for the point constructor. The computation rule for point `base` is declared as a rewrite rule using `{-# REWRITE , ...#-}` pragma. The computation rule for the path constructor `loop` is postulated using reduction rule `loop`. The operator `ap` is frequently referred to as `cong`, because it expresses that propositional equality is a congruence. However, when viewed through a homotopy type theory lens, it is often called `ap`, as it describes the action of a function on paths. In a higher inductive type, `ap` should compute new paths from old ones.

```
postulate
  _↦_ : ∀ {i} {A : Set i} → A → A → Set i
{-# BUILTIN REWRITE _↦_ #-}
module Circle where
  postulate
    S : Set
    base : S
    loop : base ≡ base
  postulate
    recS : S → (C : Set) → (cbase : C) → (cloop : cbase ≡ cbase) → C
    βbase : (C : Set) → (cbase : C) → (cloop : cbase ≡ cbase) →
      recS base C cbase cloop ↦ cbase
  {-# REWRITE βbase #-}
  postulate
    βloop : (C : Set) → (cbase : C) → (cloop : cbase ≡ cbase) →
      ap (λ x → recS x C cbase cloop) loop ≡ cloop
  postulate
    indS : (x : S) → (C : S → Set) →
      (cbase : C base) → (cloop : transport C loop cbase ≡ cbase) → C x
    iβbase : (C : S → Set) →
      (cbase : C base) → (cloop : transport C loop cbase ≡ cbase) →
      indS base C cbase cloop ↦ cbase
  {-# REWRITE iβbase #-}
  postulate
    iβloop : (C : S → Set) →
      (cbase : C base) → (cloop : transport C loop cbase ≡ cbase) →
      apd (λ x → indS x C cbase cloop) loop ≡ cloop
```

Fig. 2. A HIT encoded using rewrite rules

$$
\begin{aligned}
&\text{ap} : \{A\ B : Set\} → \{x\ y : A\} → \\
&\quad (f : A → B) → \\
&\quad (p : x ≡ y) → \\
&\quad f\ x ≡ f\ y
\end{aligned}
$$

In addition to describing the constructors of the points and paths of S, Fig. 2 additionally demonstrates the dependent eliminator (that is, the induction rule) indS and its computational meaning. The dependent eliminator relies on another operation on identifications, called transport, that coerces an inhabitant of a family of types at a particular index into an inhabitant at another index. Outside of homotopy type theory, transport is typically called subst or replace, because it also expresses that substituting equal elements for equal elements is acceptable.

$$
\begin{aligned}
&\text{transport} : \{A : Set\} → \{x\ y : A\} → \\
&\quad (P : A → Set) → \\
&\quad (p : x ≡ y) → \\
&\quad P\ x → P\ y
\end{aligned}
$$

In the postulated computation rule for indS, the function apd is the dependent version of ap: it expresses the action of dependent functions on paths.

$$
\begin{aligned}
&\text{apd} : \{A : Set\} → \{B : A → Set\} → \{x\ y : A\} → \\
&\quad (f : (a : A) → B\ a) → \\
&\quad (p : x ≡ y) → \\
&\quad \text{transport}\ B\ p\ (f\ x) ≡ f\ y
\end{aligned}
$$

Using our library, the user can automate the generation of recS, βbase, βloop, indS, iβbase, and iβloop. Further handling of the HIT should proceed normally as if the rules were declared manually.

2.2 Agda Reflection

Agda [24] is a functional programming language with full dependent types and dependent pattern matching. Agda's type theory has gained a number of new features over the years, among them the ability to restrict pattern matching to that subset that does not imply Streicher's Axiom K [14], which is inconsistent with univalence. The convenience of programming in Agda, combined with the ability to avoid axiom K, makes it a good laboratory for experimenting with the idioms and techniques of univalent programming while more practical implementations of univalent type theories are under development.

Agda's reflection library enables compile-time metaprogramming. This reflection library directly exposes parts of the implementation of Agda's type checker and elaborator for use by metaprograms, in a manner that is similar to Idris's elaborator reflection [11,12] and Lean's tactic metaprogramming [18]. The type checker's implementation is exposed as effects in a monad called TC.

Agda exposes a representation of its syntax to metaprograms, including datatypes for expressions (called Term) and definitions (called Definition). The primitives exposed in TC include declaring new metavariables, unifying two Terms, declaring new definitions, adding new postulates, computing the normal form or weak head normal form of a Term, inspecting the current context, and constructing fresh names. This section describes the primitives that are used in our code generation library; more information on the reflection library can be found in the Agda documentation [1].

TC computations can be invoked in three ways: by macros, which work in expression positions, using the unquoteDecl operator in a declaration position, which can bring new names into scope, and using the unquoteDef operator in a declaration position, which can automate constructions using names that are already in scope. This preserves the principle in Agda's design that the system never invents a name.

An Agda *macro* is a function of type $t_1 \to t_2 \to \ldots \to$ Term $\to$ TC $\top$ that is defined inside a macro block. Macros are special: their last argument is automatically supplied by the type checker and consists of a Term that represents the metavariable to be solved by the macro. If the remaining arguments are quoted names or Terms, then the type checker will automatically quote the arguments at the macro's use site. At some point, the macro is expected to unify the provided metavariable with some other term, thus solving it.

Figure 3(a) demonstrates a macro that quotes its argument. The first step is to quote the quoted expression argument again, using quoteTC, yielding a quotation of a quotation. This double-quoted expression is passed, using Agda's new support for Haskell-style do-notation, into a function that unifies it with the hole. Because unification removes one layer of quotation, unify inserts the original quoted term into the hole. The value of sampleTerm is

```
macro                                  macro
  mc1 : Term → Term → TC ⊤               mc2 : Term → Term → TC ⊤
  mc1 exp hole =                         mc2 exp hole =
    do exp' ← quoteTC exp                  do exp' ← unquoteTC exp
       unify hole exp'                        unify hole exp'

sampleTerm : Term                      sampleSyntax : Nat → Nat
sampleTerm = mc1 (λ (n : Nat) → n)     sampleSyntax =
                                         mc2 (lam visible (abs "n" (var 0 [])))
```

(a)   (b)

Fig. 3. A macro that quotes (a) or unquotes (b) its argument

```
plus : Nat → Nat → Nat
plus zero b = b
plus (suc n) b = suc (plus n b)
```

Fig. 4. Addition on natural numbers

```
lam visible (abs "n" (var 0 []))
```

The constructor `lam` represents a lambda, and its body is formed by the abstraction constructor `abs` that represents a scope in which a new name `"n"` is bound. The body of the abstraction is a reference back to the abstracted name using de Bruijn index 0.

The `unquoteTC` primitive removes one level of quotation. Figure 3(b) demonstrates the use of `unquoteTC`. The macro `mc2` expects a quotation of a quotation and substitutes its unquotation for the current metavariable.

The `unquoteDecl` and `unquoteDef` primitives, which run `TC` computations in a declaration context, will typically introduce new declarations by side effect. A function of a given type is declared using `declareDef`, and it can be given a definition using `defineFun`. Similarly, a postulate of a given type is defined using `declarePostulate`. Figure 4 shows an Agda implementation of addition on natural numbers, while Fig. 5 demonstrates an equivalent metaprogram that adds the same definition to the context.

In Fig. 5, `declareDef` declares the type of `plus`. The constructor `pi` represents dependent function types, but a pattern synonym is used to make it shorter. Similarly, `def` constructs references to defined names, and the pattern synonym `'Nat` abbreviates references to the defined name `Nat`, and `vArg` represents the desired visibility and relevance settings of the arguments. Once declared, `plus` is defined using `defineFun`, which takes a name and a list of clauses, defining the function by side effect. Each clause consists of a pattern and a right-hand side. Patterns have their own datatype, while right-hand sides are `Terms`. The name `con` is overloaded: in patterns, it denotes a pattern that matches a particular constructor, while in `Terms`, it denotes a reference to a constructor.

The next section introduces the necessary automation features by describing the automatic generation of eliminators for a variant on Dybjer's inductive

```
pattern vArg x = arg (arg-info visible relevant) x
pattern _'⇒_ a b = pi (vArg a) (abs "_" b)
pattern 'Nat = def (quote Nat) []

unquoteDecl plus =
  do declareDef (vArg plus) ('Nat '⇒ 'Nat '⇒ 'Nat)
     defineFun plus
       (clause (vArg (con (quote zero) []) ::
                    vArg (var "y") ::
                    [])
              (var 0 []) ::
         clause (vArg (con (quote suc)
                          (vArg (var "x") :: [])) ::
                    vArg (var "y") ::
                    [])
              (con (quote suc)
                (vArg (def plus
                          (vArg (var 1 []) ::
                           vArg (var 0 []) :: [])) ::
            [])) :: [])
```

Fig. 5. Addition, defined by metaprogramming

families. Section 4 then generalizes this feature to automate the production of eliminators for higher inductive types using the rewrite mechanism.

3   Code Generation for Inductive Types

An inductive type D is a type that is freely generated by a finite collection of constructors. The constructors of D accept zero or more arguments and have D as the co-domain. The constructors can also take an element of type D itself as an argument, but only *strictly positively*: any occurrences of the type constructor D in the type of an argument to a constructor of D must not be to the left of any arrows. Type constructors can have a number of *parameters*, which may not vary between the constructors, as well as *indices*, which may vary.

In Agda, constructors are given a function type. In Agda's reflection library, the constructor **data-type** of the datatype **Definition** stores the constructors of an inductive type as a list of **Names**. The type of a constructor can be retrieved by giving its **Name** as an input to the **getType** primitive. In this section, we discuss how to use the list of constructors and their types to generate code for the elimination rules of an inductive type.

3.1   Non-dependent Eliminators

In Agda, we define an inductive type using **data** keyword. A definition of an inductive datatype declares its type and specifies its constructors. While Agda supports a variety of ways to define new data types, we will restrict our attention to the subset that corresponds closely to Dybjer's inductive families. In general,

```
data Vec (A : Set) : Nat → Set where
  []    : Vec A zero
  _::_  : {n : Nat} → (x : A) →
          (xs : Vec A n) → Vec A (suc n)
```

Fig. 6. Length-indexed lists

the definition of an inductive datatype D with constructors $c_1 \ldots c_n$ has the following form:

$$\textbf{data } D\,(a_1 : A_1) \ldots (a_n : A_n) : (i_1 : I_1) \to \ldots \to (i_m : I_m) \to \textsf{Set } \textbf{where}$$
$$c_1 : \Delta_1 \to D\,a_1 \ldots a_n\,e_{11} \ldots e_{1m}$$
$$\vdots$$
$$c_r : \Delta_n \to D\,a_1 \ldots a_n\,e_{r1} \ldots e_{rm}$$

where the index instantiations $e_{k1} \ldots e_{km}$ are expressions in the scope induced by the telescope Δ_k. Every expression in the definition must also be well-typed according to the provided declarations. A telescope $\Delta = (x_1 : B_1) \ldots (x_n : B_n)$ is a sequence of types where later types may depend on elements of previous types.

As an example, the datatype Vec (Fig. 6) represents lists of a known length. There is one parameter, namely (A : Set), and one index, namely Nat. The second constructor, _: : _, has a recursive instance of Vec as an argument.

While inductive datatypes are essentially characterized by their constructors, it must also be possible to eliminate their inhabitants, exposing the information in the constructors. This section describes an Agda metaprogram that generates a non-dependent recursion principle for an inductive type; Sect. 3.2 generalizes this technique to fully dependent induction principles.

For Vec, the recursion principle says that, in order to eliminate a Vec A n, one must provide a result for the empty Vec and a means for transforming the head and tail of a non-empty Vec combined with the result of recursion onto a tail into the desired answer for the entire Vec. Concretely, the type of the recursor recVec is given as follows.

```
recVec : (A : Set) →
         {n : Nat} →
         Vec A n →
         (C : Set) →
         (base : C) →
         (step : {n : Nat} → (x : A) →
                 (xs : Vec A n) → C → C) →
         C
```

The recursor recVec maps the constructor [], which takes zero arguments, to base. It maps (x : : xs) to (step x xs (recVec xs C base step)). Because step is applied to a recursive call to the recursor, it takes one more argument than the constructor _: : _.

Based on the schematic presentation of inductive types D earlier in this section, we can define a schematic representation for their non-dependent eliminators D_{rec}.

$$
\begin{aligned}
D_{rec} : \; & (a_1 : A_1) \to \ldots \to (a_n : A_n) \to \\
& (i_1 : I_1) \to \ldots \to (i_m : I_m) \to \\
& (tgt : D\ a_1 \ldots a_n\ i_1\ \ldots\ i_n) \to \\
& (C : \mathsf{Set}) \to \\
& (f_1 : \Delta_1' \to C) \to \ldots \to (f_r : \Delta_r' \to C) \to \\
& C
\end{aligned}
$$

The type of f_i, which is the method for fulfilling the desired type C when eliminating the constructor c_i, is determined by the type of c_i. The telescope Δ_i' is the same as Δ_i for non-recursive constructor arguments. However, Δ_i' binds additional variables when there are recursive occurrences of D in the arguments. For instance, if Δ_i has an argument $(y : B)$, where B is not an application of D or a function returning such an application, Δ_i' binds $(y : B)$ directly. If B is an application of D, then an additional binding $(y' : C)$ is inserted following y. Finally, if B is a function type $\Psi \to D$, the additional binding is $(y' : \Psi \to C)$.

To construct the type of `recVec`, we need to build the types of `base` and `step`. These are derived from the corresponding types of `[]` and `_::_`, which can be discovered using reflection primitives. Since `[]` requires no arguments, its corresponding method is `(base : C)`. The constructor `pi` of type `Term` encodes the abstract syntax tree (AST) representation of `_::_`. We can retrieve and traverse the AST of `_::_`, and add new type information into it to build a new type representing `step`. Once the AST for `step`'s type has been found, it is possible to build the type of `recVec`. To quantify over the return type `(C : Set)`, we use the `Term` constructor `agda-sort` to refer to `Set`.

In general, when automating the production of D_{rec}, all the information that is needed to produce the type signature is available in the `TC` monad by looking up D's definition. The constructor `data-type` contains the number of parameters occurring in a defined type. It also encodes the constructors of the type as a list of `Names`. Metaprograms can retrieve the index count by using the type and the number of parameters. The constructors of D refer to the parameter and the index using de Bruijn indices.

The general schema for the computation rules corresponding to D_{rec} and constructors $c_1, \ldots, c_n$ is as follows:

$$
D_{rec}\ a_1\ \ldots\ a_n\ i_1\ \ldots\ i_m\ (c_1\ \Delta_1)\ C\ f_1 \ldots f_r = \mathsf{RHS}\,(f_1, \Delta_1')
$$

$$
\vdots
$$

$$
D_{rec}\ a_1\ \ldots\ a_n\ i_1\ \ldots\ i_m\ (c_r\ \Delta_r)\ C\ f_1 \ldots f_r = \mathsf{RHS}\,(f_r, \Delta_r')
$$

Here, Δ_j' is the sequence of variables bound in Δ_j. RHS constructs the application of the method f_j to the arguments of c_j, such that C is satisfied. It is defined by recursion on Δ_j. $\mathsf{RHS}\,(f_j, \cdot)$ is f_j, because all arguments have been accounted for. $\mathsf{RHS}\,(f_j, (y : B)\Delta_k)$ is $\mathsf{RHS}\,(f_j\ y, \Delta_k)$ when B does

```
generateRec, generateInd : Arg Name → (indType : Name) → TC ⊤

generateβRec, generateβInd : Arg Name → List (Arg Name) →
    (indType : Name) → (param : Nat) → (points : List Name) → TC ⊤

generateRecHit, generateIndHit : Arg Name →
    (indType : Name) → (baseElim : Name) → (param : Nat) →
    (points : List Name) → (paths : List Name) → TC ⊤

generateβRecHitPath, generateβIndHitPath : Name → List (Arg Name) →
    (indType : Name) → (baseElim : Name) → (param : Nat) →
    (points : List Name) → (paths : List Name) → TC ⊤
```

Fig. 7. Library for generating dependent and non-dependent eliminators

not mention D. RHS $(f_j, (y : D)(y' : C)\Delta_k)$ is RHS $(f_j\ y\ (D_{rec} \ldots y \ldots), \Delta_k)$, where the recursive use of D_{rec} is applied to the recursive constructor argument as well as the appropriate indices, and the parameters, result type, and methods remain constant. Higher-order recursive arguments are a generalization of first-order arguments. Finally, RHS $(f_j, (y : \Psi \to D)(y' : \Psi \to C)\Delta_k)$ is RHS $\left(f_j\ y\ \left(\lambda\overline{\Psi}.D_{rec} \ldots \left(y\ \overline{\Psi}\right) \ldots\right), \Delta_k\right)$ where the recursive use of D_{rec} is as before.

After declaring recVec's type using declareDef, it is time to define its computational meaning using the schematic rules defined above. The computation rule representing the action of function recVec on [] and _: : _ is defined using clause. The first argument to clause encodes variables corresponding to the above type, and it also includes the abstract representation of the constructors [] and _: : _ on which the pattern matching should occur. The second argument to clause, which is of type Term, refers to the variables in the first argument using de Bruijn indices, and it encodes the output of recVec when the pattern matches. The computation rules for recVec are given as follows.

```
recVec []          C base step = base
recVec (x :: xs) C base step = step x xs (f xs C base step)
```

generateRec (Fig. 7) builds the computation and elimination rules respectively. The recursion rule generated by generateRec is brought into scope using unquoteDecl. The first argument to generateRec is the quoted Name of the recursor encoded inside Arg, and the second argument is the quoted Name of the inductive type.

3.2 Dependent Eliminators

The dependent eliminator for a datatype, also known as the *induction principle*, is used to eliminate elements of a datatype when the type resulting from the elimination mentions the very element being eliminated. The type of the induction principle for D is:

$$
\begin{aligned}
D_{ind} : {}& (a_1 : A_1) \to \ldots \to (a_n : A_n) \to \\
& (i_1 : I_1) \to \ldots \to (i_m : I_m) \to \\
& (tgt : D\ a_1 \ldots a_n\ i_1\ \ldots\ i_m) \to \\
& (C : (i_1 : I_1) \to \ldots \to (i_m : I_m) \to \\
& \qquad\quad D\ a_1 \ldots a_n\ i_1\ \ldots\ i_n \to \mathsf{Set}) \to \\
& (f_1 : \Delta_1' \to C\ e_{11} \ldots e_{1p}\ (c_1\ \overline{\Delta_1})) \to \\
& \quad\vdots \\
& (f_r : \Delta_r' \to C\ e_{r1} \ldots e_{rp}\ (c_r\ \overline{\Delta_r})) \to \\
& C\ i_1\ \ldots\ i_n\ tgt
\end{aligned}
$$

Unlike the non-dependent recursion principle D_{rec}, the result type is now computed from the target and its indices. Because it expresses the reason that the target must be eliminated, the function C is often referred to as the *motive*. Similarly to D_{rec}, the type of each method f_i is derived from the type of the constructor c_i—the method argument telescope Δ_k' is similar, except the arguments that represent the result of recursion now apply the motive C to appropriate arguments. If Δ_i has an argument $(y : B)$, where B is not an application of D or a function returning such an application, Δ_i' still binds $(y : B)$ directly. If B is an application of D to parameters $a \ldots$ and indices $e \ldots$, then an additional binding $(y' : C\ e \ldots\ y)$ is inserted following y. Finally, if B is a function type $\Psi \to D\ a \ldots\ e \ldots$, the additional binding is $(y' : \Psi \to C\ e \ldots (y\ \overline{\Psi}))$.

Following these rules, the induction principle for Vec can be defined as follows.

```
indVec : (A : Set) →
         {n : Nat} →
         (xs : Vec A n) →
         (C : {n : Nat} → Vec A n → Set) →
         (base : C []) →
         (step : {n : Nat} → (x : A) →
                 (xs : Vec A n) → C xs → C (x :: xs)) →
         C xs
```

Automating the production of the dependent eliminator is an extension of the procedure for automating the production of the non-dependent eliminator. The computation rules for the induction principle are automated using the same approach as for the recursion principle. The generation of induction principles is carried out using `generateInd` (Fig. 7).

4   Code Generation for Higher Inductive Types

In Agda, there are no built-in primitives to support the definition of higher inductive types. However, we can still define a higher inductive type using rewrite rules, as described in Sect. 2.1. In this section, we discuss the automation of code generation for the elimination and the computation rules of higher inductive types. While the general formulation of higher inductive types is a subject of active research [17,19,21], we stick to a schema that follows a pattern similar to Basold et al.'s [7] general rules for higher inductive types.

4.1   Non-dependent Eliminators for HITs

The recursion principle of a higher inductive type G maps the points and paths of G to points and paths in an output type C. We extend the general schema of the recursion principle given in Sect. 3.1 by adding methods for path constructors (Fig. 8(a)).

$$
\begin{aligned}
G_{rec} : (a_1 : A_1) &\to \ldots \to (a_n : A_n) \to \\
(i_1 : I_1) &\to \ldots \to (i_m : I_m) \to \\
(tgt : G\, a_1 &\ldots a_n\, i_1\, \ldots\, i_n) \to \\
(C : Set) &\to \\
(f_1 : \Delta_1' \to C) &\ldots (f_r : \Delta_r' \to C) \to \\
(k_1 : \Delta_1' &\to (f_i \ldots) \equiv (f_j \ldots)) \to \\
&\vdots \\
(k_q : \Delta_q' &\to (f_i \ldots) \equiv (f_j \ldots)) \to \\
C&
\end{aligned}
$$

$$
\begin{aligned}
\beta G_{rec} : (a_1 : A_1) &\to \ldots \to (a_n : A_n) \to \\
(C : Set) &\to \\
(f_1 : \Delta_1' \to C) &\ldots (f_r : \Delta_r' \to C) \to \\
(k_1 : \Delta_1' &\to (f_i \ldots) \equiv (f_j \ldots)) \to \\
&\vdots \\
(k_q : \Delta_q' &\to (f_i \ldots) \equiv (f_j \ldots)) \to \\
ap\, (\lambda\, x.G_{rec}\, x\, C\, f_1\, &\ldots\, f_r\, k_1\, \ldots\, k_q) \\
(p_i \ldots) &\equiv (k_i \ldots)
\end{aligned}
$$

(a)   (b)

Fig. 8. Generic schema for recursion (a) and computation rule (b)

The schematic definition of G_{rec} supports only one-dimensional paths. The type of the method f_i for a point constructor g_i in G_{rec} is built the same way as for the normal inductive type D, as described in Sect. 3.1. The code generator builds the type of k_i, method for path constructor p_i in G_{rec}, by traversing the AST of p_i. The arguments of k_i are handled the same way as for the point constructor's method f_i. During the traversal, the code generator uses the base type recursor D_{rec} to map the point constructors g_i of G in the codomain of p_i to f_i. Determining the computation rules corresponding to points g_i is similar to the computation rules corresponding to constructors c_i of the inductive type D, except that there are additional methods to handle paths. Paths compute new paths; the computation rules that govern the interaction of recursors and paths p_i are named and postulated. They identify the action of the recursor on the path with the corresponding method. The computation rules corresponding to paths p_i are postulated as given in Fig. 8(b).

As an example, if the code for the circle HIT from Sect. 2.1 has been generated, and the type is called S, then the recursor needs a method for base and one for loop. The method for base should be an inhabitant of C. If it is called cbase, then the method for loop should be a path cbase $\equiv$ cbase. The types of the path methods depend on the values of the point methods. The code generator builds the type of loop's method by traversing the AST of loop's type, replacing references to point constructors with the result of applying the base type's recursor to the point methods. The recursion rule recS follows this pattern.

```
recS : S →
        (C : Set) →
        (cbase : C) →
        (cloop : cbase ≡ cbase) →
        C
```

The code generator builds the computation rule for the point constructor base using the same approach as described in Sect. 3.1 as if it were for the base type. Additionally, it includes variables in the clause definition for the path constructor loop. The code generator postulates the following computation rule βloop for the path constructor loop:

```
βloop : (C : Set) →
         (cbase : C) →
         (cloop : cbase ≡ cbase) →
         ap (λ x → recS x C cbase cloop) loop ≡ cloop
```

The application of function recS to the path loop substitutes the point base for the argument x and it evaluates to the path cloop in the output type C. In the tool, generateRecHit is used to build the elimination rule and the computation rules for points, and generateβRecHitPath is used to build the computation rules for paths (Fig. 7). The third argument to generateRecHit is the base type's recursor built using generateβRec that constructs the computation rules for points using rewrite rules. The parameter count is passed as the fourth argument.

4.2   Dependent Eliminators for HITs

The dependent eliminator for a higher inductive type G is a dependent function that maps an element g of G to an output type $C\,g$. The general schema for the induction principle of G is given in Fig. 9(a).

Similar to G_{rec}, the type of f_i is built the same way as for the normal inductive type D. The code generator builds the type of the method for path constructor p_i, called k_i, in G_{ind}, by traversing the AST of p_i. During the traversal, the code generator uses the base eliminator D_{ind} to map the point constructors g_i of G in the codomain of p_i to f_i. In the first argument to the identity type in the codomain of k_i, the code generator adds an application of transport to the motive C and the path p_i. The arguments of k_i are handled the same way as for f_i. The computation rules corresponding to paths p_i are postulated as given in Fig. 9(b).

For the type S with point constructor base and path constructor loop, to define a mapping indS : (x : S) → C x, we need cbase : C base and cloop : transport C loop cbase ≡ cbase, where cloop is a heterogeneous path transported over loop. The code generator builds the type of cloop by adding relevant type information to the type of loop. The type of the method for the path constructor cloop is derived by inserting a call to transport with arguments C, loop, and cbase. The code generator applies the base eliminator to map the point base to cbase during the construction of the codomain of cloop. The following declaration gives the type of indS.

$$G_{ind} : (a_1 : A_1) \to \ldots \to (a_n : A_n) \to$$
$$(i_1 : I_1) \to \ldots \to (i_m : I_m) \to$$
$$(tgt : G\, a_1 \ldots a_n\, i_1\ \ldots\ i_n) \to$$
$$(C : (i_1 : I_1) \to \ldots \to (i_m : I_m) \to$$
$$G\, a_1 \ldots a_n\, i_1 \ldots\ i_n \to$$
$$\text{Set}) \to$$
$$(f_1 : \Delta_1' \to C\, j_{11} \ldots j_{1p}\, (c_1\, \overline{\Delta_1})) \to$$
$$\vdots$$
$$(f_r : \Delta_r' \to C\, j_{r1} \ldots j_{rp}\, (c_r\, \overline{\Delta_r})) \to$$
$$(k_1 : \Delta_1' \to \text{transport}\, C\, p_1\, (f_i \ldots)$$
$$\equiv (f_j \ldots)) \to$$
$$\vdots$$
$$(k_q : \Delta_q' \to \text{transport}\, C\, p_q\, (f_i \ldots)$$
$$\equiv (f_j \ldots)) \to$$
$$C\, i_1 \ldots i_n\, tgt$$

(a)

$$\beta G_i : (a_1 : A_1) \to \ldots \to (a_n : A_n) \to$$
$$(C : (i_1 : I_1) \to \ldots \to (i_m : I_m) \to$$
$$G\, a_1 \ldots a_n\, i_1\ \ldots\ i_n \to$$
$$\text{Set}) \to$$
$$(f_1 : \Delta_1' \to C\, j_{11} \ldots j_{1p}\, (c_1\, \overline{\Delta_1})) \to$$
$$\vdots$$
$$(f_r : \Delta_r' \to C\, j_{r1} \ldots j_{rp}\, (c_r\, \overline{\Delta_r})) \to$$
$$(k_1 : \Delta_1' \to \text{transport}\, C\, p_1\, (f_i \ldots)$$
$$\equiv (f_j \ldots)) \to$$
$$\vdots$$
$$(k_r : \Delta_r' \to \text{transport}\, C\, p_r\, (f_i \ldots)$$
$$\equiv (f_j \ldots)) \to$$
$$\text{apd}\, (\lambda\, x\, .\, G_{ind}\, x\, C\, f_1\ \ldots\ f_r\, k_1\ \ldots\ k_r)$$
$$(p_i \ldots) \equiv (k_i \ldots)$$

(b)

Fig. 9. Generic schema for induction (a) and computation rule (b)

```
indS : (circle : S) →
       (C : S → Set) →
       (cbase : C base) →
       (cloop : transport C loop cbase ≡ cbase) →
       C circle
```

The computation rule for base, which defines the action of indS on base, is built using the same approach as for the non-dependent eliminator recS. The postulated computation rule iβloop for the path loop uses apd which gives the action of dependent function indS on the path loop.

```
iβloop : (C : S → Set) →
         (cbase : C base) →
         (cloop : transport C loop cbase ≡ cbase) →
         apd (λ x → indS x C cbase cloop) loop ≡ cloop
```

generateIndHit is used to build the elimination rule and the computation rules for points, and generateβIndHitPath is used to build the computation rules for paths (Fig. 7).

5 Applications

5.1 Patch Theory Revisited

We reimplemented Angiuli et al.'s patch theory [6] using our code generator[1] in Agda. We implemented basic patches such as the insertion of a string as line l_1 in a file and deletion of a line l_2 from a file. The functions implementing insertion

---

[1] Please see https://github.com/pavenvivek/WFLP-18.

and deletion in the universe are not bijective. So, we used Angiuli et al.'s patch history approach to encode non-bijective functions. According to this approach, we developed a separate higher inductive type `History` which serves as the types of patches. We also implemented patches involving encryption or decryption with cryptosystems like RSA and Paillier. In addition to easing the implementation difficulties of higher inductive types, the code generator greatly reduced the code size. The type definitions shrank from around 1500 to around 70 lines, resulting in a 60% decrease in the overall number of lines of code in the development.

5.2   Cryptographic Protocols

Vivekanandan [30] models certain cryptographic protocols using homotopy type theory, introducing a new approach to formally specifying cryptographic schemes using types. The work discusses modeling cryptDB [26] using a framework similar to Angiuli et al.'s patch theory. CryptDB employs layered encryption techniques and homomorphic encryption. We can implement cryptDB by modeling the database queries as paths in a higher inductive type and mapping the paths to the universe using singleton types [6]. The code generator can be applied to generate code for the higher inductive type representing cryptDB and its corresponding elimination and computation rules. By using the code generator, we can decrease the length and increase the readability of the definitions, hopefully making it more accessible to the broad cryptographic community.

6   Related Work

Kokke and Swierstra [20] implemented a library for proof search using Agda's old reflection primitives, from before it had elaborator reflection. They describe a Prolog interpreter in the style of Stutterheim et al. [28]. It employs a hint database and a customizable depth-first traversal, with lemmas to assist in the proof search.

Van der Walt and Swierstra [32] and van der Walt [31] discuss automating specific categories of proofs using proof by reflection. A key component of this proof technique is a means for converting an expression into a quoted representation. They automate this process, giving a user-defined datatype. Van der Walt [31] also gives an overview of Agda's old metaprogramming tools.

Datatype-generic programming [4,10,22] via representation types allows defining a single function over an entire class of datatypes at once, saving developers the effort of implementing the operation for datatypes specific to their programs. As Agda's reflection library evolves and the internal representation of datatypes changes, the tool described in this paper requires maintenance work. A future direction would be to work with a representation type extended with support for higher inductive types. In such case, the only metaprograms necessary are those that convert to and from the representation type. The metaprograms automating the elimination rules do not need to change as long as the representation type is kept the same.

Ongoing work on cubical type theories [5,15,16] provides a computational interpretation of univalence and HITs. We strenuously hope that these systems quickly reach maturity, rendering our code generator obsolete. In the meantime, however, these systems are not yet as mature as Agda.

7   Conclusion and Future Work

We presented a code generator that generates the encodings of higher inductive types, developed using Agda's new support for Idris-style elaborator reflection. In particular, the tool generates the dependent and non-dependent elimination rules and the computational rules for 1-dimensional higher inductive types. This syntax is greatly simplified with respect to writing the encoding by hand. We demonstrated an extensive reduction in code size by employing our tool. Next, we intend to extend the tool to support higher-dimensional paths in the definition of HITs, bringing its benefits to a wider class of problems.

Acknowledgements. The author is greatly indebted to David Christiansen for his contributions and advice, and the anonymous reviewers for their valuable review comments.

References

1. Agda's Documentation (2018). http://agda.readthedocs.io/en/latest/language/reflection.html
2. Abbott, M., Altenkirch, T., Ghani, N.: Containers: constructing strictly positive types. Theor. Comput. Sci. **342**(1), 3–27 (2005)
3. Altenkirch, T.: Containers in homotopy type theory, talk at Mathematical Structures of Computation, January 2014
4. Altenkirch, T., McBride, C., Morris, P.: Generic programming with dependent types. In: Backhouse, R., Gibbons, J., Hinze, R., Jeuring, J. (eds.) SSDGP 2006. LNCS, vol. 4719, pp. 209–257. Springer, Heidelberg (2007). https://doi.org/10.1007/978-3-540-76786-2_4
5. Angiuli, C., Harper, R., Wilson, T.: Computational higher-dimensional type theory. In: Proceedings of the 44th ACM SIGPLAN Symposium on Principles of Programming Languages, POPL, Paris, France, pp. 680–693, January 2017
6. Angiuli, C., Morehouse, E., Licata, D.R., Harper, R.: Homotopical patch theory. In: Proceedings of the 19th ACM SIGPLAN International Conference on Functional Programming, ICFP, Gothenburg, Sweden, September 2014
7. Basold, H., Geuvers, H., van der Weide, N.: Higher inductive types in programming. J. Univ. Comput. Sci. **23**(1), 63–88 (2017)
8. Brunerie, G.: Custom definitional equalities in agda, talk at Univalent Foundations and Proof Assistants session of the 5th International Congress on Mathematical Software, July 2016
9. Cavallo, E., Harper, R.: Computational higher type theory iv: inductive types, July 2018. arXiv:1801.01568
10. Chapman, J., Évariste Dagand, P., McBride, C., Morris, P.: The gentle art of levitation. In: Proceedings of the 15th ACM SIGPLAN International Conference on Functional Programming, ICFP, Baltimore, USA, September 2010

11. Christiansen, D.: Practical reflection and metaprogramming for dependent types. Ph.D. thesis, IT University of Copenhagen (2016)
12. Christiansen, D., Brady, E.: Elaborator reflection: extending Idris in Idris. In: Proceedings of the 21st ACM SIGPLAN International Conference on Functional Programming, ICFP, Nara, Japan, September 2016
13. Cockx, J., Abel, A.: Sprinkles of extensionality for your vanilla type theory. In: 22nd International Conference on Types for Proofs and Programs, May 2016
14. Cockx, J., Devriese, D., Piessens, F.: Pattern matching without K. In: Proceedings of the 19th ACM SIGPLAN International Conference on Functional Programming, ICFP, Gothenburg, Sweden, pp. 257–268, September 2014
15. Cohen, C., Coquand, T., Huber, S., Mörtberg, A.: Cubical type theory: a constructive interpretation of the univalence axiom. In: Proceedings of the 21st International Conference on Types for Proofs and Programs, Tallinn, Estonia, May 2015
16. Coquand, T., Huber, S., Mörtberg, A.: On higher inductive types in cubical type theory (2018). arXiv:1802.01170
17. Dybjer, P., Moeneclaey, H.: Finitary higher inductive types in the groupoid model. Electro. Notes Theor. Comput. Sci. **336**, 119–134 (2018)
18. Ebner, G., Ullrich, S., Roesch, J., Avigad, J., de Moura, L.: A metaprogramming framework for formal verification. In: Proceedings of the 22nd ACM SIGPLAN International Conference on Functional Programming, ICFP, September 2017
19. Kaposi, A., Kovács, A.: A syntax for higher inductive-inductive types. In: Proceedings of the 3rd International Conference on Formal Structures for Computation and Deduction, FSCD, Oxford, UK, July 2018
20. Kokke, P., Swierstra, W.: Auto in agda. In: Hinze, R., Voigtländer, J. (eds.) MPC 2015. LNCS, vol. 9129, pp. 276–301. Springer, Cham (2015). https://doi.org/10.1007/978-3-319-19797-5_14
21. Lumsdaine, P.L., Shulman, M.: Semantics of higher inductive types, May 2017. arXiv:1705.07088
22. Löh, A., Magalhães, J.P.: Generic programming with indexed functors. In: Proceedings of the 7th ACM SIGPLAN Workshop on Generic Programming, WGP, September 2011
23. Mimram, S., Giusto, C.D.: A categorical theory of patches. Electron. Notes Theor. Comput. Sci. **298**, 283–307 (2013)
24. Norell, U.: Towards a practical programming language based on dependent type theory. Ph.D. thesis, Chalmers University of Technology, Göteborg, Sweden (2007)
25. Pelayo, A., Warren, M.: Homotopy type theory and Voevodsky's univalent foundations, October 2012. arXiv:1210.5658
26. Popa, R.A., Redfield, C.M., Zeldovich, N., Balakrishnan, H.: CryptDB: protecting confidentiality with encrypted query processing. In: Proceedings of the 23rd ACM Symposium on Operating Systems Principles, SOSP, Cascais, Portugal (2011)
27. Roundy, D.: Darcs: distributed version management in haskell. In: Proceedings of the 2005 ACM SIGPLAN Workshop on Haskell, September 2005
28. Stutterheim, J., Swierstra, W., Swierstra, S.D.: Forty hours of declarative programming: teaching prolog at the junior college utrecht. Electron. Proc. Theor. Comput. Sci. **106**, 50–62 (2013)
29. The Univalent Foundations Program: Homotopy Type Theory: Univalent Foundations of Mathematics. Institute for Advanced Study (2013). https://homotopytypetheory.org/book

30. Vivekanandan, P.: HoTT-Crypt: a study in homotopy type theory based on cryptography. In: Short Paper proceedings of the 22nd International Conference on Logic for Programming, Artificial Intelligence and Reasoning, LPAR-22, Ethiopia, November 2018. https://doi.org/10.29007/tvpp
31. van der Walt, P.: Reflection in agda. Master's thesis. Utrecht University, Utrecht, Netherlands (2012)
32. van der Walt, P., Swierstra, W.: Engineering proof by reflection in agda. In: Hinze, R. (ed.) IFL 2012. LNCS, vol. 8241, pp. 157–173. Springer, Heidelberg (2013). https://doi.org/10.1007/978-3-642-41582-1_10

Debugging and Testing

Measuring Coverage of Prolog Programs
Using Mutation Testing

Alexandros Efremidis[1], Joshua Schmidt[1](✉) [iD], Sebastian Krings[2] [iD],
and Philipp Körner[1] [iD]

[1] Institut für Informatik, Universität Düsseldorf,
Universitätsstr. 1, 40225 Düsseldorf, Germany
{alefr101,joshua.schmidt,p.koerner}@uni-duesseldorf.de
[2] Niederrhein University of Applied Sciences, Mönchengladbach, Germany
sebastian.krings@hs-niederrhein.de

Abstract. Testing is an important aspect in professional software development, both to avoid and identify bugs as well as to increase maintainability. However, increasing the number of tests beyond a reasonable amount hinders development progress. To decide on the completeness of a test suite, many approaches to assert test coverage have been suggested. Yet, frameworks for logic programs remain scarce.

In this paper, we introduce a framework for Prolog programs measuring test coverage using mutations. We elaborate on the main ideas of mutation testing and transfer them to logic programs. To do so, we discuss the usefulness of different mutations in the context of Prolog and empirically evaluate them in a new mutation testing framework on different examples.

1 Introduction and Motivation

Testing is an important aspect in professional software development, both to avoid and identify bugs as well as to increase maintainability. However, tests themselves again consist of source code and possibly further artifacts that need to be maintained. In modern software systems, code only needed for testing purposes can contribute between 33 and 50% to the overall source code of a project [5,19]. In consequence, increasing the number of tests beyond a reasonable amount again hinders development progress. The key to an efficient test suite is to assert the code coverage of existing tests. That means, to measure to what extent production code is tested. Afterwards, one can remove tests that do not cover additional aspects and add tests where code is uncovered. In Sect. 2, we present different approaches to measure code coverage.

This paper makes two contributions: Firstly, we discuss several program transformations used for mutation testing in Sect. 3, inspired by Toaldo and Vergilio [23], and argue whether we deem them to be sensible or not. Secondly, we provide an implementation of a framework featuring several mutations. Our framework is publicly available for SWI and SICStus Prolog and is presented

© Springer Nature Switzerland AG 2019
J. Silva (Ed.): WFLP 2018, LNCS 11285, pp. 39–55, 2019.
https://doi.org/10.1007/978-3-030-16202-3_3

in Sect. 4. In Sect. 5, this framework is used to evaluate whether our intuitive classification of mutations as sensible or foolish is correct by measuring the test coverage of several selected examples. Finally, we discuss related and future work in Sects. 6 and 7.

2   Code Coverage Metrics

Different metrics for code coverage, mostly differing in granularity, have been suggested and are at least partially applicable to Prolog:

Predicate, Clause, Sub-Goal Coverage: A simple way to gain some insight into code coverage is to execute tests and trace which code was executed. This can be done on different levels, that is, on the level of sub-goals, clauses or predicates. Moreover, there are different metrics to decide whether a specific level is covered. For instance, a sub-goal, clause or predicate can be regarded as covered if it succeeded at some point during execution. In this paper, we use a more restricted metric. We regard a clause to be covered if all sub-goals are covered, and, analogously, regard a predicate to be covered if all clauses are covered. Success on each level can be traced, for instance, by inserting tracing code via term expansion (source-to-source transformation) as done by Krings [8], using hooks into the Prolog interpreter (as done in SWI-Prolog's [24] testing framework PlUnit) or executing the code in a meta-interpreter.

Branch Coverage: Instead of considering individual program points covered if reached, branch coverage considers if branching points such as if-statements have been executed both ways. In particular, this implies that each condition has been evaluated to both true and false at least once. For Prolog, this could be implemented either on the level of conditions, but also on the level of individual calls. In this case, we would expect the test suite to make each call fail and succeed at least once. This would be harder to reach than the predicate coverage introduced above, given that each predicate would additionally have to fail at least once. In case of Prolog, one also has to decide if and how redos of predicates should be counted.

Path Coverage: Path coverage abstracts further from individual program points. Instead of enforcing each condition to be evaluated in both directions, path coverage considers all combinations of decision, that is, all paths through a predicate. As above, one has to decide how redos should be counted, that is, if each combination of redo and later succeed is an individual path.

MC/DC Analysis: A more sophisticated and popular approach is coverage analysis via MC/DC (modified condition/decision coverage). In order for code to be considered covered by MC/DC, all conditions and decisions have to take all outcomes and each condition of a decision has to independently influence the overall outcome of the decision. MC/DC analysis can be implemented via term expansion as well.

2.1 Mutation Testing

The idea behind *mutation testing* is to determine the test coverage by asserting the effectiveness of a test suite on modified versions of the source code under test. To do so, syntactically not equivalent versions of the source code, called *mutants*, are generated which are intended to be semantically not equivalent to the original code. We view two programs to be semantically not equivalent if they produce a different output for the same input at least once. For instance, a mutant is generated by replacing an equality with an inequality. Afterwards, all tests are executed.

Once a semantically not equivalent mutant is considered, we expect at least one test to change its outcome. That means, at least one positive test fails or a negative test succeeds. If this is the case, the mutant is called *dead*, indicating that the test suite covers the mutated clause. Otherwise, the mutant is called *alive*, indicating a lack of coverage.

To finally determine the coverage, a mutation testing tool will run the tests on the mutant, check the result and reset the mutant to the original code for the next iteration. This workflow continues until no further mutation is possible. Afterwards, the so-called *mutation score*, i.e., the number of dead mutants divided by the number of generated mutants, is computed. The mutation score can be used as a measure for the test coverage.

As one can see, it is crucial to compute mutants that are indeed not equivalent regarding their semantics, as a semantically equivalent mutant will always be considered alive. In consequence, the mutation score becomes less meaningful with an increasing amount of semantically equivalent mutants. However, deciding whether two programs are semantically equivalent is, in general, undecidable [18].

To counter this, it is possible to approximate the equivalence of two source code snippets by constraining the domains of used arguments, as for example suggested by Offutt and Pan [16]. Afterwards, their equivalence is checked exhaustively within these restricted domains. Of course, this might result in detecting false positives depending on the chosen domains.

In consequence, special care has to be taken when selecting mutation operators to be applied to the source code [6]. While it is only seldom possible to find mutation operators without risk of generating semantically equivalent mutants, the risk of semantically identical mutants differs between operators.

Libraries of useful mutations have been suggested for other languages, such as the Javalanche framework [20] and PIT [3] for Java, Mull [4] for LLVM, MuCheck [12] for Haskell, and many more [7]. Of course, some mutations like changing relational and arithmetic operators or constant values are similar in different programming languages. However, due to the different nature of Prolog, those libraries cannot easily be adapted to Prolog. In Prolog, a predicate is either true or false and values are input and output via its arguments. Instead of writing a sequence of instructions like in imperative programming languages, one describes the solution for a problem declarative. Prolog predicates do not determine which arguments are inputs or outputs and can possibly be used in several directions like the predicate append/3. If calling append([1], [2], R), the two lists are concatenated and we derive R = [1, 2]. If calling append(A, B, [1, 2]), we derive ground lists A and B that can be concatenated to the list [1, 2]. Here, we are able to derive all solutions via backtracking. To that effect, a mutation like changing return values as PIT suggests for Java is not applicable in Prolog by default. Besides that, there are more mutations that are specific for certain programming languages like replacing constructor calls with null values in Java or type-aware function replacements in Haskell.

3 Mutation Operators

In the following, we introduce our selection of mutation operators, which is based on the selection suggested by Toaldo and Vergilio [23]. We distinguish between *sensible* operators, which we expect to yield semantically different programs, and *foolish* operators, where programs are expected to retain the original semantics in most cases. For most mutations, examples that represent idiomatic Prolog code are given. In all cases, we expect existing test cases to be reasonable: for example, if the actual test initially fails, backtracking should be avoided and the test should fail. Furthermore, the test should compare with a (mostly) ground term instead of allowing unification generously. Test cases can either prove or disprove a goal. When applying mutation testing, we expect all tests to succeed. A test disproving a goal should also succeed by checking for failure.

3.1 Sensible Mutations

From our experience, we consider the following transformations to be sensible:

Predicate Removal: Deleting a predicate ϕ, more precisely all clauses of ϕ with the same arity, is a sensible mutation because at least one test should fail, otherwise ϕ is not tested at all. As long as ϕ is not dead code, the semantics change by removing ϕ due to the occurring existence error. This mutation is comparable to predicate coverage, as we expected at least one test to call ϕ.

Disjunction to Conjunction: By mutating a disjunction to a conjunction, only a subset of queries can succeed: now, they have to satisfy both branches. Similar to branch coverage, we expect tests to cover each branch individually. In particular, there should exist a test where the first alternative fails whereas the second succeeds. An example is given in Fig. 1.

In propositional logic, replacing a disjunction with a conjunction does not necessarily change the semantics since a disjunction also provides the case where both arguments are true. Prolog, on the other hand, does not execute the case

```
is_empty(L) :-                          is_empty(L) :-
    L == [], ! ; fail.                      L == [], ! , fail.
```

Fig. 1. Changing semantics by replacing a disjunction with a conjunction.

that both disjuncts are true. Instead, Prolog introduces a choice point leading to backtracking when searching for another solution. This choice point is not retained by the mutant. In practice, the calls within a disjunction often refer to the same variables providing alternative results. To that effect, we expect replacing a disjunction with a conjunction to alter the semantics in most cases, and, thus, to be sensible in Prolog.

Conjunction to Disjunction: Replacing a conjunction by a disjunction does not necessarily change the semantics in propositional logic. For instance, if $A \wedge B$ is true, the disjunction $A \vee B$ will be true as well. If $A \wedge B$ is false, the disjunction will be true if A or B is true, which changes the semantics for all interpretations but $A = \bot \wedge B = \bot$. In Prolog however, the data flow of a predicate often consists of passing arguments between predicates within a conjunction as can be seen in Fig. 2. In this context, replacing a conjunction by a disjunction will most likely change the semantics since the execution of this predicate will terminate after executing the first argument of a disjunction but initializing a choice point. This choice point also applies if a disjunction fails. In case both arguments fail or succeed and do not pass arguments among each other or depend on any shared state, this mutation will not change the semantics like in propositional logic.

```
flatten([L|Ls], FlatL) :-               flatten([L|Ls], FlatL) :-
    flatten(L, NewL),                       flatten(L, NewL) ;
    flatten(Ls, NewLs),                     flatten(Ls, NewLs) ,
    append(NewL, NewLs, FlatL).             append(NewL, NewLs, FlatL).
```

Fig. 2. Changing semantics by replacing a conjunction with a disjunction.

Atom or Variable to Anonymous Variable: Turning an atom or a variable to an anonymous variable causes that certain values are no longer ground which most likely changes the semantics. Yet, tests may still pass if recursive cases are not tested. Nevertheless, the predicate might be too complicated, taking a variable as parameter that is not used within a clause. Moreover, a variable might be a singleton one. In both cases, replacing this variable by an anonymous one will not necessarily change the semantics of this specific clause as can be seen in Fig. 3. However, assuming that a clause does not define singleton or unnecessary variables, this mutation will change the semantics in most cases. These false positives still bear meaning about code quality, where singleton variables and unnecessary parameters qualify as "code smell" that should be avoided.

```
remove_dups([X,X|T],W,Res) :-          remove_dups([X,X|T],_,Res) :-
    remove_dups([X|T],W,Res).              remove_dups([X|T],_,Res).
```

Fig. 3. A predicate retaining its semantics when replacing a variable with an anonymous one.

Interchanging Arithmetic Operators: When replacing two arithmetic operators with each other (e.g. replacing + with *), a sensible mutant is likely to be created. Since there are many operators to choose from it is important to not create multiple mutants to avoid a disproportional impact on the overall mutation score. For instance, if an arithmetic operation is well tested, every mutation should fail. Using several mutations would lead to a higher mutation score, although the branch is already ensured to be covered by a single mutation. On the other hand, other branches without heavy arithmetic, where only few sensible mutation are applicable, would be valued lower due to the branch's lower amount of mutations.

Interchanging Relational Operators: The mutation of relational operators is also sensible but not in every case. It is not necessarily sensible to mutate A \== B to A > B because multiple cases exist where the semantics do not change, that is, every case where A > B is true. Moreover, we would need to know the types of the arguments in order to implement this mutation since arithmetic operators are only defined for integers, whereas non-equality is defined for all Prolog terms as well. A sensible mutant is created by negating relational operators (e.g. < to >=). By negating a relational operator, the semantics is inverted: every case which was true before will be false now and vice versa.

Furthermore, we decided to independently check edge cases of relational operators. For instance, by mutating A >= B to A == B. We then expect at least one test case to fail. Otherwise, no test case uses any values where A and B are not equal, which is either a bug or uncovered behavior. If only negating the relational operator for this example, a single test case using the same values for A and B will always lead to a dead mutant although there is no test case using different values for A and B. We thus deem the mutations covering the edge cases of relational operators to be sensible.

Negating a Predicate: In Prolog, the negation of a predicate is implemented using negation as failure [2]. For instance, the goal \+(p,q) succeeds iff (p,q) cannot be proven by resolution. In propositional logic, the goal could be simplified by applying De Morgan's laws resulting in a disjunction with negated literals. Hence, we decided to directly negate operators where applicable instead of using Prolog's negation. For instance, we change disjunctions to conjunctions or negate relational operators as described above.

The data flow of a predicate in Prolog is usually defined by passing data among predicates within a conjunction. Disjunctions can be used to provide different clauses for a predicate. Negating a predicate within a conjunction or disjunction likely manipulates a program's data flow due to the forced backtracking and possibly occurring side effects (see Fig. 4). We thus negate predicates within conjunctions or disjunctions using Prolog's negation as failure. In this context, we do not negate predicates which we have considered independently like relational operators in case Prolog's negation has the same effect. For instance, mutating a predicate A >= B to A < B and \+(A >= B) would result in equivalent mutations. We restrict this mutation to predicates within conjunctions or disjunctions since negating the only goal within a predicate's body would be equivalent to removing the whole predicate in case the goal has no side effects.

```
rev([H|T],Rev) :-              rev([H|T],Rev) :-
    rev(T,NT) ,                    \+ rev(T,NT) ,
    append(NT,[H],Rev).            append(NT,[H],Rev).
```

Fig. 4. An example for negating a predicate resulting in different semantics.

3.2   Foolish Mutations

There are also several mutations suggested by Toaldo and Vergilio that we consider to be foolish. Our reasoning is the following:

Clause Reversal: By reversing the order of clauses of a given predicate, semantically different mutants are most likely just an infinite loop in case a predicate is non-deterministic (see Fig. 5). The creation of a non-terminating loop has no value for calculating the mutation score, because one cannot tell whether the mutated branch is tested or not due to the non-termination. Therefore, we consider the result of a test that exceeds a reasonable time limit and a failing test to be different. Otherwise, the mutation score would possibly be corrupted.

Furthermore, reversing the order of a predicate's clauses does not change the semantics in case the predicate is purely logical and deterministic, that is, each clause of the predicate validates its inputs (see Fig. 6).

```
add_to_list(L, _, 0, L).          add_to_list(L, E, C, R) :-
add_to_list(L, E, C, R) :-            CC is C - 1,
    CC is C - 1,                      LL = [E|L],
    LL = [E|L],                       add_to_list(LL, E, CC, R).
    add_to_list(LL, E, CC, R).    add_to_list(L, _, 0, L).
```

Fig. 5. An example for a non-terminating loop with reversed clause ordering.

```
is_list([]).                        is_list([_|T]) :-
is_list([_|T]) :-                       is_list(T).
    is_list(T).                     is_list([]).
```

Fig. 6. An example for an equivalent program with reversed clause ordering.

Cut Transformations: Inserting, removing and permuting cuts often does not cause a change in semantics. In Prolog, there are two kinds of cuts: A cut is called *red*, when its removal would create a semantically not equivalent program. Predicates with red cuts are, thus, not pure in a logical sense and, per definition, behave differently without their cuts. All other cuts are called *green*: while not affecting the semantics of the program, they are used in order to increase performance. In practice however, it is difficult to efficiently decide whether a cut is red or green.

In the context of mutation testing, we only want to mutate red cuts in order to change the semantics. Shifting a red cut to a subsequent position is unlikely to change the semantics since the condition of the cut has still been evaluated. Thus, shifting red cuts to a prior position within the predicate is most likely to be reasonable for mutation testing, because the original condition after which a cut is called has not been evaluated. By preventing backtracking, the semantics of the predicate is likely to be changed as can be seen in Fig. 7.

```
filter(Pred,[H|T],[H|NT]) :-        filter(Pred,[H|T],[H|NT]) :- ! ,
    call(Pred,H) , ! ,                  call(Pred,H) ,
    filter(Pred,T,NT).                  filter(Pred,T,NT).
```

Fig. 7. An example for moving a red cut resulting in different semantics.

4   A Mutation Testing Framework

In the following, we will take a closer look at the implementation of our framework. As it relies on term expansion, the framework must be loaded before the module under test. Before the tool is able to begin with the mutation testing process, some setup routines are executed: in order to generate sensible mutants, the tool collects the source code's predicates during term expansion. Moreover, the term expander adds a *dynamic* declaration for all predicates that may be modified, in order to be able to use retraction and assertion to create mutants. Then, the actual tests are executed on the original code to ensure that every test passes. Otherwise, the criterion that tests pass on the mutant is obviously flawed. Furthermore, the overall runtime of the tests is stored in order to derive a reasonable timeout. As mutations might result in infinite loops, tests must be executed with a timeout on mutants.

The process can be divided into the following procedures (also cf. Fig. 8):

1. find a suitable mutant, i.e., a predicate where a new mutation is applicable
2. generate a mutated predicate
3. retract the predicate and assert the mutated one
4. run the tests and check for failing tests or timeouts
5. restore the original predicate

This workflow continues until no other suitable mutation can be found.

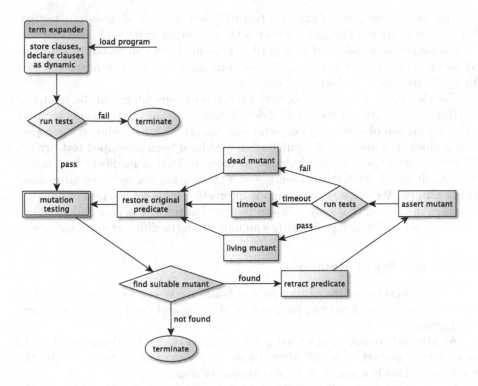

Fig. 8. The framework's workflow diagram.

Particular care has to be taken when manipulating a single clause of a predicate: the order of all clauses should (usually) be retained, but new facts can only be asserted either at the top or bottom of the predicate. The tool thus retracts and re-asserts the entire predicate, i.e., all of its clauses, at once.

The mutation score is later calculated on the basis of all collected results. Mutants are labeled either as *dead* when at least a single test has failed or as *alive* when all tests have passed.

However, a mutation may have caused an infinite loop. To counter this, tests on a mutant are executed with a timeout which is defined by doubling the original runtime. Mutants which exceeded their test runtime are labeled as *timeouts*. In general, it is undecidable whether an actual infinite loop was encountered or if the mutant just runs significantly longer.

To calculate the mutation score, mutants labeled as timeouts are not considered. We thus deem the result of a test exceeding a time limit to be different from a failing test. Otherwise, the mutation score might be corrupted in case of detecting false positives caused by a significantly longer runtime.

5 Empirical Evaluation

In this section, we aim to evaluate two different aspects of mutation testing. Firstly, we verify our claims from Sect. 3 by measuring living and dead mutants on several pieces of code that we regard as reasonably tested. Secondly, the overall mutation scores for these programs are compared with the coverage computed by predicate, clause and sub-goal coverage.

For the evaluation, we use several Prolog programs which can be found on GitHub[1] along with a more detailed description. Most of the programs are part of an evaluation of different interpreter designs [11]. We have chosen these programs since they are part of a publication and have been developed test driven. Therefore, we expect these programs to have at least a mediocre test coverage. Additionally, we test the coverage of a translation between two formalisms (`alloy2b`) [9]. We think this program is interesting for a comparison of different coverage metrics since it only contains integration tests. The code will thus not be tested in detail which probably has an impact on the different coverage scores.

5.1 Sensibility of Mutations

A detailed overview of the results for our benchmarks can be found in Table 1, where for each considered file, the amount of living and dead mutants are given per mutation.

As claimed, removing a tested predicate always creates dead mutants. In cases where mutants are still alive, there simply existed no test case for the predicates. This is a mutation that is obviously sensible.

In our benchmarks, disjunctions have been fairly scarce; this is due to the fact that usually two separate clauses are preferred. However, no mutants on the few disjunctions survived the testing, so it seems to be as sensible as claimed. Changing conjunctions to disjunctions, however, generates more living mutants than expected. Apparently, this mutation is not as sensible as assumed.

There are a few instances of living mutants after negating a unification: e.g., in the case of the `fifteen_puzzle` data set, the only unification unifies a potential solution to the actual solution as a condition to terminate. Since the implemented algorithms are expected to always find a solution, terminating with a wrong solution after mutation is not caught. Overall, it still seems to be a sensible mutation for most applications.

For the considered programs, negating predicates within conjunctions and disjunctions results in a very small amount of living mutants. As this is fairly

---

[1] https://github.com/hhu-stups/prolog-mutation-testing.

Table 1. Overview of living (first number)/dead (second number) mutants in real-world examples. Timeouts are not considered.

Mutation	ast_interpreter	compiler	parser	rational_trees	rt_bytecode	alloy2b	fifteen_puzzle
remove predicate	0/3	4/11	0/5	0/5	0/4	8/68	4/17
; to ,	0/2	0/2	0/3	0/2	0/1	1/15	1/0
, to ;	0/30	10/34	1/14	4/12	12/31	38/245	22/22
= to \=	0/1	0/2	0/0	0/1	0/0	4/51	1/0
\= to =	0/0	0/0	0/0	0/0	0/0	0/1	0/0
=:= to =\=	0/0	0/0	0/0	0/0	0/0	0/0	0/0
=\= to =:=	0/0	0/0	0/0	0/0	0/0	0/0	0/0
== to \==	0/2	0/0	0/0	0/3	0/1	1/2	0/0
\== to ==	0/0	0/0	0/0	0/0	0/0	0/0	0/0
> to =<	0/0	0/0	0/0	0/0	0/0	0/2	1/2
>= to <	0/0	0/4	0/7	0/0	0/0	0/0	0/0
< to >=	0/0	0/2	0/0	0/0	0/0	0/1	0/1
=< to >	0/0	0/0	2/5	0/0	0/0	0/0	0/1
+ to -	0/0	0/6	0/0	0/0	0/0	0/2	0/2
- to +	0/0	4/35	0/0	0/5	0/0	0/1	0/2
* to +	0/0	0/0	0/0	0/0	0/0	0/0	0/0
/ to -	0/0	0/0	0/0	0/0	0/0	0/0	0/0
> to ==	0/0	0/0	0/0	0/0	0/0	0/2	1/2
>= to ==	0/0	0/4	2/5	0/0	0/0	0/0	0/0
< to ==	0/0	0/2	0/0	0/0	0/0	0/1	0/1
=< to ==	0/0	0/0	2/5	0/0	0/0	0/0	0/1
increase number	0/0	10/34	11/3	0/0	0/15	9/151	2/30
decrease number	0/0	9/35	12/2	0/0	1/14	10/151	4/28
negate predicate	0/19	6/24	0/7	0/9	2/29	15/102	6/22
true to false	0/3	0/2	0/0	0/2	0/0	1/2	0/0
false to true	0/3	1/2	0/0	0/0	0/0	8/0	0/0
var to _	33/184	122/245	0/69	5/103	133/252	244/1327	95/138
atom to _	0/0	1/2	0/0	0/4	1/3	48/185	3/0
[] to _	0/1	12/6	3/0	0/1	2/1	42/51	11/1
permute cut	1/0	4/1	0/1	2/0	16/0	18/21	1/3
reverse predicate	3/0	13/2	3/2	5/0	4/0	38/22	18/0

close to sub-goal coverage, we think that they might be created by uncovered code instead of false positives.

Changing variables to anonymous variables results in a fairly large amount of mutants in many cases, yet the mutation is applicable in a significantly larger amount of places as well. There is a good chance that tests do not cover all variables, in particular where entire predicates remain uncovered. Overall, this mutation seems to be sensible as well.

As expected, permuting cuts to an earlier position and reversing clauses of a predicate often results in semantically equivalent code.

Unfortunately, the selected examples do not use many arithmetic or relational operators. For most of these examples, however, there is no difference between negating a relational operator and using only the edge case. Only the mutation >= to == seems to be more sensible than using the negated operator for the parser example, that is >= to <. Here, two mutations stay alive indicating that there is indeed code that is not covered by any test.

Overall, our reasoning in Sect. 3 seems to be supported by our measurements. The only unexpected outcome is changing conjunctions to disjunctions. We think that specific tests are not as good as we initially expected and succeed for not equivalent mutations that cause variables being uninstantiated. For instance, if a unit test verifies the value of a variable using the Prolog unification (=/2) rather than equality (==/2), a predicate returning a variable will pass this test. When passing arguments between two predicates within a conjunction, the choice point introduced by a disjunction possibly causes uninstantiated variables. Another reason could be that arguments are not passed directly within a single but several conjunctions. Then, the mutation of a single conjunction does not necessarily change the semantics.

Yet, for example, mutations concerning arithmetic or relational operators are not covered by our benchmarks representatively. For these transformations, further code examples are required.

5.2   Comparison with Predicate and Clause Coverage

In the following, we compare the coverage of different Prolog modules using the coverage tools of SWI[2] and SICStus[3] Prolog as well as the introduced mutation testing framework. To give a short impression of the complexity of a program, we list the number of predicates, clauses and lines of code for each Prolog program in Table 2.

The coverage tool of SICStus Prolog measures how many times specific parts of the program, referred to as coverage sites, were executed. According to the documentation of SICStus, a coverage site corresponds to all predicate calls like in *trace* mode. In consequence, there are different ways of interpreting the coverage results of the SICStus Prolog coverage analysis. First, we compute the coverage on the level of clauses, that is, we view a predicate's clause to be uncovered if any coverage site within this clause is indicated to be uncovered. Second, we compute the coverage on the level of predicates which we view as uncovered if they contain an uncovered clause. Third, we compute a more detailed sub-goal coverage where we view each sub-goal independently.

The coverage tool of SWI Prolog behaves similarly and computes the predicate coverage. In the following, we will thus only refer to clause and predicate coverage without distinguishing between SWI and SICStus Prolog.

For two source files, we encountered technical issues with our mutation testing framework. Both programs rely on writing and consulting Prolog files at runtime. Yet, when mutating the code, the corresponding streams might not be closed properly, resulting in an error caused by holding too many file handles simultaneously.

---

[2] http://www.swi-prolog.org/pldoc/man?section=cover.

[3] https://sicstus.sics.se/sicstus/docs/4.3.2/html/sicstus/Coverage-Analysis.html.

Table 2. Comparison of prolog coverage tools

Prolog file	LoC	Predicates	Clauses	Clause coverage	Predicate coverage	Sub-goal coverage	Mutation coverage
ast_interpreter	107	2	20	100.00%	100.00%	100.00%	88.10%
compiler	165	15	42	80.95%	62.50%	86.04%	69.90%
parser	80	38	16	100.00%	100.00%	100.00%	92.20%
rational_trees	39	4	10	100.00%	100.00%	100.00%	96.50%
rt_bytecode	105	4	33	93.93%	50.00%	95.24%	70.10%
alloy2b	725	74	198	84.41%	75.95%	87.68%	80.20%
fifteen_puzzle	161	21	44	77.27%	67.10%	82.28%	70.40%

Overall, the results are non-binary. In most cases, the results are similar to the clause coverage approach. For some files, our framework reports a higher score than predicate coverage. Yet, it is able to find uncovered instances where all other approaches claim perfect coverage. In general, no approach can fully substitute the others. Thus, we recommend to use mutation testing as an additional tool.

A rather unsatisfying result, however, is that for now living mutants require manual review in order to determine whether they are semantically equivalent to the original code. While this problem is generally undecidable, techniques from *declarative debugging*[4] [15] could be used to offer tool support as follows.

The idea behind declarative debugging in Prolog is to examine the proof tree [14] computed during execution. Each node inside the tree represents an atomic goal that succeeded. Calls are nested, i.e., the children of a node are the successful subgoals taken from the body of the predicate used to prove said goal.

Declarative debugging now classifies these nodes as either being *correct* (i.e., the goal is valid and all instances are true with respect to the intention of the programmer) or *erroneous* (i.e., not valid). Using this information, a declarative debugger can identify bugs, i.e., instances which are not supposed to be true in the intended interpretation, yet they are. Furthermore, it can use the proof tree to trace the location of programming errors.

In the context of mutation testing, we know several goals to be *correct*, as they have been traversed by the initial, successful, test run. Furthermore, we know where mutations took place and which calls should not be *errorneous*. Hence, the results of mutation testing can be used to provide input to a declarative debugger which could now be used to identify the root cause of a mutation being alive and help to distinguish between foolish mutations and missing test cases.

6   Related Work

As already stated in Sect. 3, different mutation operators for Prolog have been outlined by Toaldo and Vergilio [23]. We have evaluated each reasonable mutation independently using several examples in order to classify them as either

---

[4] Initially named *algorithmic debugging* by Shapiro [21].

sensible or foolish in Sect. 3. Our evaluation performed in Sect. 5.1 has shown that not all of these mutations are efficient, for instance, they might generate numerous semantically equivalent mutants. We have compared our implementation with several different coverage metrics in Sect. 5.2. Moreover, we have incorporated new mutations and made our implementation publicly available both for SICStus and SWI Prolog.

Of course, mutation testing can be performed on other, non-logical, languages as well. Among the most prominent tools is PIT [3], a mutation testing tool for Java. Imperative languages aside, mutation testing has been considered for declarative and functional languages as well [13]. Usable tools exist, for instance, for Haskell [12].

Since generating and testing redundant mutants makes up the majority of the runtime of mutation testing, plenty of work, e.g., by Offutt et al. [17], has been done on finding a set of mutants that is as small as possible but still finds all uncovered code. Ammann et al. [1] compare two different sets of mutation operations for PIT. We are not aware that comparisons of the amount of generated alive and dead mutants per mutation rule has been done for other languages.

This might be because in "traditional" languages, e.g., Java, C or even Assembly, control flow is usually linear, rendering selection of mutation operations fairly straightforward. In Prolog however, it is easier to manipulate control flow, e.g., changing conjunctions to disjunctions basically introduces if-then-else constructs. Futhermore, for many possible mutations, it is hard to predict how the program will be influenced, e.g., moving cuts forwards or backwards. An empirical study as shown in this paper renders it easier to reason about these transformations which simply are not possible in other programming languages.

Regarding test coverage, several measurement tools are available and integrated into the most common Prolog interpreters such as SWI [24] and SICStus [22]. While they provide basic code coverage metrics, they usually only report on reached ports, that is, call, exit, redo and fail during execution. As discussed in the introduction and shown in our empirical evaluation, this can lead to different results compared to calculating coverage based on mutation testing. Of course, this does not imply that one metric is better than the other but rather that a combination of multiple approaches yields the best results.

7   Future Work

Even though we have improved the selection of mutation operators, our approach still generates mutations semantically equivalent to the program under test. As an equivalent mutation does not lead to a failing test by definition, each equivalent mutation causes a false positive to be reported. With our current implementation, deciding whether a mutation is semantically equivalent is done after the test results are reported. In particular, the decision is made manually by the programmer as mentioned at the end of Sect. 5.2.

To improve the efficiency of our test framework, techniques to detect semantically equivalent mutations should be incorporated in the future. For instance, we are able to approximate the check for equivalence of two programs by restricting the domains of the arguments and using constraint solving to search for a counter example. However, Prolog is a dynamic language not providing types which hampers constraint solving. To counter this, we could try to detect the types of a predicate's arguments at runtime. Unfortunately, this is not possible in general, for instance, if an argument is a variable which is not unified within a specific predicate call. *plspec* [10], for example, offers a simple and easily extensible domain specific language for type annotations. If a predicate is annotated using *plspec*, we are able to derive the types of arguments as well as their role, that is, whether they act as an input or output of a predicate. One downside of approximating the equivalence of two programs is that we do not consider possible side-effects of a predicate. Nevertheless, in practice, we expect an approximation with appropriate domains to exclude more false positives than true positives. The meaningfulness of mutation testing will thus probably increase.

Another line of future work is the integration of automated test case generation in the mutation testing framework. Again, we need to be able to derive the types of the arguments of a predicate (e.g., assume that *plspec* has been used). We gain a lot of information about a program under test during mutation testing. In case a mutation is alive, we might be able to use the mutated and the original code to generate an appropriate test case covering the mutated clause. For instance, we could mutate a predicate p using two arguments while the first argument acts as an input and the second one as an output. The predicate is mutated to p_{mut} and the mutation stays alive. Assuming the mutation did change the semantics of p, we know that our test case needs to satisfy a call to p and has to fail for p_{mut}.

We can then use techniques such as fuzzing to generate randomized inputs until a set of parameters has been found. Furthermore, we can use constraint solving to search for appropriate arguments. Doing so, we can, on the one hand, search for any arguments that cause different behavior on the level of the predicate call. That means, the arguments satisfy the constraint $\exists a, b : p(a, b) \land \neg p_{mut}(a, b)$. On the other hand, in case we know which arguments are inputs and outputs, we can probably generate a more detailed test case by searching for input values that cause different output values. In the context of our example that results to asserting $\exists a : p(a, b) \land p_{mut}(a, \bar{b}) \land b \neq \bar{b}$ to hold. Of course, the implementation of the predicate p might be faulty. We thus cannot automatically determine a generated test case to be correct. However, we can present generated test cases to the user who can validate the behavior.

Additionally, as discussed in Sect. 5, not all mutations were covered by our benchmarks. Therefore, the impact of these mutations should be measured on other Prolog programs.

8   Conclusion

We have presented a framework for performing mutation testing on Prolog code. Starting from the discussion of mutation rules by Toaldo and Vergilio [23], we have devised a set of mutation rules we deem sensible, i.e., we suspect them to mostly compute semantically different mutations. Our testing framework is available both for SICStus and SWI Prolog and can be downloaded from https://github.com/hhu-stups/prolog-mutation-testing.

We have shown empirically, that our mutation testing framework can handle different Prolog programs. In particular, we tested it on large examples, showing both applicability and performance of our approach. Furthermore, we have shown that mutation testing indeed reports different coverage statistics than the ones provided by the coverage analysis tools shipping with SICStus and SWI. We do not want to start a discussion on whether predicate coverage, path coverage or MC/DC analysis is better or worse than mutation testing. Instead, we argue that any further knowledge about test coverage and the validity of a test suite helps to improve the overall implementation.

References

1. Ammann, P., Delamaro, M.E., Offutt, J., et al.: Establishing theoretical minimal sets of mutants. In: IEEE International Conference on Software Testing, Verification, and Validation, vol. 7. IEEE Computer Society (2014)
2. Clark, K.L.: Negation as failure. In: Gallaire, H., Minker, J. (eds.) Logic and Data Bases, pp. 293–322. Springer, Boston (1978). https://doi.org/10.1007/978-1-4684-3384-5_11
3. Coles, H., Laurent, T., Henard, C., Papadakis, M., Ventresque, A.: PIT: a practical mutation testing tool for Java (Demo). In: International Symposium on Software Testing and Analysis, ISSTA 2016, pp. 449–452. ACM (2016)
4. Denisov, A., Pankevich, S.: Mull it over: mutation testing based on LLVM. In: 2018 IEEE International Conference on Software Testing, Verification and Validation Workshops (ICSTW), pp. 25–31, April 2018
5. Deursen, A.V., Moonen, L., Bergh, A., Kok, G.: Refactoring test code. In: International Conference on Extreme Programming and Flexible Processes in Software Engineering, pp. 92–95 (2001)
6. Grün, B.J., Schuler, D., Zeller, A.: The impact of equivalent mutants. In: IEEE International Workshop on Mutation Analysis, pp. 192–199. IEEE (2009)
7. Jia, Y., Harman, M.: An analysis and survey of the development of mutation testing. IEEE Trans. Softw. Eng. 37(5), 649–678 (2011)
8. Krings, S.: Code coverage analysis for prolog. Bachelor's thesis, Heinrich-Heine-University, Duesseldorf, Germany (2010)
9. Krings, S., Schmidt, J., Brings, C., Frappier, M., Leuschel, M.: A translation from alloy to B. In: Butler, M., Raschke, A., Hoang, T.S., Reichl, K. (eds.) ABZ 2018. LNCS, vol. 10817, pp. 71–86. Springer, Cham (2018). https://doi.org/10.1007/978-3-319-91271-4_6
10. Körner, P., Krings, S.: plspec - A specification language for prolog data. In: Seipel, D., Hanus, M., Abreu, S. (eds.) Declare 2017, vol. 499, Technical report. University of Würzburg (2017)
11. Körner, P., Schneider, D., Leuschel, M.: Evaluating interpreter design in prolog. In: Kolloquium Programmiersprachen und Grundlagen der Programmierung KPS, Schriftenreihe des Instituts für Computersprachen (2015)

12. Le, D., Alipour, M., Gopinath, R., Groce, A.: MuCheck: an extensible tool for mutation testing of haskell programs. In: International Symposium on Software Testing and Analysis, ISSTA (2014)
13. Le, D., Alipour, M.A., Gopinath, R., Groce, A.: Mutation testing of functional programming languages. Technical report. Oregon State University, School of Software Engineering and Computer Science (2014)
14. Lloyd, J.W.: Foundations of Logic Programming. Springer, Heidelberg (1984). https://doi.org/10.1007/978-3-642-96826-6
15. Naish, L.: A declarative debugging scheme. J. Funct. Logic Program. **1997**(3) (1997). http://danae.uni-muenster.de/lehre/kuchen/JFLP/articles/1997/A97-03/A97-03.html
16. Offutt, A.J., Pan, J.: Automatically detecting equivalent mutants and infeasible paths. Softw. Testing Verif. Reliab. **7**(3), 165–192 (1997)
17. Offutt, A.J., Rothermel, G., Zapf, C.: An experimental evaluation of selective mutation. In: International Conference on Software Engineering, pp. 100–107. IEEE Computer Society Press (1993)
18. Papadimitriou, C.H.: A note the expressive power of prolog. Bull. EATCS **26**(21–23), 61 (1985)
19. Sangwan, R.S., LaPlante, P.A.L.: Test-driven development in large projects. IT Prof. **8**(5), 25–29 (2006)
20. Schuler, D., Zeller, A.: Javalanche: efficient mutation testing for Java. In: Joint Meeting of the European Software Engineering Conference and the ACM SIGSOFT Symposium on the Foundations of Software Engineering, ESEC/FSE 2009, pp. 297–298. ACM (2009)
21. Shapiro, E.Y.: Algorithmic Program Debugging. MIT Press, Cambridge (1983)
22. SICS, Kista, Sweden. SICStus Prolog User's Manual. http://www.sics.se/isl/sicstuswww/site/documentation.html
23. Toaldo, J.R., Vergilio, S.R.: Applying mutation testing in prolog programs. In: VII Workshop de Testes e Tolerância a Falhas. Biblioteca Digital Brasileira de Computação (2006)
24. Wielemaker, J., Schrijvers, T., Triska, M., Lager, T.: SWI-prolog. Theory Pract. Logic Program. **12**(1–2), 67–96 (2012)

Runtime Verification in Erlang by Using Contracts

Lars-Åke Fredlund[1], Julio Mariño[1], Sergio Pérez[2(✉)], and Salvador Tamarit[2]

[1] Babel Group, Universidad Politécnica de Madrid, Madrid, Spain
{lfredlund,jmarino}@fi.upm.es
[2] Departament de Sistemes Informàtics i Computació,
Universitat Politècnica de València, Valencia, Spain
{serperu,stamarit}@dsic.upv.es

Abstract. During its lifetime, a program regularly undergoes changes that seek to improve its functionality or efficiency. However, such modifications may also introduce new errors. In this work, we use the *design-by-contract* approach to allow programmers to formally state, in the code, some of the knowledge and assumptions originally made when the code was first written. Such contracts can then be checked at runtime, to ensure that modifications made to a program did not violate those assumptions. Applying these principles we have designed a runtime verification system for the Erlang language, permitting to specify as annotations the contracts needed for both sequential and concurrent code. As a second contribution we extend the commonly used Erlang gen_server behaviour (a design pattern) permitting to specify declaratively when a server is ready to service a client request. The ideas presented in this paper have been implemented in a tool named EDBC. Its source code is available at github.com as an open-source and free project.

Keywords: Runtime verification · Design-By-Contract · Program instrumentation · Concurrency

1 Introduction

Developing software is not an easy task and, consequently, errors (*bugs*) are present in most software artefacts. Companies usually rely on program testing to check that programs behave as expected. There are also programming languages, e.g., Haskell and Rust, that provide robust static type systems which can help discover errors during program compilation. Once a bug is found, the

This work has been partially supported by MINECO/AEI/FEDER (EU) under grant TIN2016-76843-C4-1-R, by the *Comunidad de Madrid* under grant S2013/ICE-2731 (*N-Greens Software*), and by the *Generalitat Valenciana* under grant PROMETEO-II/2015/013 (*SmartLogic*). Salvador Tamarit was partially supported by the *Conselleria de Educación, Investigación, Cultura y Deporte de la Generalitat Valenciana* under grant APOSTD/2016/036.

J. Silva (Ed.): WFLP 2018, LNCS 11285, pp. 56–73, 2019.
https://doi.org/10.1007/978-3-030-16202-3_4

debugging process can start in order to find the *cause* or source of the bug. Even in a program language which lacks a static type system, programmers can make the process of locating the cause of a bug easier by annotating code with implicit assumptions made – e.g., concerning type of parameters to methods or functions. For instance, consider a function that will divide a number by zero if one of its parameters has a non-expected value. Normally such an error is manifest when the division by zero occurs. However, the true source of the bug is the function call. Defensive programming is a way to eliminate unexpected behaviours, e.g., division by zero, by checking the validity of arguments before operations are attempted. However, in mainstream programming this style is not a recommendable practice for various reasons, such as the need to add *boiler-plate* code which obscures the program logic, and because of the execution time overhead caused by such checks. In fact, the language considered in this article, Erlang, is infamous for its stance that defensive programming is to be avoided – "let it crash".

Erlang has a number of innovative mechanisms for error detection and recovery,[1] but these features are supposed to be used only for errors that are hard to avoid (i.e., because static type systems are not strong enough to characterise full program behaviour). Unfortunately, not all the errors fall in this category. Some errors are rather easy to detect, and should ideally be detected at "compile time" instead of being detected and corrected when a software is operational. Erlang, as Python or JavaScript, is a dynamic programming language. This means that the program compiler does relatively few checks during compilation to help prevent errors when the program is later run. For this reason, static analysis techniques, popularised primarily by the Dialyzer tool [12], have been successfully and widely adopted by Erlang practitioners. Dialyzer can analyse the code and report some errors without requiring annotating program code in any way. However, the capability of Dialyzer to detect program bugs can be considerably improved by the use of type contracts [10]. Note that such contracts are not only used by Dialyzer to implement static type checking, but also serve to document the developed code, which improves the maintainability of the resulting software.

Even when the Dialyzer tool is used, and when programmers provide e.g. EUnit test cases (an Erlang testing tool) to further check program behaviour, program bugs can still remain. In this work, we propose a mechanism to further structure and strengthen such "defensive" programming tasks, i.e., the Erlang Design-By-Contract (EDBC) system, a runtime verification framework based on the Design-By-Contract [14] philosophy. The EDBC system is available as free and open-source software at https://github.com/tamarit/edbc.

In typical design-by-contract frameworks, there are different types of contracts, with most of them being related to program functions or methods. The most common contracts are *pre-* and *postconditions*. Preconditions are conditions that should hold before evaluating a function or method, while postconditions

---

[1] For example, process links help structure fault detection and fault recovery in complex applications.

should hold after its evaluation. In addition to these, the EDBC system includes type contracts, decreasing-argument contracts to help analyse program termination, execution-time contracts to document bounds for the execution time of a function, and purity contracts which prohibit side effects such as Erlang process-to-process communication. All these contracts can be used in any Erlang program, regardless whether the program is purely functional, or structured as a concurrent system, composed of a number of concurrent processes. To avoid the traditional execution overhead associated with the use of contracts, normally they are checked only during software production and maintenance. The EDBC library provides a mechanism to disable such checks for running product code.

The article is structured as follows: Sect. 2 describes the contracts supported by our annotations, regardless whether the code is purely functional or implements concurrent behaviours. This section contains a number of examples (Sect. 2.1), and also gives details on the implementation of contracts by means of program instrumentation in Sect. 2.2. In Sect. 3.2 we focus on concurrency, extending the frequently used Erlang "behaviour" gen_server, a client–server design pattern. The extension permits to specify declaratively when the server is ready to service a particular client request, in contrast with the standard behaviour where such functionality has to be programmed explicitly using queues. The new behaviour is illustrated with examples in Sects. 3.3 and 3.4. Finally, Sect. 4 presents an overview of related work, and Sect. 5 concludes and provides directions for future research and development.

2   Contracts in Erlang

In this section, we first introduce the contracts provided by the EDBC system, and show how they can be used to check program behaviour at runtime in Sect. 2.1. Then, we present some implementation details in Sect. 2.2.

2.1   The Contracts

Precondition Contracts. With the macro[2] ?PRE/1 we can define a precondition that a function should hold. The macro should be placed before the first clause of the annotated function. The single argument of this macro is a function without parameters, e.g. fun pre/0 or an anonymous function fun() -> ... end, that we call *precondition function*. A precondition function is a plain Erlang function. Its only particularity is that it includes references to the function parameters. In Erlang, a function can have more than one clause, so referring to the parameter using the user-defined names can be confusing for both EDBC and for the user. In order to avoid these problems, in EDBC we refer to the parameters by their position. Additionally, the parameters are rarely single variables but can be more

---

[2] As an implementation decision, we have chosen to use Erlang macros to represent all contracts. The reason is that similar tools like EUnit also use macros for assert definitions.

complex terms like a list or a tuple (since Erlang permits pattern matching). For these reasons we use the EDBC's macro ?P/1 to refer to the parameters. The argument of this macro should be a number that ranges from 1 to the arity of the annotated function. For instance, ?P(2) refers to the second parameter of the function. A precondition function should return a boolean value which indicates whether the precondition of the annotated function holds or not. The precondition is checked during runtime before actually performing the call. If the precondition function evaluates to false, the call is not performed and a runtime exception is raised.

As an example, imagine a function find(L,K) which searches for the position of a value K in a list L, and returns -1 if the value is not found. Figure 1a shows the usage of a precondition contract which expresses that the first parameter list should not be empty.

In case the precondition is violated, an Erlang exception is raised. For instance, if we consider the function call find([], 3), which fails the precondition check because the length of the list argument is 0, the resulting error message is shown in Fig. 1b.

Postcondition Contracts. Similar to preconditions, the macro ?POST/1 is used to define a postcondition that a function should satisfy. The macro should be placed after the last clause of the annotated function. Its argument is a function without parameters, which we call the *postcondition function*. For checking postconditions referring to the result of the function is essential; the macro ?R permits this. Additionally, as in the ?PRE/1 precondition function the ?P/1 macros can be used to refer to the actual parameters of the annotated function. The result of a postcondition function is also a boolean value. Postcondition functions are checked after a call terminates, and a runtime error is raised if the postcondition function evaluates to false. Figure 1c shows an example of a postcondition contract associated with the function find/2. In this contract, an error is raised if the index returned by find/2 is greater than the length of the list. Suppose an implementation of find/2 returns the value 5 to the call find([1,2,3],3). In this case, the execution would raise the error shown in Fig. 1d.

Decreasing-Argument Contracts. These contracts are meant to be used in recursive functions, and check that (some) arguments are always decreasing in nested calls[3]. There are two types of macros to define these contracts: ?DECREASE/1 and ?SDECREASE/1. They both operate exactly in the same way with the exception that the ?SDECREASE/1 macro indicates that the argument should be strictly smaller in each nested call, while the ?DECREASE/1 macro also permits the argument to be equal. The argument of both macros can be either a single ?P/1 macro or a list containing several ?P/1 macros. These contracts should be placed before the first clause of the function. Decreasing-argument contracts are checked each

---

[3] Note that decreasing-argument contracts only guarantee termination if the sequence is strictly decreasing and well founded, i.e. values cannot go below a certain limit.

```
1 ?PRE(fun() -> length(?P(1)) > 0 end).
2 find(L, K) -> ...
```

(a) Erlang function `find/2` annotated with contracts.

```
** exception error: {"Precondition does not hold.
Call find([], 3), the list is empty."}
```

(b) Precondition contract violation.

```
1 find(L, K) -> ...
2 ?POST(fun() -> ?R < 0 orelse
3           ?R < length(?P(1)) end).
```

(c) Erlang function `find/2` with contract annotations.

```
** exception error: {"Postcondition does not hold.
Call find([1,2,3], 3), returned value 5."}
```

(d) Postcondition contract violation.

```
?SDECREASES(?P(1)).
-spec fib(integer()) -> integer().
fib(0) -> 0;
fib(1) -> 1;
fib(N) -> fib(N - 1) +  fib(N + 2).
```

(e) Erlang function `fib/1` annotated.

```
** exception error: {"Decreasing condition does
not hold. Previous call: fib(2).
Current call: fib(4).", [{ex,fib,1,[]},...
```

(f) Decrease contract violation.

```
1 ?EXPECTED_TIME(fun() ->
2     20 + lists:sum([case (I rem 2) of
3       0 -> 100; 1 -> 200 end || I <- ?P(1)]) end)
4 f_time(L) -> [f_time_run(E) || E <- L].
5 f_time_run(N) when (N rem 2) == 0 ->
  timer:sleep(100);
6 f_time_run(N) when (N rem 2) /= 0 ->
  timer:sleep(200).
```

(g) Function with time contracts.

```
** exception error: {"The execution of
ex:f_time2([1,2,3,4,5,6,7,8,9,10]) took too
much time. Real: 1509.913 ms.
Expected: 1020 ms. Difference: 489.913 ms)
```

(h) Execution-time contract report.

```
1 fold1(Fun, Acc, Lst) -> lists:fold(Fun, Acc, Lst).
2 fold2(Lst, Fun) -> fold1(Fun, 1, Lst).
3 g3() -> fold1(fun erlang:put/2, ok,
4            [computer, error]).
5 ?PURE.
6 g4() -> fold2([2, 3, 7], fun erlang:'*'/2).
```

(i) Example taken from PURITY [15].

```
** exception error: {"The function is not pure.
Last call: ex:g3().
It has called the impure BIF erlang:put/2
when evaluating g3().",[{ex,g3,0,[]}]}
```

(j) Pure contract report.

Fig. 1. Several examples of contract annotations.

time a recursive function call is made, by comparing the arguments of the current call with the nested call just before performing the actual nested recursive call. In case the argument expected to decrease is not actually decreasing, a runtime error is raised and the call is not performed. To exemplify the functionality of this contract, we use a wrong implementation of the Erlang program calculating the Fibonacci numbers shown (Fig. 1e). When executing the function call `fib(2)`, the error message in Fig. 1f is shown.

Execution-Time Contracts. EDBC introduces two macros that allow users to define contracts concerning execution times: `?EXPECTED_TIME/1` and `?TIMEOUT/1`. The macros should be placed before the first clause of the annotated function. The argument of these macros is a function without parameters called the *execution-time function.* An execution-time function should evaluate to an integer which defines the expected execution time in milliseconds. Within the body of an execution-time function we can use ?P/1 macros to refer to the arguments. Permitting the execution-time function to refer to arguments is particularly useful when dealing with lists or similar structures where the expected execution time of the function is related to the sizes of arguments. Both macros have a similar semantics, the only difference is that with macro ?EXPECTED_TIME/1 the EDBC system waits till the evaluation of the call finishes to check whether the call takes the expected time, while with macro ?TIMEOUT/1 EDBC raises an exception if the function call does not terminate before the timeout limit is reached. As an example of time contracts, we consider a function which performs a list of tasks. Each task has its type (even or odd), and the allowed execution time is defined by this type (100 and 200 ms, respectively). Figure 1g shows the function and its associated time contract. Supposing we change the execution-time function to, for instance, fun() -> 20 + (length(?P(1)) * 100) end, we would obtain the contract-violation report shown in Fig. 1h.

Purity Contracts. When we say that a function is pure we mean that its execution does not cause any side effects, i.e., it does not perform I/O operations, nor does it send messages, etc. That a function is "pure" can be declared by using the macro ?PURE/0 before its first clause. The purity checking process is performed in two steps. First, before a call to a function declared to be pure is performed, a tracing process is started. Then, once the evaluation of the annotated function call finishes, the trace is inspected. If a call to an impure function or operation has been made, a runtime exception is raised. Note that due to the use of tracing we can provide exact purity checks, ensuring that there are neither false positives nor false negative reports.

Note that purity checking is not compatible with execution-time contracts, since checking execution times does require performing impure actions. In order to illustrate the checking of purity contracts we take a simple example used to present PURITY [15], i.e., an analysis that statically decides whether a function is pure or not. The example the authors presented is depicted in Fig. 1i. We only added the contract ?PURE in the test case g4/0, because the other test case, i.e. g3/0, performs the impure operation erlang:put/2. When g4/0 is run, no contract violation is reported as expected. If we added the contract ?PURE to g3/0, then the execution will fail showing the error in Fig. 1j.

Invariant Contracts. This contract is meant to be used in Erlang behaviours which have an internal state. An invariant contract is defined by using the macro ?INVARIANT/1. This macro can be placed anywhere inside the module implementing the behaviour. The argument of the ?INVARIANT/1 macro is a function, named *invariant function*, with only one parameter that represents the current state of the behaviour. Then, an invariant function should evaluate to a boolean value which indicates whether the given state satisfies the invariant or not. The invariant function is used to check the invariant contract each time a call to a

```
** exception error: {"The spec precondition does not hold.
Last call: ex:fib(a).
The value a is not of type integer().", ...}
```

Fig. 2. spec contract-violation report.

```
method Find(a: array<int>, key: int)
   returns (index: int)
   requires a != null
   ensures 0 <= index ==> index < a.Length &&
      a[index] == key
   ensures index < 0 ==> forall k ::
      0 <= k < a.Length ==> a[k] != key
{...}
```

```
1  ?PRE(fun() -> length(?P(1)) > 0 end).
2  ?SDECREASES(?P(1))
3  find(L, K) -> ...
4  ?POST(fun() -> ?R < 0 orelse
5        (?R < length(?P(1))
6           andalso lists:nth(?R, ?P(1)) == ?P(2))
7     end).
8  ?POST(fun() -> ?R > 0 orelse
9        lists:all(fun(K) -> K /= ?P(2) end,
10          ?P(1))
11    end).
```

(a) Function Find/2 annotated in Dafny.

(b) Function find/2 annotated in Erlang/EDBC.

Fig. 3. Contracts for function find/2 in Dafny and Erlang.

function which is permitted to change the state finishes, e.g., when a call by the gen_server behaviour to the handle_call/3 callback function finishes (see Sect. 3.2 for a description of the behaviour). Note that invariant contracts can be used to check for the absence of problems in concurrent systems such as e.g. starvation. Examples of invariant contracts are presented in Sect. 3.2.

Type Contracts. Erlang has a dynamic type system, i.e., types are not checked during compilation but rather at runtime. Even though, the language still permits to specify type contracts (represented by spec attributes) which serves both as code documentation, and as aid to static analysers such as Dialyzer [12]. However, such type contracts are not checked at runtime by the Erlang interpreter, because of the potential associated cost in execution time. However, for programs still in production, checking such type contracts during runtime can be helpful to detect unexpected behaviour. For this reason, before a function is evaluated, EDBC checks the type contract of its parameters (if any), while its result is checked after its evaluation. If a type error is detected, a runtime exception error is raised. Note that EDBC does not use any special macro to check type contracts, the standard spec attributes are used instead. Figure 2 shows an error that would be shown in case of calling fib(a) for the program defined in Fig. 1e.

Note that the EDBC system can be used to define quite advanced contracts. As a comparison point, the Dafny tool [11], which was an inspiration for EDBC, permits the use of quantifiers to define conditions for input lists. Figure 3a shows an example of how quantifiers are used in Dafny to characterise the function Find/2.

Such contracts with quantifiers can be represented in EDBC too. Instead of using a special syntax like in Dafny, we can check conditions with quantifiers using a common Erlang function such as `lists:all/2`, which checks whether a given predicate is true for all the elements of a given list. Figure 3b shows how the contracts in Fig. 3a are represented in EDBC. If we implemented this function as a recursive one, the list would be decreasing between calls. Then, we could also add the contract `?SDECREASE(?P(1))` to the function.

Contracts added by users can also be used to generate documentation. Erlang OTP includes the tool `EDoc` [6] which generates documentation for modules in HTML format.

We have modified the generation of HTML documents to also include information concerning EDBC contracts. As an example the EDoc-generated documentation for the function `find/2`, with information of its contracts (some in Fig. 3b and some new), and its type specification, is depicted in Fig. 4. Finally, it is important to note that the contract checking performed by EDBC does not cause incompatibilities with other Erlang analysis tools. For instance, users can both define EDBC contracts, and include EUnit [3] test case assertions, in the same function.

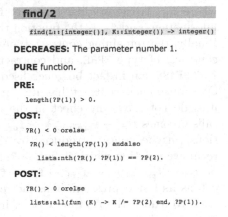

find/2

```
find(L::[integer()], K::integer()) -> integer()
```

DECREASES: The parameter number 1.

PURE function.

PRE:
```
length(?P(1)) > 0.
```

POST:
```
?R() < 0 orelse
?R() < length(?P(1)) andalso
lists:nth(?R(), ?P(1)) == ?P(2).
```

POST:
```
?R() > 0 orelse
lists:all(fun (K) -> K /= ?P(2) end, ?P(1)).
```

Fig. 4. EDoc for the annotated function `find/2`.

2.2 Implementation Details

In this section we explain how the code is instrumented to support contract checking at runtime. Note that the code produced by the instrumentation process is normal Erlang code, which is executed by the standard Erlang runtime system in a completely normal fashion. Technically the instrumentation is performed using so called Erlang "parse transforms", which permit defining syntactic transformations on Erlang code.

Consider a module with a number of annotated functions. The instrumentation process replaces such annotated functions with a copy of the (possibly modified) original functions, together with a number of helper functions which are synthesised from the contracts. The instrumentation is performed in three steps:

1. First, if a function has an associated contract, then an instrumentation to store the relevant information regarding function calls (function name, arguments and stack trace) is performed. This creates a new function which becomes the function entry point, and the original function is renamed. When the new function is called, it stores the call information, and proceeds to call the original function.

2. Then, contracts of type ?DECREASES/1 (including ?SDECREASES/1) are processed. This instrumentation creates a function which checks if the size of its parameters have decreased between recursive calls. If they are decreased, delayed calls are executed, and if they are not, a contract violation exception is raised. During the instrumentation the original function is also modified by replacing all the recursive calls to calls to the new created function. Note that, due to this instrumentation and the previous one, we have changed the call cycle of a recursive call from $f_{ori} \rightarrow f_{ori}$ to $f_{si} \rightarrow f_{ori} \rightarrow f_{dc} \rightarrow f_{si}$, where f_{ori} is the original function, f_{si} is the function that stores the call information, and f_{dc} is the function that checks the decreasing of arguments.

3. Finally, the remaining contract types are processed distinguishing between contracts of type ?PRE, and contracts of type ?POST. All contracts except ?DECREASE can in fact be generalised to one of these two types of contract. Of course, each contract has its particularities, however, these particularities do not have any effect in the instrumentation process. The chain of calls becomes $f_{si} \rightarrow f_{pre/post}* \rightarrow f_{ori}$, where $f_{pre/post}*$ are a number of functions (maybe none) introduced by ?PRE/?POST contracts. In the case of a recursive function which defines a ?DECREASE contract, the call chain would be $f_{si} \rightarrow f_{pre/post}* \rightarrow f_{ori} \rightarrow f_{dc} \rightarrow f_{si}$. Most of the helper functions have a call as its last expression. This fact enables the so called last call optimisations to reduce the runtime cost of instrumenting code. The only exception is the functions generated for postconditions, which needs to be stacked until internal calls are completely evaluated.

Finally, contract checking can be easily disabled or enabled using a special compilation flag, thus e.g. permitting production code to be compiled and run without instrumentation.

3   Concurrency

Most Erlang programmers do not write concurrent code from scratch, but rather rely heavily on proven concurrent Erlang behaviours (which can be considered a form of *design pattern*) present in the Erlang/OTP standard library. As we shall see, the contracts in Sect. 2 are very useful to ensure that the generic behaviour is instantiated properly.

3.1   Erlang Behaviours

Erlang behaviours formalise common programming patterns. The idea is to divide the code for a process in a generic part (a behaviour Erlang module), which is never changed, and a specific part (a callback Erlang module), which is used to tailor the process for the particular application being implemented. Thus, the behaviour module is part of the Erlang/OTP standard library, and the callback module is implemented by the programmer. Such behaviours provide standard mechanisms to implement concurrent behaviours: the generic part provides a proven implementation of an often complex concurrent coordination task, which permits programmers to focus on the easier task on how to adapt this generic behaviour to the particular application at hand.

3.2 The gen_server Behaviour, and How to Improve It

One of the most commonly used Erlang behaviours – especially in industrial applications – is the gen_server, which provides a standard way to implement a client–server architecture. A callback module for this behaviour needs to define the specific parts of the server (process), e.g., what is the initial state of the server (e.g., implementing the Erlang function init/0), and handling specific client requests (e.g., implementing the Erlang functions handle_call/3 for blocking client calls, and handle_cast/2 for non-blocking client calls), etc.

Given the regular nature of specific parts of this behaviour, the use of the contracts defined in Sect. 2 is highly useful. For instance, invariants (as expressed by the ?INVARIANT/1 contract explained in Sect. 2) constrain the (persistent) state of the underlying server process. Moreover, for the server to function correctly, the generic parts of the service require the programmer writes specific parts of the behaviour to satisfy a number of properties expressible as contracts: calls to handle_call/3 (or handle_cast) must normally be side effect free (as the generic part handles replying to server requests) as expressed by the ?PURE/0 contract, and the code implementing handle_call/3 should be efficient expressed in order to fulfil a defined ?EXPECTED_TIME/1 contract.

In practice, this behaviour has a number of shortcomings which are addressed in EDBC by extending it to handle client requests which arrive when the server is not capable of servicing them, a common situation in asynchronous concurrent systems. A programmer using the normal gen_server behaviour must manually handle such asynchronous requests by implementing a queuing policy in the specific behaviour part. In EDBC a modified gen_server is available, where the generic behaviour part handles such asynchronous requests according to a simple rule, implementing a flexible queuing policy, thus providing a behaviour which is far easier to use.

Specifically, we have added a new callback function that the behaviour's specific part must implement: cpre/3. This function should return a boolean value indicating whether the server is ready or not to serve a given request. The rest of the gen_server callbacks are not modified. The three parameters of the callback function cpre/3 are (1) the request, (2) the *from of the request*[4] and (3) the current server state. The function cpre/3 should evaluate to a tuple with two elements. The first tuple element is a boolean value which indicates if the given request can be served or not, and the second tuple element is the new server state.

---

[4] The *from of the request* has the same form as in the handle_call/3 callback, i.e., a tuple {Pid,Tag}, where Pid is the process identifier of the client issuing the request, and Tag is a unique tag.

The `gen_server_cpre` behaviour behaves in the same way as the `gen_server` behaviour except for a significant difference. Each time the server receives a client request, it calls to `cpre/3` callback before calling the actual `gen_server` callback, i.e., `handle_call/3`. Then, according to the value of the first element of the tuple that `cpre/3` returns, either the request is actually performed (when the value is `true`) or it is queued to be served later (when the value is `false`). In both cases, the server state is updated with the value returned in the second element of the tuple.

EDBC includes two implementations of the `gen_server_cpre` behaviour, each one treats the queued requests in a different way. The less complicated implementation resends to itself a client request that cannot be served in the current server state, i.e., a request for which function `cpre/3` returns `{false, ...}`. Since mailboxes in Erlang are ordered according to the arrival time of messages (i.e., in FIFO order), the postponed request will be the last request in the queue of incoming requests. The problem with this implementation is that it does not respect the arrival order of the requests. For instance, if the state of the server changes permitting a postponed request to be served, the server will serve new client requests before it. This way, a request that have arrived later than the postponed one would be served before.

The EDBC framework also provides a more fair version of the `gen_server_cpre` behaviour. In this version, three queues are used to ensure that older requests are served first: $queue_{current}$, $queue_{old}$, and $queue_{new}$. Each time the server is ready to listen for new requests, the $queue_{current}$ is inspected. If it is empty, then the server proceeds as usual, i.e., by receiving a request from its mailbox. Otherwise, if it is not empty, a request from $queue_{current}$ is served, removing it from the queue. The queues are also modified by adding requests to $queue_{old}$ and $queue_{new}$. This is done when function `cpre/3` returns `{false, ...}`. Depending on the origin of the request it is added to $queue_{old}$ (when it comes from $queue_{current}$) or to $queue_{new}$ (when it comes from the mailbox). Finally, each time a request is completely served, the server state could have been modified. A modification in the server state can enable postponed requests to be served. Therefore, each time the server state changes, $queue_{current}$ is rebuilt as follows: $queue_{old}$ + $queue_{current}$ + $queue_{new}$.

3.3   Selective Receives

In public forums such as https://stackoverflow.com and the erlang-questions mailing list[5], there have been a number of questions regarding the limitations of the standard `gen_server` implementation. Most of them concern how to implement a server which has the ability to delay some requests. For example, one question posted on stackoverflow.com[6] asks whether it is possible to implement a server which performs a selective receive while using a `gen_server` behaviour.

---

[5] See http://erlang.org/mailman/listinfo/erlang-questions.

[6] See https://stackoverflow.com/questions/1290427/how-do-you-do-selective-receives-in-gen-servers.

None of the provided answers is giving an easy solution. Some of them suggest that the questioner should not use a gen_server for this, and directly implement a *low-level* selective receive. Other answers propose to use gen_server but delay the requests *manually*. This solution involves storing the request in the server state and returning a no_reply in the handle_call/3. Then, the request should be revised continually, until it can be served and use gen_server:reply/2 to inform the client of the result. Our solution is closer to the last one, but all the management of the delayed requests is completely transparent to the user.

Figure 5 shows the function handle_call/2 of the gen_server that the questioner provided to exemplify the problem. When the request test is served, it builds ten processes, each one performing a {result, N} request, with N ranging from 0 to 9. Additionally, the server state is defined as a list which also ranges from 0 to 9

```
1  handle_call(test, _From, _State) ->
2    List = [0,1,2,3,4,5,6,7,8,9],
3    lists:map(fun(N) -> spawn(fun() ->
4      gen_server:call(?MODULE, {result, N}) end)
5      end, lists:reverse(List)),
6    {reply, ok, List};
7  handle_call({result, N}, _From, [N|R]) ->
8    io:format("result: " ++ integer_to_list(N) ++ "~n"),
9    {reply, ok, R}.
```

Fig. 5. handle_call/2 for selective receive.

(Fig. 5, lines 2 and 6). The interesting part of the problem is how the {result, N} requests need to be served. The idea of the questioner is that the server should process the requests in the order defined by the state. For instance, the request {result, 0} can only be served when the head of the state's list is also 0. However, there is a problem in this approach. The questioner explains it with the sentence: *when none of the callback function clauses match a message, rather than putting the message back in the mailbox, it errors out*. Although this is the normal and the expected behaviour of a gen_server, the questioner thinks that some easy alternative should exist. However, as explained above, the solutions proposed in the thread are not satisfactory enough.

With the enhanced versions of the gen_server behaviour we propose in this paper, users can define conditions for each request by using function cpre/3. Figure 6 depicts a definition of the function cpre/3

```
1  cpre(test, _, State) -> {true, State};
2  cpre({result, N}, _, [N|R]) -> {true, [N|R]};
3  cpre({result, N}, _, State) -> {false, State}.
```

Fig. 6. cpre/3 for selective receive.

that solves the questioner's problem without needing to redefine function handle_call/3 of Fig. 5. The first clause indicates to the gen_server_cpre server that the request test can be served always. In contrast, {result, N} requests only can be served when N coincides with the first element of the server's state.

3.4   Readers-Writers Example

In this section we define a simple server that implements the readers-writers problem, as a second example of the use of the extended `gen_server_cpre` behaviour. We start by introducing a naive implementation of the problem, that does not take into account its synchronization conditions, by using the standard `gen_server` behaviour. The server state is

```
1  handle_call(request_read, _, State) ->
2      NState = State#state{readers = State#state.readers + 1},
3      {reply, pass, NState};
4  handle_call(request_write, _, State) ->
5      NState =  State#state{writer = true}},
6      {reply, pass, NState}.
7
8  handle_cast(finish_read, State) ->
9      NState = State#state{readers = State#state.readers - 1},
10     {noreply, NState};
11 handle_cast(finish_write, State) ->
12     NState = State#state{writer = false},
13     {noreply, NState}.
```

Fig. 7. Readers-writers request handlers.

a record defined as `-record(state, readers = 0, writer = false)`. The requests that it can handle are four: `request_read`, `request_write`, `finish_read` and `finish_write`. The first two requests are blocking (because clients need to wait for a confirmation) while the latter two do not block the client (clients do not need confirmation). Figure 7 shows the handlers for these requests. They basically increase/decrease the counter `readers` or switch on/off the flag `writer`.

Having defined all these components, we can already run the readers-writer server. It will start serving requests successfully without any noticeable issue. However, the result in the shared resource is a mess, mainly because we are forgetting an important problem: its invariant, i.e. $!writer \lor readers = 0$.

We can define an invariant for the readers-writers server by using the macro `?INVARIANT/1` introduced in Sect. 2. Figure 8 shows how the macro is used and the helper function which actually checks the invariant.

```
1  ?INVARIANT(fun invariant/1).
2
3  invariant(#state{ readers = Readers, writer = Writer}) ->
4      is_integer(Readers) andalso Readers >= 0
5      andalso is_boolean(Writer)
6      andalso ((not Writer) orelse Readers == 0).
```

Fig. 8. Readers-writers invariant definition.

Apart from the standard invariant, i.e., `(not Writer) orelse Readers == 0`, the function also checks that the state field `readers` is a positive integer and that the state field `writer` is a boolean value.

If we run the server with the invariant defined, we obtain feedback on whether the server is behaving as expected. In this case, the server is clearly not a correct implementation of the problem. Therefore, an error should be raised due to the violation of the invariant. An example of the errors is shown in Fig. 9.

The error is indicating that the server state was `{state,0,true}` when the server processed a `request_read` which led to the new state `{state,1,true}` which clearly violates the defined invariant. The information provided by the error report can be improved by returning a tuple `{false, Reason}` in the invariant function, where `Reason` is a string to be shown in this invariant-violation report after the generic message.

```
=ERROR REPORT====
** Generic server readers_writers terminating
** Last message in was request_read
** When Server state == {state,0,true}
** Reason for termination ==
** {{"The invariant does not hold.",Last call: readers_writers:handle_call(
      request_read, ..., {state,0,true}). Result: {reply, pass,{state,1,true}}",
      [{readers_writers,handle_call,3,...},...]}, ...}
```

Fig. 9. Failing invariant report.

In order to correctly implement this feature, we use the function `cpre/3` to control when a request can be served or not. Figure 10 shows a function `cpre/3` which makes the server's behaviour correct and avoids violations of the invariant. It enables `request_read` requests as long as the flag `writer` is switched off. Similarly, the `request_write` requests also require the flag `writer` to be switched off and also the counter `readers` to be 0. If we rerun now the server, no more errors due to invariant violations will be raised.

Although this implementation is already correct, it is unfair for writers as they have less chances to access the shared resource. The EDBC code repository[7] includes a number of implementations of the example, which implement various fairness criteria.

```
1  cpre(request_read, _, State = #state{writer = false}) ->
2      {true, State};
3  cpre(request_read, _, State) ->
4      {false, State};
5  cpre(request_write, _,
6        State = #state{writer = false, readers = 0}) ->
7      {true, State};
8  cpre(request_write, _, State) ->
9      {false, State}.
```

Fig. 10. Readers-writers `cpre/3` definition.

4   Related Work

Our contracts are similar to the ones defined in [1], where the function specifications are written in the same language, i.e., Curry, so they are executable. Being executable enables their usage as prototypes when the real implementation is not provided. Their contracts are functions in the source code instead of macros, so it is not clear whether they could be removed in the final release. One of the authors extended this work in [8], where static analysis performed by an SMT solver at compile time was used to check the contracts. This analysis discharged the overhead produced by the dynamic verification of these contracts. In these works, there is not any mention about whether their contracts are integrated with a documentation tool like our contracts are with EDoc. Moreover, they only allow to define basic precondition and postcondition contracts, while we are providing alternative ones like decreasing or time contracts. Finally, Curry is a pure functional logic language not targeting on concurrent computations. For that reason, contracts for purity checking or concurrency behaviours would not be very useful in a language like Curry.

---

[7] https://github.com/tamarit/edbc/tree/master/examples/readers_writers.

The work in [15] presents a static analysis which infers whether a function is pure or not. Since the focus on the article is on static analysis whereas ours is on dynamic analysis, the purity checking is performed in completely different ways in each work. However, we can benefit from their results by, for instance, avoiding to execute functions that are already known to be impure, reporting earlier to the user a purity-contract violation. In the same way, our system can be used in their approach to check the validity of statically-inferred results.

The type contract language for Erlang [10] allows to specify the intended behaviour of functions. Their usage is twofold: (i) as a documentation in the source code which is also used to generate EDoc, and (ii) to refine static analyses provided by tools such as Dialyzer. The contract language allows for singleton types, unions of existing types and the definition of new types. However, these types and function specifications do not guarantee type safety. This guarantee comes with Erlang which incorporates strong runtime typing with type errors detected and reported at runtime. Although such a static analysis is quite capable in detecting typing violations, strong typing usually detects unexpected behaviour too far from its source. Therefore, when debugging a program, providing the feature to detect violations of such type contracts at runtime can be a useful aid to provide more precise error locations.

The concurrency behaviours follow the same philosophy as the specifications defined in [7,9]. Indeed, our function `cpre/3` takes its name and inspiration from these works. Although these works were more focused on enabling the use of formal methods, or testing techniques, to verify nontrivial properties of realistic systems, in this paper we demonstrate that they can be used to concisely program server applications which are forced to deal with asynchronous requests that must be delayed, and moreover are also useful for runtime verification.

Dafny [11] is a language which allows to define invariants and contracts in their programs. The main difference between their approach and ours is that their contracts are not checked during runtime, but during compile-time. Additionally, as we have explained in Sect. 2, we can replicate the same type of contracts in EDBC. However, our approach does not need an extra syntax or functionality to define complex contracts as Dafny does.

The aspect-oriented approach for Erlang (`eAOP`) presented in [4] shares some similarities with our work. eAOP allows the instrumentation of a program with a user-defined tracing protocol (at an expression level). This is able to report events to a monitor (asynchronous) as well as to force some part of the code to block waiting for information from the monitor (synchronicity). Our system could be used to a similar purpose but only at the function level. However, combining our concurrency behaviours with some of the ideas in [13] could be an interesting line for future work.

Also in Erlang, the work [5] defines a runtime monitoring tool which helps to detect messages which do not match a given specification. These specifications are defined through an automaton, which requires an extra knowledge from the user concerning both the syntax of the specification, and in the whole system operation. We propose a clear and easy way to define the conditions for when to accept a request without needing any user input.

Finally, JErlang [16] enables so called joins in Erlang. This is achieved by modifying the syntax of Erlang receive patterns to permit expressing matching of multiple subsequent messages. Although our goal and theirs are different, both approaches can simplify the way programmers solve similar kinds of problems. Indeed, we could simulate joins by adding a forth parameter to the function cpre/3. This additional parameter would represent the still unserved pending requests. When the last request of a user-defined sequence (*join*) is received, the pending requests should be examined to check whether the required join can be served. A similar modification is needed to the callback handle_call/3 interface so that the pending requests could be served using the gen_server:reply/2 call.

5 Conclusions

We have developed a new framework EDBC which permits annotating Erlang code (functions) with a number of different code contracts, ranging from classical ones such as function pre- and post-conditions to more novel ones, e.g., whether functions are side-effect free, and which can express limits on the execution time of function calls. Such contracts help programmers to formally document otherwise undocumented contextual assumptions regarding how functions may be used. Such a feature can, we believe, for instance reduce the number of bugs introduced when programs are rewritten to add new functionality, as contracts permit checking that new code interfaces correctly with the old code. An additional advantage that code contracts provide is improved API documentation. Our framework includes a feature to include runtime contract as part of the automatically generated documentation of Erlang functions.

The code contracts supported by EDBC are checked at runtime, and can be easily disabled for deployed code to avoid the runtime overhead of checking contracts, if so desired. Moreover our contracts use plain Erlang, without the need for defining new syntax or requiring supporting libraries.

As a second contribution of the article we have also provided the implementation of a new design pattern for an important class of client–server based concurrent systems. In Erlang such concurrent design patterns are manifest as so called "behaviours". Our improved concurrent behaviour permits programmers to state, in a declarative fashion, when asynchronous client requests can be served by the server, and when they must be postponed as the server is incapable of responding to them in its current state. The EDBC provides an implementation of this behaviour, essentially freeing an Erlang programmer from having to explicitly manage a set of queues to properly coordinate client requests, a nontrivial task.

There are multiple extensions of this work. For instance, contracts can be modified to return a default value instead of an error when a contract is violated, to permit more flexible policies for how contract violations are signalled, and recovered from. Another item for future work is to generalise the "decrease" contracts, which are used to ensure that recursive functions progress.

We can also use EDBC to control starvation of concurrent systems. The idea is to use a mapping from types of requests to waiting requests which represents the fact that a delayed request is waiting for a concrete event to occur. An invariant can then be used to control starvation. Another useful extension concerning concurrency behaviours would be to cleanly communicate the fact that a server process fails a precondition check to the client process that issued the failing request. This extension would protect the server process while communicating the error to the responsible party.

More generally, we can extend our system to translate EDBC contracts to EUnit tests cases, or to property test generators for property-based testing tools like Quviq QuickCheck [2]. Finally, we are trying to establish a relation between so called liquid types [17] and our approach as there are a number of similarities.

References

1. Antoy, S., Hanus, M.: Contracts and specifications for functional logic programming. In: Russo, C., Zhou, N.-F. (eds.) PADL 2012. LNCS, vol. 7149, pp. 33–47. Springer, Heidelberg (2012). https://doi.org/10.1007/978-3-642-27694-1_4
2. Arts, T., Hughes, J., Johansson, J., Wiger, U.T.: Testing telecoms software with quviq QuickCheck. In: Proceedings of the 2006 ACM SIGPLAN Workshop on Erlang, pp. 2–10. ACM (2006)
3. Carlsson, R., Rémond, M.: EUnit: a lightweight unit testing framework for Erlang. In: Feeley, M., Trinder, P.W. (eds.) Proceedings of the 2006 ACM SIGPLAN Workshop on Erlang, p. 1. ACM (2006)
4. Cassar, I., Francalanza, A., Aceto, L., Ingólfsdóttir, A.: eAOP: an aspect oriented programming framework for Erlang. In: Chechina, N., Fritchie, S.L. (eds.) Proceedings of the 16th ACM SIGPLAN International Workshop on Erlang, pp. 20–30. ACM (2017)
5. Colombo, C., Francalanza, A., Gatt, R.: Elarva: a monitoring tool for Erlang. In: Khurshid, S., Sen, K. (eds.) RV 2011. LNCS, vol. 7186, pp. 370–374. Springer, Heidelberg (2012). https://doi.org/10.1007/978-3-642-29860-8_29
6. Ericsson AB: EDoc (2018). http://erlang.org/doc/apps/edoc/chapter.html
7. Fredlund, L., Mariño, J., Alborodo, R.N., Herranz, Á.: A testing-based approach to ensure the safety of shared resource concurrent systems. Proc. Inst. Mech. Eng. Part O: J. Risk Reliab. 230(5), 457–472 (2016)
8. Hanus, M.: Combining static and dynamic contract checking for curry. In: Fioravanti, F., Gallagher, J.P. (eds.) LOPSTR 2017. LNCS, vol. 10855, pp. 323–340. Springer, Cham (2018). https://doi.org/10.1007/978-3-319-94460-9_19
9. Herranz, Á., Mariño, J., Carro, M., Moreno Navarro, J.J.: Modeling concurrent systems with shared resources. In: Alpuente, M., Cook, B., Joubert, C. (eds.) FMICS 2009. LNCS, vol. 5825, pp. 102–116. Springer, Heidelberg (2009). https://doi.org/10.1007/978-3-642-04570-7_9
10. Jimenez, M., Lindahl, T., Sagonas, K.: A language for specifying type contracts in Erlang and its interaction with success typings. In: Thompson, S.J., Fredlund, L. (eds.) Proceedings of the 2007 ACM SIGPLAN Workshop on Erlang, Freiburg, Germany, 5 October 2007, pp. 11–17. ACM (2007)
11. Leino, K.R.M.: Dafny: an automatic program verifier for functional correctness. In: Clarke, E.M., Voronkov, A. (eds.) LPAR 2010. LNCS, vol. 6355, pp. 348–370. Springer, Heidelberg (2010). https://doi.org/10.1007/978-3-642-17511-4_20

12. Lindahl, T., Sagonas, K.: Detecting software defects in telecom applications through lightweight static analysis: a war story. In: Chin, W.-N. (ed.) APLAS 2004. LNCS, vol. 3302, pp. 91–106. Springer, Heidelberg (2004). https://doi.org/10.1007/978-3-540-30477-7_7

13. Lorenz, D.H., Skotiniotis, T.: Extending design by contract for aspect-oriented programming. CoRR, abs/cs/0501070 (2005)

14. Meyer, B.: Applying "Design by Contract". IEEE Comput. **25**(10), 40–51 (1992)

15. Pitidis, M., Sagonas, K.: Purity in Erlang. In: Hage, J., Morazán, M.T. (eds.) IFL 2010. LNCS, vol. 6647, pp. 137–152. Springer, Heidelberg (2011). https://doi.org/10.1007/978-3-642-24276-2_9

16. Plociniczak, H., Eisenbach, S.: JErlang: Erlang with joins. In: Clarke, D., Agha, G. (eds.) COORDINATION 2010. LNCS, vol. 6116, pp. 61–75. Springer, Heidelberg (2010). https://doi.org/10.1007/978-3-642-13414-2_5

17. Rondon, P.M., Kawaguci, M., Jhala, R.: Liquid types. In: PLDI 2008, pp. 159–169. ACM (2008)

Enhancing POI Testing Through the Use of Additional Information

Sergio Pérez[(✉)] and Salvador Tamarit

Departament de Sistemes Informàtics i Computació,
Universitat Politècnica de València, Camí de Vera s/n, 46022 València, Spain
{serperu,stamarit}@dsic.upv.es

Abstract. Recently, a new approach to perform regression testing has been defined: the point of interest (POI) testing. A POI, in this context, is any expression of a program. The approach receives as input a set of relations between POIs from a version of a program and POIs from another version, and also a sequence of entry points, i.e. test cases. Then, a program instrumentation, an input test case generation and different comparison functions are used to obtain the final report which indicates whether the alternative version of the program behaves as expected, e.g. it produces the same outputs or it uses less CPU/memory. In this paper, we present a method to improve POI testing by including additional context information for a certain type of POIs. Concretely, we use this method to obtain an enhanced tracing of calls. Additionally, it enables new comparison modes and a categorization of unexpected behaviours.

Keywords: Code evolution control · Automated regression testing ·
Call traces · Tracing

1 Introduction

During its useful lifetime, a program might evolve many times. Each evolution is often composed of several changes that produce a new release of the software. Software developers usually define test suites to detect any *unexpected behaviour* (UnB) in new program releases. These suites help developers to notice the errors, but detecting an error is just the beginning of the debugging process.

Let us suppose that we are running our test suite and some test fails. Our next step would probably be to start a debugging process in order to find the bug. This process requires our knowledge and cannot be done without it. We are going to start observing intermediate results until the origin of the bug is found. We need to interpret each one of these intermediate results, until we locate the

This work has been partially supported by MINECO/AEI/FEDER (EU) under grant TIN2016-76843-C4-1-R, and by the *Generalitat Valenciana* under grant PROMETEO-II/2015/013 (SmartLogic). Salvador Tamarit was partially supported by the *Conselleria de Educación, Investigación, Cultura y Deporte de la Generalitat Valenciana* under grant APOSTD/2016/036.

© Springer Nature Switzerland AG 2019
J. Silva (Ed.): WFLP 2018, LNCS 11285, pp. 74–90, 2019.
https://doi.org/10.1007/978-3-030-16202-3_5

one that makes no sense. However, in this process there is a lot of information that is available, but is not usually exploited by users. All this information comes from previous versions of the code which, in a continuous integration scheme, will be very similar to the latest version or exactly the same.

First of all, the mentioned information can be used to establish relations between the expressions of the last version of the code and its predecesor. Once these relations are created, we can run the failing test using as observation point all the expressions that form these relations. We should run the test on both versions, and observe and compare the results obtained on each of these auto-generated observation points[1]. However, most of the times, the compared values are going to be very similar, so why do not automatise the comparison process as well? These principles (expression relation across versions and comparison of execution results) are the basis of *Point of interest* (POI) testing (briefly described in Sect. 2).

POI testing tries to help users in comparing the behaviour of their code across versions by observing specific points of a program. A POI can be any expression of the code whose behaviour wants to be observed, e.g. the POI (module, 5, (var, 'A'), 2) refers to the second occurrence[2] of variable A in the fifth line of the file module. We can establish these relations between points of both programs versions and search for errors with our defined tests suites but, what happens if the observed points does not reveal any incoherence when running our test suite? or, even worse, what happens if we do not have any test suite? This is also solved in our approach by auto-generating (a lot of) test cases that focus on the observation points (POIs) when deciding what to use as concrete data inside the test. Thus, it enables the comparison of versions without needing a user-defined test-suite or reuses the existing one to create similar ones that explore the behaviour of the POIs for different program executions.

POI testing, as mentioned previously, can be a very powerful tool that eases the debugging process and reuses a lot of information that is available in common repositories, such as Git repositories. However, its first and current definition does not use all the available information when running a test. For this reason, the user needs to do some extra work to locate the source of a bug. In this paper we present a framework that allows to reuse more available information to ease the task of the user in the debugging process (Sect. 3). As an example, we present a concrete usage of the framework by increasing the information provided by POIs placed at function calls (Sect. 4) in the context of the functional programming language Erlang[3] [1]. Let's see Example 1 to better understand the framework and its usage.

---

[1] Although current implementation of POI testing does not still support auto-generation of observation points, it is a key feature that will be part of next release.

[2] The occurrence argument (2 in the example) can be omitted, selecting in that case the first occurrence of the variable in the indicated line.

[3] More information about Erlang and how we implemented a POI tester for this language are further discussed in Sect. 4.

Example 1. Consider the code (in any specific language) shown in Fig. 1 which represents three lines of a program that show some differences between versions.

```
PREVIOUS       NEW
x = g()        x = h()      →  Expression changed, no relation built.
y = i()        y = i()      →  Expression unchanged, relation built.
lib.f(x,y)     lib.f(x,y)   →  f is in a library (lib) that has completely
                               changed due to some severe refactoring. Re-
                               lation built.
```

Fig. 1. Two different versions of a source code

In the new version, a severe refactoring on function f has been done. Suppose that in the new version h() computes the value 5, while g() computes 4. Then, when running our test suite, an error raises. Then we run POI testing, which builds the relations between code versions as explained in Fig. 1.

This means that, until comparing the values computed by each call to f, we would not know that the call is uncovering the UnB. Our first reaction would be to blame function f and start the debugging process for f, comparing completely different versions of the same algorithm, that stands a hard and arduous task. The framework presented in this paper can be used to add to our POI testing the knowledge of the call arguments. These arguments, are integrated as another expression in the plain POI testing, so they can be used when comparing values computed on the POIs across versions.

2   POI Testing

In POI testing, (i) the programmer identifies a POI and a set of *entry points*. Then, by using some automatic test case generation technique, (ii) the approach automatically generates a test suite which tries to cover all possible paths that reach the POI (trying also to produce execution paths that evaluate this POI several times). Therefore, in POI testing, the *input of a test case* (ITC) is defined as a call to a particular function (defined as an entry point) with some specific arguments. On the other hand, the output of a test case is the sequence of values that the POIs are evaluated to for an ITC. For the sake of simplicity, in the rest of the paper we use the term *traces* to refer to these sequences of values. Next, (iii) the test suite is used to automatically check whether the behaviour of the program remains unchanged across new versions[4]. Finally, (iv) the user is provided with a report about the success or failure of these test cases.

---

[4] Steps (ii) and (iii) could also be executed in parallel. Here, for the sake of simplicity, we only consider the sequential execution of these steps.

Note that this technique allows the definition of multiple POIs [9]. With this feature, users can trace several (and maybe unrelated) functionalities in a single run. Additionally, users can strengthen the quality of their test suite by checking behaviour preservation in more than one point. Finally, this feature is required in those cases where a POI in one version is associated with more than one POI in another version (e.g., when a POI is associated with two or more POIs due to a refactoring or a removal of duplicated code).

An example of a POI tester is the tool SecEr (*Software Evolution Control for Erlang*), which is publicly available at https://github.com/mistupv/secer. The analyses performed by SecEr are transparent to the user. The only task in SecEr that requires user intervention is identifying suitable POIs in both old and new versions of a program. SecEr allows to define test configuration files to ease all this process and also to make it reusable. The interested readers are referred to [9] where they will find an extensive discussion about the similarities with other tools and how to deal with concurrency.

	Program P$_1$	Program P$_2$
1	main(X, Y) ⇒	main(X, Y) ⇒
2	A = X + Y,	S = diff(X, Y),
3	D = X - Y,	A = add(X, Y),
4	RETURN A * D.	RETURN A * S.
5		add(X, Y) ⇒
6		RETURN X + Y.
7		diff(Y, X) ⇒
8		RETURN X - Y.

Fig. 2. Two versions of the same program

In the following, we introduce the approach with the help of the example presented in Fig. 2. There are three main parts in POI testing:

- **Inputs:** POI testing requires at least two parameters to be able to operate: a sequence of *POI relations* and a set of *entry points*. Additionally, POI testing can also be run with some specific comparison and report functions. The comparison and report functions are explained within the internals and the outputs of the approach, respectively.
  - *POI relations* connect POIs from two different versions of the same program. A POI relation is represented by a set of pairs. Each pair contains two POIs, one of each version of the program. For instance, the POI relation ((P$_1$, 3, (var, D)), (P$_2$, 2, (var, S), 1)) defines a relation between the two POIs contained at lines 3 and 2 respectively, in Fig. 2. This POI relation indicates that the variable D in line 3 has been renamed to S, and moved to line 2.
  - *Entry points* determine the beginning of the execution. They are represented by a set of function names with their arity. For example, the set {main/2} defines an entry point for the approach in the example of

Fig. 2, i.e. all the ITCs generated for the approach are calls to function main/2. Concretely, this function requires the generation of specific arguments which are not provided by the user. This is further discussed in the internals of the approach.

– **Internals:** There are three main stages of the approach. First, how traces are built, then how they are compared, and finally how new ITCs are generated.

- *Trace building.* The basis of POI testing is the tracing of some POIs during the evaluation of a concrete ITC. For this reason, it is needed a way to create and collect these traces. This process is performed by means of a program instrumentation (like the one defined in [9] for Erlang). The instrumentation builds tuples of the form $(POI, value)$ and sends them to a trace server which collects and sorts all the tuples, producing the final trace. For example, when we run the program P_1 with the ITC main(4,2), the trace obtained for the previously defined POI (P_1, 3, (var, D)) would be $\{2\}$[5].

- *Trace comparison.* Once traces are generated and stored, the next step is to compare them in order to infer if there is any UnB[6]. In the case that some UnB is found, it shows the corresponding UnB type with and an associated UnB report. There are several ways of comparing traces. The most relevant techniques to compare multi-POI traces are described in [9], where the authors distinguish between two main forms of comparison: (i) the traces are compared as a whole or (ii) the traces are compared independently for each POI. For example, consider both versions of the program shown in Fig. 2. Consider also the set of POI relations

$$\{((P_1, \ 3, \ (var, \ D)), \ (P_2, \ 2, \ (var, \ S))),$$
$$((P_1, \ 2, \ (var, \ A)), \ (P_2, \ 3, \ (var, \ A)))\}$$

represented from now on as $\{(P_1\_D, \ P_2\_S), \ (P_1\_A, \ P_2\_A)\}$, and the ITC main(5,1). When running this ITC, the generated traces are

$$P_1: \ \{(P_1\_A, \ 6), \ (P_1\_D, \ 4)\}$$
$$P_2: \ \{(P_2\_S, \ -4), \ (P_2\_A, \ 6)\}$$

If they are compared as a whole, an UnB is raised reporting that a trace from P_2_A was expected, but a trace of P_2_S was found instead. In this comparison, the elements of both traces must be generated in the same order for both executions. On the other hand, when they are compared separately, independent traces are generated for each POI relation. Therefore, for this example, there is an UnB found when comparing the traces of the (P_1_D, P_2_S) POI relation (i.e., value 4 was expected but

---

[5] Note that a trace consists of a sequence of values since a variable can be evaluated several times. Each evaluation is represented by an element of the sequence.

[6] The observed UnBs are represented and identified using literals, e.g. the atom greater could be used to represent an UnB that occurs when an expression is evaluated to a greater value in the new version than in the old one. The UnB representations are defined during the comparison process as it is then when the UnBs are found.

value −4 was found). There is an optional input parameter that allows users to define their own comparison functions. This function should receive two traces and must return either *true* or a tuple of the form (UnB_Type, UnB_Report), where UnB_Type is a label representing the UnB and UnB_Report is the message shown when this type of UnB is reported.

- *ITC generation.* POI testing starts by generating an ITC for each entry point. However, in order to reinforce the obtained UnB report, each time an ITC is run, new ITCs may be derived from it according to the comparison result. This way, if an UnB is found when running a particular ITC, we can generate new ITCs based on it, so that they are more conducive to generate the same or other UnBs. In [9], an ITC generation based on the mutation of the arguments of the ITC is described. Alternative generators can be used, but they should take into account the result of the trace comparison in order to obtain better results for POI testing.

- **Outputs:** The output of POI testing consists of a collection of ITCs together with the result of their trace comparisons. When none of the ITCs evaluated have generated an UnB, users are informed of the successful result by adding also some additional information such as the number of ITCs evaluated. On the contrary, when one or more UnBs have been observed, users get a report that can be configured in several ways. For example, the program of Fig. 2 when using the POI relation $\{(P_1\_D, P_2\_S)\}$ would result in a report similar to the one shown in Fig. 3.

```
Generated test cases: 259
Mismatching test cases: 234 (90.35%)
*** Detected Error ***
Call: main(5,1)
Error Type: Unexpected trace value
POI: (P₁_D) trace: [4]
POI: (P₂_S) trace: [-4]
```

Fig. 3. Example of an error report

3   Enhancing POI Testing with Additional Information

This section introduces a general overview of the enhancement that we have defined for POI testing. In order to include this enhancement, extensions have been incorporated in some of the stages of the approach introduced in Sect. 2. Concretely, the trace building stage, the trace comparison stage, and the output stage. Therefore, Sect. 4 is a special case of the general methodology explained here.

3.1   Augmenting Traces with Additional Information

POI testing uses POI traces to check whether some UnBs exist across several program versions. We represent each element of this trace as a tuple $(POI, value)$.

In this paper, we propose an extension where some additional information is attached to each *trace element*. Thus, we have extended the concept of trace element to a triplet $(POI, value, ai)$ where ai is a mapping function containing any kind of information we add about the program context when tracing a POI.

Then, a concrete implementation of an enhanced POI testing should be able to construct these trace element triplets and handle them during the whole process. As mentioned in Sect. 2, the trace elements are sent when the instrumented code is executed. Then, they are collected and stored by the tracer which produces the final trace. Thus, the task of any concrete enhancement proposed for POI testing is to build these triplets, storing in ai all the desired execution information (e.g. the arguments of a function call), and manage its usage in the trace comparison and UnB report stages. In other words, for each enhancement we need to modify the code instrumentation and add some extra tracing functionality.

3.2   Using Augmented Traces to Compare Program Behaviour

POI testing allows using any comparison function. This feature gives users a complete freedom to configure the testing and/or debugging process in the best way according to their needs.

In order to maximize the customization level of the comparison, users can define their own comparison functions. Each comparison function is defined by a set of connected functions that cover the different aspects of the comparison. Thus, the input part of the approach is extended with two extra

Fig. 4. Comparison function structure

functions. The connection between these functions is illustrated in Fig. 4. The outer black box represents the general comparison function (it receives the whole traces of both executions as parameters, TO and TN), while the gray and white boxes represent the new mentioned functions, that are used inside the general comparison function. Their behaviour is explained below[7].

- **Value-extractor function** (VEF) : This function works at the trace element level. Its target is to extract for any trace element only the parts that the user wants to compare. For example, function:

$$\texttt{VEF(POI, value, ai)} \Rightarrow \texttt{RETURN (POI, value, ai(args))}$$

  extracts from a trace element only the arguments information related to call POIs and ignores the rest of additional information[8].

---

[7] All functions presented in Sect. 3 are written in pseudocode. In a particular implementation, all functions should be implemented in the target language.

[8] We use the notation *ai(key)* to refer to access some specific information previously stored in the ai mapping. In this case *ai(args)* represent the arguments of a POI placed in a function call.

– **Trace element comparison function** (TECF): In order to allow users to check UnBs in different ways and not only a plain equality function, i.e. operator ==, we add a comparison function for each pair of trace elements. This function iteratively receives pairs of trace elements contained in the whole traces, and it is the one in charge of comparing them. In order to compare two trace elements, it uses the VEF function to extract their values, perform a defined comparison, and, if an UnB is found, it returns an UnB type notifying about it. For example, function:

```
TECF(TOE, TNE) ⇒
    CASE compare(VEF(TOE),VEF(TNE)) OF
        gt → RETURN true
        eq → RETURN same
        lt → RETURN downgrade
    ENDCASE
```

is an example of a TECF, where function compare/2 is used to check whether a reduction in some performance indicator is obtained. Then, when it is not obtained, either a same or a downgrade UnB type is returned.

3.3   Reporting Customized Error Types

When an UnB is detected, a specific report should be generated, i.e. a message should be provided to users. In order to further define these error messages, we have added to the approach a way to specify how the POI tester should react to a particular UnB. In this case, we have added an extra input parameter called *unexpected-behaviour report mapping* (UnBRM). We use a mapping, because it allows easy redefinitions and additions of UnBs reports. The mapping returns a function for a given UnB type. The returned function should build a string that will be the report message. For example, expression UnBRM(downgrade) may return a function similar to the one shown in Fig. 5, where a custom message is shown[9] when an UnB of this type is found during the execution.

```
DOWNGRADE(TEO, TEN, History) ⇒
    RETURN "There has been a downgrade in the new version"
```

Fig. 5. Example of a function providing a customized error message

3.4   POI Testing Configurations

There are several ways of using the additional information stored in the trace elements, and all these modes are defined by the added resources introduced in the previous subsections (TECF, VEF and UnBRM). In this section, we show three different modes which will be more useful for users.

---

[9] The function presented in Fig. 5, does not make use of parameters TEO, TEN and History to define the message content. However, more complex functions that treat the information stored in these parameters can be defined to obtain a more elaborated message, like the one shown in Fig. 7.

– **Additional information is not used during comparison (NUAI).** In this mode, the traced values are the only data used when comparing the trace elements. This is the mode that should be used when the additional information is expected to vary due to the differences between program versions or simply due to the type of data it contains. Additionally, this mode can also be used to ease the comparison process. This mode will use a value-extractor function like VEF(POI, V, AI) $\Rightarrow$ RETURN (POI, V) or a particular variant, where additional information is simply ignored. According on how additional information is used, we have identified three submodes.

  • **Additional information is only used to define UnB types (NUAI-T).** The additional information is only used to define new types of UnBs, but it will not appear in the UnB report. This mode is really convenient in such cases where the additional information is too complex or large, so it will not give a significant feedback to the user. In such cases, when an UnB is found, it is interesting to define a new type of UnB (e.g., diff_value_same_args can represent those UnBs where the values of two POIs placed at function calls differ when their call arguments are the same). The TECF is the one that should be defined to use this mode. For example, Fig. 6 shows a TECF which distinguishes between those unexpected values for call POIs where the arguments are the same and those where the arguments are different[10]. Categorizing different types of UnBs has several benefits in POI testing. First of all, these types can be considered in the ITC generation as a criterion to decide whether an ITC should be mutated or not. In the example above, if we do not distinguish between diff_value_same_args and diff_value_diff_args, once a diff_value type has been mutated it can have less chances of being selected to be mutated again. However, with this distinction, each one is treated separately, so that both mutate as separated entities. Additionally, if the final report is enriched with several UnB types, users have more feedback that can help while finding the source of the UnB.

  • **Additional information is only used in the UnB report (NUAI-R).** If we consider that the additional information is not representative enough to categorize new types of UnBs, we can use its data only in the

```
TECF(TOE, TNE) ⇒
    IF VEF(TOE) == VEF(TNE) THEN
        RETURN true
    ELSE
        IF get_ai(TOE)(args) == get_ai(TNE)(args) THEN
            RETURN diff_value_same_args
        ELSE
            RETURN diff_value_diff_args
        ENDIF
    ENDIF
```

Fig. 6. TECF which returns different UnB types

---

[10] Function get_ai is defined as get_ai(POI,value,ai) $\Rightarrow$ RETURN ai.

reports. This is a less intrusive way of using the additional information, but still a useful way to obtain richer feedback in the final report of each UnB. We should add to the UnBRM a new function associated to each UnB type that could benefit from the stored additional information. For example, in the UnBRM, we can store the function of Fig. 7 associated with the default error key diff_value. In this example, each time we find a difference in the results of two call POIs, we also get feedback on their arguments.

```
DIFF_VALUE({POI1, value1, ai1}, {POI2, value2, ai2}, History) ⇒
    RETURN "Value for POI1 (value1) and for POI2 (value2) differ.
        Their call arguments were:
            ai1(args)
            ai2(args)"
```

Fig. 7. Example of UnBRM error function associated to error key diff_value

- **Additional information is used to categorize and report UnBs (NUAI-TR).** This submode takes the advantages of both previous submodes. It also involves specific trace-element comparison functions and additions in the UnB report mapping.
- **Additional information is used during comparison (UAI).** This mode is the one that gives a major relevance to the additional information. By using this mode, the value and the additional information is compared as a whole. This means that, for instance, even if the compared values are the same, when any pair of elements of the additional information differs, the ITC is reported to be generating an UnB. This mode is very convenient to uncover some UnBs earlier. It can also be used for performance checking, e.g. the values of the trace elements are equal but a performance indicator included in the additional information is revealing some downgrade. This mode uses a VEF function and a TECF which takes into account all or some parts of the additional information. The amount of information that is finally used to build the UnB reports is left to user's choice.
- **The additional information is not attached to the trace element, instead considered as an independent one (AIT).** Finally, in this completely different mode, the additional information is considered as a separated entity and constitutes a single trace element as the ones that are generated for the POIs. This mode can be similar to plain POI testing, however it requires a special instrumentation (to send the new trace elements), tracing (to receive and store the new trace elements) and maybe some special comparison functions (to take into account their singularities). This mode is very convenient in such cases where the additional information can be directly used to uncover an UnB, avoiding in this way the comparison of several subcomputations. For instance, if we place a POI in a call, and the call parameters are compared before comparing the call result, all intermediate trace elements are not compared. Additionally, this mode can be combined in such a way that other

additional information is attached to these special trace elements forming a hybrid mode suitable for some specific scenarios.

Program P	Program P'
1 main(X, Y) ⇒	main(X, Y) ⇒
2 ...	...
3 foo(X),	foo(X),
4 ...	...

Fig. 8. Two versions of a program with a call to the foo function

4   Enhancement by Using Improved Call Tracing

In this section we explain how call tracing has been improved and how the enhanced call traces have been incorporated to POI testing for Erlang.

Erlang [1] is a concurrent, functional programming language. It implements the actor model approach for concurrency, and allows concurrency based on message passing. Although one of the main features of Erlang is its potential for distributed programming, in this paper we have just focused on the non-distributed part. The sequential subset of the Erlang language supports eager evaluation and dynamic typing. In our case, the order of evaluation (eager or lazy) is not relevant for the approach, because POI testing is interested in the values of the evaluation, not in the order the expressions are evaluated. On the other hand, the dynamic typing supposed an important drawback for the ITC generation due to all possible types that needed to be considered in the generation process. This problem does not exist in static typed languages, as we know exactly the types of the value we need to generate. Additionally, all the Erlang libraries prepared to perform a live instrumentation of the code, make it a suitable language for implementing POI testing.

In this section, we also present a use case, using our tool (SecEr) that implements the POI testing methodology. In the use case, we compare the results provided by both the initial and the enhanced version of the tool.

4.1   Motivation

As it is usual in testing, after finding an UnB, we still have to find its source to fix it, i.e. we have to start a debugging process. Unfortunately, POI testing is not an exception. Consider the programs P and P' shown in Fig. 8, and both foo calls at line 3 as related POIs presenting an UnB. The information provided by plain POI testing for this scenario is shown in Fig. 9. This report contains a list with the set of values each function call is evaluated to, but without any context information (e.g., the parameters of each call, the Erlang dictionary of the process, etc.). Thus, it might be difficult to determine whether the source of the error is located in the arguments of the call or inside the function called.

In the new approach, the POIs placed at function calls will be treated in a special way. This special treatment augments the information given in the report, allowing us to specify where the source of the UnB can be found. This is the main benefit of using an enhanced tracing for calls.

```
*** Detected Error ***
Call: main(6,9)
Error Type: Unexpected trace value
POI: (P, (call, foo), line 3) trace: [12]
POI: (P', (call, foo), line 3) trace: [7]
```

Fig. 9. Report returned for programs P and P'

4.2 Implementation Details of the Call Tracing

When we place a POI in a call, we are saying that we are interested in comparing the result of this call, so the standard behaviour of a POI tester is to trace only these values. In this work, we want to create an enhanced trace where not only the result of the call, but also its arguments, are traced. Therefore, this enhancement adds to the additional information mapping a new element whose key is ca and whose value is a list that contains the call arguments.

In order to obtain the improved call traces, we have to define a way for sending, receiving and merging those traces. The main idea is to send the argument traces before actually performing the call and its result just after that. Thus, we should define how the code instrumentation is extended to create these enhanced trace elements, and also we should define how the tracer deals with them.

```
e(e̅ᵢ) ⇒ begin
          fv_ref = make_ref(),
          [fv_v|fv_vᵢ] = [e|e̅ᵢ],
          tracer!{add_i, POI, fv_ref, fv_v},
          tracer!{add_i, POI, fv_ref, fv_i},
          fv = fv_v(fv_vᵢ),
          tracer!{add, POI, fv_ref, fv},
          fv
        end
```
(a) Instrumentation rule for call tracing

```
1  tracer({Stack, Trace}) ->
2      receive
3          {add_i, POI, Ref, V} ->
4              tracer({[{Ref, V} | Stack], Trace});
5          {add, POI, Ref, V} ->
6              {CalleeArgs, NStack} =
7                  remove_same_ref(Ref, Stack),
8              tracer({NStack,
9                      [{POI, V, store(ca, CalleeArgs)}
10                     | Trace]});
11         {add, POI, V} ->
12             tracer({Stack, [{POI, V} | Trace]})
13     end.
```
(b) Simplified tracing server

Fig. 10. Elements of our proposed call tracer enhancement in Erlang

The sending process is done thanks to a program instrumentation that enables this double tracing for the call in two steps, i.e. arguments before performing the call and the result just after the call. We show in Fig. 10a how this instrumentation can be done for the programming language used, i.e. Erlang.

When the code instrumentation process finds a call, i.e. $e(\overline{e_i})$, the expression is then replaced by the block expression (begin-end) on the right-hand side.

This instrumentation (i) creates a set of auxiliar free variables[11] to store all the evaluated context of the call (callee and arguments), (ii) sends to the tracer of these defined variables, (iii) performs the actual call using the value of the callee and the arguments, (iv) sends the result of the call to the trace server, and (v) return the result of the call to make the block return the expected result.

All the information sent while running the instrumented code is received and merged by the tracer. In Erlang, the tracer is a server which is continuously receiving trace elements until the end of the execution or until a timeout is raised. Figure 10b shows a simplification of the Erlang function `tracer/1` which is in charge of this tracing process. The server state is a tuple containing: (1) a stack, where the callee and arguments are stored in the order they are received, and (2) the trace generated so far. Its body is a receive expression with three clauses: the first one is for the information sent by function calls' callees and arguments, the second one is for the result of the function call, and the third one is for the rest of trace elements, i.e. those that do not come from a function call. When a callee or an argument value is received, it is simply stacked. When the call result is received, all its arguments, which are at the top of the stack, are unstacked (function `remove_same_ref/2`), and stored in the additional information of the call trace element. Finally, the rest of trace elements are simply added to the current trace with an empty additional information structure.

4.3   Using the Enhanced Call Tracing to Compare Traces

In this section, we describe the specific requirements needed to use the implemented enhancement of Sect. 4.2. To this end, we use two executions of our POI tester `SecEr`, one execution previous to our proposed enhancement and another one after it. In concrete, we compare two versions of an Erlang program that aligns columns of a string with multiple lines. The code of both versions is shown in Fig. 11. While `align_columns_ok.erl` version code is implemented using line 19, the `align_columns.erl` version replaces that line of code with line 20. Due to space limitations, the implementation of some trusted methods is omitted, and some changes have been done. Both full program versions are part of the benchmarks used in EDD (Erlang Declarative Debugger) [3], and their originals can be found at https://github.com/tamarit/edd/tree/master/examples/align_columns.

These programs export a function with zero parameters, that can be considered a unit case. Our selected entry pointwill be function `align_left/0`. In order to test both `SecEr` implementations, we need to define also a POI relation. Our POI relation, defined in our configuration file is shown in Fig. 12.

Additionally, for enhanced POI testing, a configuration mode must be selected among the ones shown in Sect. 3.4. In our case, we have selected **NUAI-TR** mode, providing the Erlang implementation of the TECF function shown in Fig. 6 and an UnBRM that reports also the callee and the args of a function

---

[11] All free variables used in the rule are represented as fv_*. Each one of these free variables is unique and different to all the original variables of the module.

```
1  -module (align_columns_ok). / -module (align_columns).
2  -export([align_left/0]).
3
4  align_left()-> align_columns(left).
5  align_columns(Alignment) ->
6      Lines = ["Weak$people$revenge",
7               "Strong$people$forgive",
8               "Intelligent$people$ignore"],
9      Words = [ string:tokens(Line, "$") || Line <- Lines ],
10     Words_length = lists:foldl( fun max_length/2, [], Words),
11     [prepare_line(Words_line, Words_length, Alignment) || Words_line <- Words].
12
13 max_length(Words_of_a_line, Acc_maxlength) -> ...% Trusted method
14 adjust_list(L, Desired_length, Elem) -> ... % Trusted method
15
16 prepare_line(Words_line, Words_length, Alignment) ->
17     All_words = adjust_list(Words_line, length(Words_length), ""),
18     Zipped = lists:zip(All_words, Words_length),
19     [ apply(string, Alignment, [Word, Length + 1, $\s]) % align_columns_ok
20     [ apply(string, Alignment, [Word, Length - 1, $\s]) % align_columns
21       || {Word, Length} <- Zipped ].
```

Fig. 11. Align columns program versions

```
1  poiOld() -> {'align_columns_ok.erl', 19, call}.
2  poiNew() -> {'align_columns.erl', 20, call}.
3  rel() -> [{poiOld(),poiNew()}].
4  funs() -> "[align_left/0]".
5  config() -> secer_api:nuai_tr_config(mytecf(),ubrm()).
```

Fig. 12. SecEr configuration file

call as part of the report. The configuration proposed is represented with the function config/0[12] represented by line 5 in Fig. 12. Once all the configuration requirements are fulfilled, we have run SecEr obtaining the results shown in Fig. 13.

Figure 13a shows the information provided by plain POI testing implemented by SecEr. When analysing this information, we can notice that there is not enough feedback to decide whether the bug comes from the arguments or from the function call. We do not even know the function we are calling when the UnB was raised because it is passed as an argument to function prepare_line/3. On the other hand, Fig. 13b represents the execution of SecEr after implementing the enhanced call tracing. It can be seen that the source of the error is clearly the list in the third argument of the call apply, where the second element differs for both programs. Thus, we can conclude that the error comes from the expression calculating this argument. Furthermore, we also can observe that the called function in the apply call is the function string:left/3, information that was not provided by the previous SecEr version. This is just a single example, more examples of use cases dealing with some real-life programs (e.g. https://github. com/mistupv/secer/benchmarks/rebar) can be found at our Github repository.

---

[12] In our implementation, the Erlang module secer_api provides a list of implemented functions to easily select any execution mode.

```
$ ./secer -pois "test_align:rel()"
        -funs "test_align:funs()"
        -to 5


Function: align_left/0
----------------------------
Generated test cases: 1
Mismatching test cases: 1 (100.0%)
  Error Types:
    + different_value => 1 Errors
      Example call: align_left()


------ Detected Error ------
Call: align_left()
Error Type: different_value
- - - - - - - - - - - - - -
POI: {'align_columns_ok.erl',19,call,1}
  Trace:
    ["Weak        "]
POI: {'align_columns.erl',20,call,1}
  Trace:
    ["Weak        "]
```

```
$ ./secer -pois "test_align:rel()"
        -funs "test_align:funs()"
        -to 5
        -config "test_align:config()"

Function: align_left/0
----------------------------
Generated test cases: 1
Mismatching test cases: 1 (100.0%)
  Error Types:
    + different_value_different_args => 1 Errors
      Example call: align_left()


------ Detected Error ------
Call: align_left()
Error Type: different_value_different_args
- - - - - - - - - - - - - -
POI: {'align_columns_ok.erl',19,call,1}
  Trace:
    ["Weak        "]
  Call POI Info:
    Callee: apply
    Args: [string,left,["Weak",12,32]]
POI: {'align_columns.erl',20,call,1}
  Trace:
    ["Weak        "]
  Call POI Info:
    Callee: apply
    Args: [string,left,["Weak",10,32]]
```

(a) SecEr without enhancements   (b) SecEr with call tracing enhancement

Fig. 13. Comparison of SecEr executions

5   Related Work

The orchestrated survey of methodologies for automated software test case generation [2] identifies five techniques to automatically generate test cases. POI testing could be included in the class of *adaptive random technique as a variant of random testing*. Within this class, the authors identify five approaches. POI testing mutation approach of the test input shares several similarities with some approaches like selection of best candidate as next test case or exclusion. According to a survey on test amplification [5], which identifies four categories that classify all the work done in the field, our work could be included in the category named *amplification by synthesizing (new tests with respect to changes)*. Inside this category, our technique falls into the "other approaches" subcategory.

There are other approaches that use traces to compare program versions, like the ones based on program spectra [11]. Different program spectra have been proposed (branch, execution trace or data dependence spectra), but value spectra [16] is the most similar to our call trace enhancement. In particular, value trace spectra record the sequence of the user-function executions traversed as a program executes. After the spectra recording, spectra comparison techniques are used to find value spectra differences that expose internal behavioral deviations inside the black box. However, the spectrum is generated for all the user-defined functions while in our approach users decide which functions should be compared. Additionally, POI testing allows a more flexible use of these call traces. Finally, the motivation and also some techniques of the enhanced call traces are similar to the ones of *algorithmic debugging* [12]. In fact, this approach has been successfully applied to Erlang [3].

Most of the efforts in regression testing research have been put in regression testing minimization, selection, and prioritization [17], although among practitioners it does not seem to be the most important issue [6]. In fact, in the particular case of the Erlang language, most of the works in the area are focused on this specific task [13,15]. We can find other works in Erlang that share similar goals but more are focused on checking whether applying a refactoring rule will yield to a semantics-preserving new code [10].

With respect to tracing, there are multiple approximations similar to the POI testing's. In Erlang's standard libraries, there are two tracing modules. Both are able to trace function calls and process related events (spawn, send, receive, etc.). One of these modules is oriented to trace the processes of a single Erlang node [7], allowing for the definition of filters to function calls, e.g., with names of the function to be traced. The second module is oriented to distributed system tracing [8] and the output trace of all the nodes can be formatted in many different ways. Cronqvist [4] presented a tool named redbug where a call stack trace is added to the function call tracing, making possible to trace both the result and the call stack. Till [14] implemented erlyberly, a debugging tool with a Java GUI able to trace the previously defined features but also giving the possibility to add breakpoints and trace other features such as exceptions thrown or incomplete calls. All these tools are accurate to trace specific features of the program, but none of them is able to trace the value of an arbitrary point of it. In our approach, we can trace both the already defined features and a point of the program regardless of its position.

6 Conclusions

We have presented a common framework to enhance POI testing with the addition of new information. This new information enriches the approach, allowing users to get better UnB reports and to define new UnB types. These new UnB types benefit some of the internal processes of the approach, e.g. the ITC generation. These additions need new ways to send and store this additional information and also new comparison modes. In this paper, an enhancement have been proposed by augmenting call traces. This enhancement has its particularities, but it follows the common framework presented in Sect. 3.

This work opens a way to extensions of POI testing. Following the same common framework described in this paper, we can easily include different additional information. This additional data can be other functional data, i.e. similar data to richer call traces. One interesting enhancement is to store a snapshot of the current environment for each POI, so more contextual information is available to find the UnB source. We could also store the followed conditional paths, so it could be used to improve the coverage during the ITC generation. At the same time, we are studying the use of some special additional information that enables the *mocking* of values. The idea is to execute again an ITC that leads to an UnB, but when the value that uncovers the UnB is found, replace it by the value computed by a correct version of the program. This will allow the technique to find further errors using the same ITC. The same idea can be applied when an internal call is a previously executed ITC in order to avoid its recomputation. Finally, we plan to define extensions of the approach that study non-functional data, e.g. CPU or memory usage. After some preliminary work, we have concluded that the common framework presented in this paper represents a very natural way to operate with such kind of data.

References

1. Erlang (1986). http://www.erlang.org/
2. Anand, S., et al.: An orchestrated survey of methodologies for automated software test case generation. J. Syst. Softw. **86**(8), 1978–2001 (2013)
3. Caballero, R., Martin-Martin, E., Riesco, A., Tamarit, S.: EDD: a declarative debugger for sequential erlang programs. In: Ábrahám, E., Havelund, K. (eds.) TACAS 2014. LNCS, vol. 8413, pp. 581–586. Springer, Heidelberg (2014). https://doi.org/10.1007/978-3-642-54862-8_49
4. M. Cronqvist. redbug (2017). https://github.com/massemanet/redbug
5. Danglot, B., Vera-Perez, O., Yu, Z., Monperrus, M., Baudry, B.: The emerging field of test amplification: a survey. CoRR, abs/1705.10692 (2017)
6. Engström, E., Runeson, P.: A qualitative survey of regression testing practices. In: Ali Babar, M., Vierimaa, M., Oivo, M. (eds.) PROFES 2010. LNCS, vol. 6156, pp. 3–16. Springer, Heidelberg (2010). https://doi.org/10.1007/978-3-642-13792-1_3
7. Ericsson AB. dbg (2017). http://erlang.org/doc/man/dbg.html
8. Ericsson AB. Trace tool builder (2017). http://erlang.org/doc/apps/observer/ttb_ug.html
9. Insa, D., Pérez, S., Silva, J., Tamarit, S.: Behaviour preservation across code versions in Erlang. Sci. Program. **2018**, 1–42 (2018)
10. Jumpertz, E.: Using QuickCheck and semantic analysis to verify correctness of Erlang refactoring transformations. Master's thesis, Radboud University Nijmegen (2010)
11. Reps, T., Ball, T., Das, M., Larus, J.: The use of program profiling for software maintenance with applications to the year 2000 problem. In: Jazayeri, M., Schauer, H. (eds.) ESEC/SIGSOFT FSE -1997. LNCS, vol. 1301, pp. 432–449. Springer, Heidelberg (1997). https://doi.org/10.1007/3-540-63531-9_29
12. Shapiro, E.Y.: Algorithmic Program Debugging. MIT Press, Cambridge (1982)
13. Taylor, R., Hall, M., Bogdanov, K., Derrick, J.: Using behaviour inference to optimise regression test sets. In: Nielsen, B., Weise, C. (eds.) ICTSS 2012. LNCS, vol. 7641, pp. 184–199. Springer, Heidelberg (2012). https://doi.org/10.1007/978-3-642-34691-0_14
14. Till, A.: erlyberly (2017). https://github.com/andytill/erlyberly
15. Tóth, I.B.M., Horváth, Z.: Reduction of regression tests for Erlang based on impact analysis (2013)
16. Xie, T., Notkin, D.: Checking inside the black box: regression testing by comparing value spectra. IEEE Trans. Softw. Eng. **31**(10), 869–883 (2005)
17. Yoo, S., Harman, M.: Regression testing minimization, selection and prioritization: a survey. Softw. Test. Verif. Reliab. **22**(2), 67–120 (2012)

Foundations of Functional Logic Programming

Synthesizing Set Functions

Sergio Antoy[1] , Michael Hanus[2]([✉]) , and Finn Teegen[2]

[1] Computer Science Department, Portland State University, Portland, OR, USA
antoy@cs.pdx.edu
[2] Institut für Informatik, CAU Kiel, 24098 Kiel, Germany
{mh,fte}@informatik.uni-kiel.de

Abstract. Set functions are a feature of functional logic programming to encapsulate all results of a non-deterministic computation in a single data structure. Given a function f of a functional logic program written in Curry, we describe a technique to synthesize the definition of the set function of f. The definition produced by our technique is based on standard Curry constructs. Our approach is interesting for three reasons. It allows reasoning about set functions, it offers an implementation of set functions which can be added to any Curry system, and it has the potential of changing our thinking about the implementation of non-determinism, a notoriously difficult problem.

1 Introduction

Functional logic languages, such as Curry and TOY, combine the most important features of functional and logic languages. In particular, the combination of lazy evaluation and non-determinism leads to better evaluation strategies compared to logic programming [2]. However, the combination of these features poses new challenges. In particular, the encapsulation of non-strict non-deterministic computations has not a universally accepted solution so that different Curry systems offer different implementations for it. Encapsulating non-deterministic computations is an important feature for application programming when the task is to show whether some problem has a solution or to compare different solutions in order to compute the best one.

A realistic example of application is Dijkstra's algorithm for the shortest path in a graph [12]. At each iteration, the algorithm selects the "current" node, finds the set of its unvisited neighbors, and calculates their tentative distances through the current node. Defining a function that takes a node and non-deterministically produces a neighboring node is particularly simple. Our work enables us to find the set of neighbors by encapsulating this non-determinism. In this way, a relatively complicated problem becomes simple.

However, encapsulating non-determinism is not straightforward. Let $S(e)$ denote the set of all the values of an expression e. The problem with such an encapsulation operator is the fact that e might share subexpressions which are defined outside $S(e)$. For instance, consider the expression

$$\texttt{let x = 0?1 in} S(x) \tag{1}$$

© Springer Nature Switzerland AG 2019
J. Silva (Ed.): WFLP 2018, LNCS 11285, pp. 93–111, 2019.
https://doi.org/10.1007/978-3-030-16202-3_6

The infix operator "?" denotes a non-deterministic choice, i.e., the expression "0?1" has *two* values: 0 or 1. Since the non-determinism of x is introduced outside $S(x)$, the question arises whether this should be encapsulated. *Strong encapsulation*, which is similar to Prolog's findall, requires to encapsulate all non-determinism occurring during the evaluation of the encapsulated expression. In this case, expression (1) evaluates to the set $\{0,1\}$. As discussed in [8], a disadvantage of strong encapsulation is its dependence on the evaluation strategy. For instance, consider the expression

$$\text{let } x = 0?1 \text{ in } (S(x), x) \tag{2}$$

If the tuple is evaluated from left to right, the first component evaluates to $\{0,1\}$ but the second component non-deterministically evaluates to the values 0 and 1 so that the expression (2) evaluates to the values $(\{0,1\},0)$ and $(\{0,1\},1)$. However, in a right-to-left evaluation of the tuple, x is evaluated first to one of the values 0 and 1 so that, due to sharing, the expression (2) evaluates to the values $(\{0\},0)$ and $(\{1\},1)$.

To avoid this dependency on the evaluation strategy, *weak encapsulation* of $S(e)$ only encapsulates the non-determinism of e but not the non-determinism originating from expressions created outside e. Thus, *weak encapsulation* produces the result values $(\{0\},0)$ and $(\{1\},1)$ of (2) independent of the evaluation strategy. Weak encapsulation has the disadvantage that its meaning depends on the syntactic structure of expressions. For instance, the expressions "let x = 0?1 in $S(x)$" and "$S(\text{let } x = 0?1 \text{ in } x)$" have different values. To avoid misunderstandings and make the syntactic structure of encapsulation explicit, *set functions* have been proposed [4]. For any function f, there is a set function f_S which computes the set of all the values f for given argument values. The set function encapsulates the non-determinism caused by the definition of f but not non-determinism originating from arguments. For instance, consider the operation

$$\text{double } x = x + x \tag{3}$$

The result of double$_S$ is always a set with a single element since the definition of double does not contain any non-determinism. Thus, double$_S$ (0?1) evaluates to the two sets $\{0\}$ and $\{2\}$.

Although set functions fit well into the framework of functional logic programming, their implementation is challenging. For instance, the Curry system PAKCS [16] compiles Curry programs into Prolog programs so that non-determinism is implemented for free. Set functions are implemented in PAKCS by Prolog's findall. To obtain the correct separation of non-determinism caused by arguments and functions, as discussed above, arguments are completely evaluated before the findall encapsulation is invoked. Although this works in many cases, there are some situations where this implementation does not deliver any result. For instance, if the complete evaluation of arguments fails or does not terminate, no result is computed even if the set function does not demand the complete argument values. Furthermore, if the set is infinite, findall does not terminate even if the goal is only testing whether the set is empty. Thus, the PAKCS implementation of set functions is "too strict."

These problems are avoided by the implementation of set functions in the Curry system KiCS2, which compiles Curry programs into Haskell programs and represents non-deterministic values in tree-like structures [9]. A similar but slightly different representation is used to implement set functions. Due to the interaction of nested non-determinism, the detailed implementation is quite complex so that a simpler implementation is desirable.

In this paper, we propose a new implementation of set functions that can be added to any Curry system. It avoids the disadvantages of existing implementations by synthesizing an explicit definition of a set function for a given function. Depending on the source code of a function, simple or more complex definitions of a set function are derived. For instance, nested set functions require a more complex scheme than top-level set functions, and functions with non-linear right-hand sides require an explicit implementation of the call-time choice semantics.

The paper is structured as follows. In the next section, we review some aspects of functional logic programming and Curry. After the definition of set functions in Sect. 3, we introduce in Sect. 4 plural functions as an intermediate step towards the synthesis of set functions. A first and simple approach to synthesize set functions is presented in Sect. 5 before we discuss in Sects. 6 and 7 the extension to non-linear rules and nested set functions, respectively. Section 8 discussed related work before we conclude in Sect. 9.

2 Functional Logic Programming and Curry

We assume familiarity with the basic concepts of functional logic programming [5,15] and Curry [17]. Therefore, we briefly review only those aspects that are relevant for this paper.

Although Curry has a syntax close to Haskell, there is an important difference in the interpretation of rules defining an operation. If there are different rules that might be applicable to reduce an expression, all rules are applied in a non-deterministic manner. Hence, operations might yield more than one result on a given input. Non-deterministic operations, which are interpreted as mappings from values into sets of values [14], are an important feature of contemporary functional logic languages. The archetype of non-deterministic operations is the choice operator "?" defined by

```
x ? _ = x
_ ? y = y
```

Typically, this operator is used to define other non-deterministic operations like

```
coin = 0 ? 1
```

Thus, the expression coin evaluates to one of the values 0 or 1. Non-deterministic operations are quite expressive since they can be used to completely eliminate logic variables in functional logic programs, as shown in [3,11]. Therefore, we ignore logic variables in the formal development below. For instance, a Boolean logic variable can be replaced by the non-deterministic *generator operation* for Booleans defined by

$$\text{aBool = False ? True} \tag{4}$$

Passing non-deterministic operations as arguments, as in the expression `double coin`, might cause a semantical ambiguity. If the argument `coin` is evaluated before calling `double`, the expression has two values, 0 and 2. However, if the argument `coin` is passed unevaluated to the right-hand side of `double` and, thus, duplicated, the expression has three different values: 0, 1, or 2. These two interpretations are called *call-time choice* and *run-time choice* [19]. Contemporary functional logic languages stick to the call-time choice, since this leads to results which are independent of the evaluation strategy and has the rewriting logic CRWL [14] as a logical foundation for declarative programming with non-strict and non-deterministic operations. Furthermore, it can be implemented by sharing which is already available in implementations of non-strict languages. In this paper, we use a simple reduction relation, equivalent to CRWL, that we sketch without giving all details (which can be found in [20]).

A *value* is an expression without occurrences of function symbols. To cover non-strict computations, expressions can also contain the special symbol $\perp$ to represent *undefined or unevaluated values*. A *partial value* is a value that might contain occurrences of $\perp$. A *partial constructor substitution* is a substitution that replaces variables by partial values. A *context* $C[\cdot]$ is an expression with some "hole". Then expressions are reduced according to the following reduction relation:

$$C[f\ \sigma(t_1)\ldots\sigma(t_n)] \to C[\sigma(r)] \qquad \text{where } f\ t_1\ldots t_n = r \text{ is a program rule}$$
$$\text{and } \sigma \text{ a partial constructor substitution}$$
$$C[e] \to C[\perp] \qquad \text{where } e \neq \perp$$

The first rule models the call-time choice: if a rule is applied, the actual arguments of the operation must have been evaluated to partial values. The second rule models non-strictness by allowing the evaluation of any subexpression to an undefined value (which is intended if the value of this subexpression is not demanded). As usual, $\overset{*}{\to}$ denotes the reflexive and transitive closure of this reduction relation. We also write $e = v$ instead of $e \overset{*}{\to} v$ if v is a (partial) value.

For the sake of simplicity, we assume that programs are already translated into a simple standard form: conditional rules are replaced by if-then-else expressions and the left-hand sides of all operations (except for "?") are *uniform* [21] i.e., either the operation is defined by a single rule where all arguments are distinct variables, or in the left-hand sides of all rules only the last (or any other fixed) argument is a constructor with variables as arguments where each constructor of a data type occurs in exactly one rule. Section 3.2 of [21] provides an algorithm for transforming the rules defining a function into a set of uniform rules defining the same function. Uniform rules are not overlapping so that non-determinism is represented by ?-expressions.

3   Set Functions

The purpose of a set function is to encapsulate only the non-determinism caused by the definition of the corresponding function. Similarly to non-determinism, set functions encapsulate failures only if they are caused by the function's definition. If `failed` denotes a failing computation, i.e., an expression without a value, the expression `double`$_S$ `failed` has no value (and not the empty set as a value). Since the meaning of failures and nested set functions has not been discussed in [4], Christiansen et al. [10] propose a rigorous denotational semantics for set functions. In order to handle failures and choices in nested applications of set functions, computations are attached with "nesting levels" so that failures caused by different encapsulation levels can be distinguished.

In the following, we use a simpler model of set functions. Formally, set functions return sets. However, for simplicity, our implementation returns multisets, instead of sets, represented as some abstract data type. Converting multisets into sets is straightforward for the representation we choose. If b is a type, $\{b\}$ denotes the type of a set of elements of type b. The meaning of a set function can be defined as follows:

Definition 1. *Given a unary (for simplicity) function* $f :: a \to b$*, the* set function *of* f*,* $f_S :: a \to \{b\}$*, is defined as follows: For every partial value t of type a, value u of type b, and set U of elements of type b,* $(f\ t) = u$ *iff* $(f_S\ t) = U$ *and* $u \in U$*.*

This definition accommodates the different aspects of set functions discussed in the introduction. If the evaluation of an expression e leads to a failure or choice but its value is not required by the set function, it does not influence the result of the set function since e can be derived to the partial value $\bot$.

Example 1. Consider the following function:

$$\text{ndconst x y = x ? 1} \tag{5}$$

The value of `ndconst`$_S$ `2 failed` is $\{2,1\}$, and `ndconst`$_S$ `(2?4) failed` has the values $\{2,1\}$ and $\{4,1\}$.

Given a function f, we want to develop a method to synthesize the definition f_S. A difficulty is that f might be composed of other functions whose non-determinism should also be encapsulated by f_S. This can be solved by introducing plural functions, which are described next.

4   Plural Functions

If $f :: b \to c$ and $g :: a \to b$ are functions, their composition $(f \circ g)$ is well defined by $(f \circ g)(x) = f(g(x))$ for all x of type a. However, the corresponding set functions, $f_S :: b \to \{c\}$ and $g_S :: a \to \{b\}$, are not composable because their types mismatch—an output of g_S cannot be an input of f_S. To support the composition of functions that return sets, we need functions that take sets as arguments.[1]

Definition 2. *Let $f :: a \to b$ be a function. We call* plural *function of* f *any function* $f_P :: \{a\} \to \{b\}$ *with the following property: for all X and Y such that $f_P\, X = Y$, (1) if $y \in Y$ then there exists some $x \in X$ such that $f\, x = y$ and (2) if $x \in X$ and $f\, x = y$, then $y \in Y$.*

The above definition generalizes to functions with more than one argument. The following display shows both the type and an example of application of the plural function, denoted by "$++_P$", of the usual list concatenation "$++$":

$$
\begin{array}{l}
(++_P) \ :: \ \{[a]\} \ \text{->} \ \{[a]\} \ \text{->} \ \{[a]\} \\
\{[1],[2]\} \ ++_P \ \{[],[3]\} \ = \ \{[1],[1,3],[2],[2,3]\}
\end{array}
\tag{6}
$$

Plural functions are unique, composable, and cover all the results of set functions (the details are available in a longer version of this paper). Since plural functions are an important step towards the synthesis of set functions, we discuss their synthesis first. To implement plural functions in Curry, we have to decide how to represent sets (our implementation returns multisets) of elements. An obvious representation are lists. Since we will later consider non-linear rules and also nested set functions where non-determinism of different encapsulation levels are combined, we instead use search trees [8] to represent choices between values. The type of a search tree parameterized over the type of elements can be defined as follows:

```
data ST a = Val a | Fail | Choice (ST a) (ST a)
```

Hence, a search tree is either an expression in head-normal form, i.e., rooted by a constructor symbol, a failure, or a choice between search trees. Although this definition does not enforce that the argument of a `Val` constructor is in head-normal form, this invariant will be ensured by our synthesis method for set functions, as presented below. For instance, the plural function of the operation `aBool` (4) can be defined as

```
aBoolP :: ST Bool
aBoolP = Choice (Val False) (Val True)
```

The plural function of the logical negation `not` defined by

$$
\begin{array}{l}
\texttt{not False = True} \\
\texttt{not True = False}
\end{array}
\tag{7}
$$

takes a search tree as an argument so that its definition must match all search tree constructors. Since the matching structure is similar for all operations performing pattern matching on an argument, we use the following generic operation

---

[1] The notion of "plural function" is also used in [22] to define a "plural" semantics for functional logic programs. Although the type of their plural functions is identical to ours, their semantics is quite different.

to apply an operation defined by pattern matching to a non-deterministic argument:[2]

```
applyST :: (a → ST b) → ST a → ST b
applyST f (Val x)       = f x
applyST _ Fail          = Fail
applyST f (Choice x1 x2) = Choice (f `applyST` x1) (f `applyST` x2)
```

Hence, failures remain as failures, and a choice in the argument leads to a choice in the result of the operation, which is also called a pull-tab step [1]. Now the plural function of `not` can be defined by (shortly we will specify a systematic translation method)

```
notP :: ST Bool → ST Bool
notP = applyST $ \x → case x of False → Val True
                                True  → Val False
```

The synthesis of plural functions for uniform programs is straightforward: pattern matching is implemented with `applyST` and function composition in right-hand sides comes for free.[3] For instance, the plural function of

```
twiceNot x = not (not x)
```

is

```
twiceNotP x = notP (notP x)
```

So far we considered only base values in search trees. If one wants to deal with structured data, like lists of integers, a representation like `ST [Int]` is not appropriate since non-determinism can occur in any constructor of the list, as shown by

```
one23 = (1?2) : ([] ? (3:[]))
```

The expression `one23` evaluates to `[1]`, `[2]`, `[1,3]`, and `[2,3]`. If we select only the head of the list, the non-determinism in the tail does not show up, i.e., `head one23` evaluates to two values 1 and 2. This demands for a representation of head-normal forms with possible search tree arguments. It can be easily derived for any algebraic data type. The head-normal forms of non-deterministic lists are the usual list constructors where the cons arguments are search trees:

```
data STList a = Nil | Cons (ST a) (ST (STList a))
```

The plural representation of `one23` is

```
one23P :: ST (STList Int)
one23P = Val (Cons (Choice (Val 1) (Val 2))
                   (Choice (Val Nil) (Val (Cons (Val 3) (Val Nil)))))
```

The plural function of `head` is synthesized as

```
headP :: ST (STList a) → ST a
headP = applyST $ \xs → case xs of Nil      → Fail
                                   Cons x _ → x
```

_____

[2] Actually, this operation is the monadic "bind" operation with flipped arguments if `ST` is an instance of `MonadPlus`, as proposed in [13]. Here, we prefer to provide a more direct implementation.

[3] This is a consequence of the fact that `ST` is a functor. A more general treatment of these structures can be found in [6].

so that `headP one23P` evaluates to `Choice (Val 1) (Val 2)`, as intended.

To provide a precise definition of this transformation, we assume that all operations in the program are uniform (see Sect. 2). The plural transformation $[\![\cdot]\!]_{\mathcal{P}}$ of these kinds of function definitions is defined as follows (where $C_{\mathcal{P}}$ denotes the constructor of the non-deterministic type, like `STList`, corresponding to the original constructor C):

$$[\![f\ x_1 \ldots x_n = e]\!]_{\mathcal{P}} \;=\; f_{\mathcal{P}}\ x_1 \ldots x_n = \;[\![e]\!]_{\mathcal{P}}$$

$$\left[\!\!\left[\begin{array}{c} f\ x_1 \ldots x_{n-1}\ (C^1\ x_{11} \ldots x_{1i_1}) = e_1 \\ \vdots \\ f\ x_1 \ldots x_{n-1}\ (C^n\ x_{n1} \ldots x_{ni_n}) = e_n \end{array}\right]\!\!\right]_{\mathcal{P}} = \begin{array}{l} f_{\mathcal{P}}\ x_1 \ldots x_{n-1} = \texttt{applyST \$}\ \backslash x \to \\ \quad \texttt{case}\ x\ \texttt{of} \\ \qquad C^1_{\mathcal{P}}\ x_{11} \ldots x_{1i_1} \to [\![e_1]\!]_{\mathcal{P}} \\ \qquad \vdots \\ \qquad C^n_{\mathcal{P}}\ x_{n1} \ldots x_{ni_n} \to [\![e_n]\!]_{\mathcal{P}} \end{array}$$

Note that x_i and x_{jk} have different types in the original and transformed program, e.g., an argument of type `Int` is transformed into an argument of type `ST Int`. Furthermore, expressions occurring in the function bodies are transformed according to the following rules:

$$\begin{aligned} [\![x]\!]_{\mathcal{P}} &= x \\ [\![C\ e_1 \ldots e_n]\!]_{\mathcal{P}} &= \texttt{Val}\ (C_{\mathcal{P}}\ [\![e_1]\!]_{\mathcal{P}} \ldots [\![e_n]\!]_{\mathcal{P}}) \\ [\![f\ e_1 \ldots e_n]\!]_{\mathcal{P}} &= f_{\mathcal{P}}\ [\![e_1]\!]_{\mathcal{P}} \ldots [\![e_n]\!]_{\mathcal{P}} \\ [\![e_1\ ?\ e_2]\!]_{\mathcal{P}} &= \texttt{Choice}\ [\![e_1]\!]_{\mathcal{P}}\ [\![e_2]\!]_{\mathcal{P}} \\ [\![\texttt{failed}]\!]_{\mathcal{P}} &= \texttt{Fail} \end{aligned}$$

The presented synthesis of plural functions is simple and yields compositionality and laziness. Thus, they are a good basis to define set functions, as shown next.

We are not overly concerned about the increase in size of a program's object code when plural functions are synthesized and added to the program. The source code of the plural function, $f_{\mathcal{P}}$, of a function f contains the same structural elements, e.g., pattern matching and nested function calls, as f. Hence the object code of $f_{\mathcal{P}}$ is expected to have a size similar to that of f regardless of the compilation technique. Since only a fraction of the functions of a program require the synthesis of the corresponding plural function, the size of the object code should increase by a factor closer to 1 than to 2.

5   Synthesis of Set Functions: The Simple Way

Plural functions take sets as arguments whereas set functions are applied to standard expressions which might not be evaluated. To distinguish these possibly unevaluated arguments from head-normal forms, we add a new constructor to search trees

```
data ST a = Val a | Uneval a | Fail | Choice (ST a) (ST a)
```
and extend the definition of `applyST` with the rule
```
applyST f (Uneval x) = f x
```
Furthermore, plural functions yield non-deterministic structures which might not be completely evaluated. By contrast, set functions yield sets of values, i.e., completely evaluated elements. In order to turn a plural function into a set function, we have to evaluate the search tree structure into the set of their values. For the sake of simplicity, we represent the latter as ordinary lists. Thus, we need an operation like
```
stValues :: ST a  →  [a]
```
to extract all the values from a search tree. For instance, the expression
```
stValues (Choice (Val 1) (Choice Fail (Val 2)))
```
should evaluate to the list [1,2]. This demands for the evaluation of all the values in a search tree (which might be head-normal forms with choices at argument positions) into its complete normal form. We define a type class[4] for this purpose:

```
class NF a where
  nf :: a  →  ST a
```
Each instance of this type class must define a method `nf` which evaluates a given head-normal form into a search tree where all `Val` arguments are completely evaluated. Instances for base types are easily defined:
```
instance NF Int where
  nf x = Val x
```
The operation `nf` is easily extended to arbitrary search trees:[5]
```
nfST :: NF a => ST a  →  ST a
nfST (Val x)        = nf x
nfST (Uneval x)     = x 'seq' nf x
nfST Fail           = Fail
nfST (Choice x1 x2) = Choice (nfST x1) (nfST x2)
```
Now we can define an operation that collects all the values in a search tree (without `Uneval` constructors) into a list by a depth-first strategy:
```
searchDFS :: ST a  →  [a]
searchDFS (Val x)        = [x]
searchDFS Fail           = []
searchDFS (Choice x1 x2) = searchDFS x1 ++ searchDFS x2
```
Thus, failures are ignored and choices are concatenated. Combining these two operations yields the desired definition of `stValues`:
```
stValues :: NF a => ST a  →  [a]
stValues = searchDFS . nfST
```

---

[4] Although the current definition of Curry [17] does not include type classes, many implementations of Curry, like PAKCS, KiCS2, or MCC, support them.

[5] The use of `seq` ensures that the `Uneval` argument is evaluated. Thus, non-determinism and failures in arguments of set functions are not encapsulated, as intended.

NF instances for structured types can be defined by moving choices and failures in arguments to the root:

```
instance NF a => NF (STList a) where
  nf Nil          = Val Nil
  nf (Cons x xs) = case nfST x of
    Choice c1 c2  →  Choice (nf (Cons c1 xs)) (nf (Cons c2 xs))
    Fail          →  Fail
    y             →  case nfST xs of
      Choice c1 c2  →  Choice (nf (Cons y c1)) (nf (Cons y c2))
      Fail          →  Fail
      ys            →  Val (Cons y ys)
```

For instance, the non-deterministic list value [1?2] can be described by the ST structure

```
nd01 = Val (Cons (Choice (Val 0) (Val 1)) (Val Nil))
```

so that stValues nd01 moves the inner choice to the top-level and yields the list

```
[Cons (Val 0) (Val Nil), Cons (Val 1) (Val Nil)]
```

which represents the set {[0], [1]}.

As an example for our first approach to synthesize set functions, consider the following operation (from Curry's prelude) which non-deterministically returns any element of a list:

```
anyOf :: [a]  →  a
anyOf (x:xs) = x ? anyOf xs
```

Since set functions do not encapsulate non-determinism caused by arguments, the expression anyOf$_S$ [0?1,2,3] evaluates to the sets {0, 2, 3} and {1, 2, 3}.

In order to synthesize the set function for anyOf by exploiting plural functions, we have to convert ordinary types, like [Int], into search tree types, like STList Int, and vice versa. For this purpose, we define two conversion operations for each type and collect their general form in the following type class:[6]

```
class ConvertST a b where
  toValST   :: a  →  b
  fromValST :: b  →  a
```

Instances for base and list types are easily defined:

```
instance ConvertST Int Int where
  toValST   = id
  fromValST = id

instance ConvertST a b => ConvertST [a] (STList b) where
  toValST []       = Nil
  toValST (x:xs) = Cons (toST x) (toST xs)

  fromValST Nil                      = []
  fromValST (Cons (Val x) (Val xs)) = fromValST x : fromValST xs
```

where the operation toST is like toValST but adds an Uneval constructor:

---

[6] Multi-parameter type classes are not yet supported in the Curry systems PAKCS and KiCS2. The code presented here is more elegant, but equivalent, to the actual implementation.

```
toST :: ConvertST a b => a → ST b
toST = Uneval . toValST
```

The (informal) precondition of `fromValST` is that its argument is already fully evaluated, e.g., by an operation like `stValues`. Therefore, we define the following operation to translate an arbitrary search tree into the list of its Curry values:

```
fromST :: (ConvertST a b, NF b) => ST b → Values a
fromST = map fromValST . stValues
```

As already mentioned, we use lists to represent multisets of values:

```
type Values a = [a]
```

However, one could also use another (abstract) data type to represent multisets or even convert them into sets, if desired.

Now we have all parts to synthesize a set function: convert an ordinary value into its search tree representation, apply the plural function on it, and translate the search tree back into the multiset (list) of the values contained in this tree. We demonstrate this by synthesizing the set function of `anyOf`.

The uniform representation of `anyOf` performs complete pattern matching on all constructors:

```
anyOf []     = failed
anyOf (x:xs) = x ? anyOf xs
```

We easily synthesize its plural function according to the scheme of Sect. 4:

```
anyOfP :: ST (STList Int) → ST Int
anyOfP = applyST $ \xs →
           case xs of Nil     → Fail
                      Cons x xs → Choice x (anyOfP xs)
```

Finally, we obtain its set function by converting the argument into the search tree and the result of the plural function into a multiset of integers:

```
anyOfS :: [Int] → Values Int
anyOfS = fromST . anyOfP . toST
```

The behavior of our synthesized set function is identical to their original definition, e.g., `anyOfS [0?1,2,3]` evaluates to the lists `[0,2,3]` and `[1,2,3]`, i.e., non-determinism caused by arguments is not encapsulated. This is due to the fact that the evaluation of arguments, if they are demanded inside the set function, are initiated by standard pattern matching so that a potential non-deterministic evaluation leads to a non-deterministic evaluation of the synthesized set function.

In contrast to the strict evaluation of set functions in PAKCS, as discussed in the introduction, our synthesized set functions evaluate their arguments lazily. For instance, the set function of `ndconst` defined in Example 1 is synthesized as follows:

```
ndconstP :: ST Int → ST Int → ST Int
ndconstP nx ny = Choice nx (Val 1)

ndconstS :: Int → Int → Values Int
ndconstS x y = fromST (ndconstP (toST x) (toST y))
```

Since the second argument of `ndconstS` is never evaluated, the expression `ndconstS 2 failed` evaluates to `[2,1]` and `ndconstS (2?4) (3?5)` yields the lists

[2,1] and [4,1]. The set function implementation of PAKCS fails on the first
expression and yields four results on the second one. Hence, our synthesized set
function yields better results than PAKCS, in the sense that it is more complete and avoids duplicated results. Moreover, specific primitive operations, like
findall, are not required.

The latter property is also interesting from another point of view. Since
PAKCS uses Prolog's findall, the evaluation strategy is fixed to a depth-first
search strategy implemented by backtracking. Our implementation allows more
flexible search strategies by modifying the implementation of stValues. Actually,
one can generalize search trees and stValues to a monadic structure, as done in
[7,13], to implement various strategies for non-deterministic programming.

A weak point of our current synthesis is the handling of failures. For instance,
the evaluation of anyOfS [failed,1] fails (due to the evaluation of the first list
element) whereas $anyOf_S$ [failed,1] = {1} according to Definition 1. To correct this incompleteness, failures resulting from argument evaluations must be
combined with result sets. This can be done by extending search trees and distinguishing different sources of failures, but we omit it here since a comprehensive
solution to this issue will be presented in Sect. 7 when nested applications of set
functions are discussed.

6   Adding Call-Time Choice

We have seen in Sect. 1 that the expression double (0?1) should evaluate to the
values 0 or 2 due to the call-time choice semantics. Thus, the set function of

```
double01 :: Int
double01 = double (0?1)
```

should yield the multiset {0, 2}. However, with the current synthesis, the corresponding set function yields the list [0,1,1,2] and, thus, implements the runtime choice. The problem arises from the fact that the non-deterministic choice
in the synthesized plural function

```
double01P :: ST Int
double01P = doubleP (Choice (Val 0) (Val 1))
```

is duplicated by doubleP. In order to implement the call-time choice, the same
decision (left or right choice) for both duplicates has to be made. Instead, the
search operation searchDFS handles these choices independently and is unaware
of the duplication.

To tackle this problem, we follow the idea implemented in KiCS2 [9] and
extend our search tree structure by identifiers for choices (represented by the
type ID) as follows:

```
data ST a = Val a | Uneval a | Fail | Choice ID (ST a) (ST a)
```

The changes to previously introduced operations on search trees, like applyST
or nfST, are minimal and straightforward as we only have to keep a choice's
identifier in their definitions. The most significant change occurs in the search
operation. As shown in [9], the call-time choice can be implemented by storing
the decision for a choice, when it is made for the first time, during the traversal

of the search tree and looking it up later when encountering the same choice again. We introduce the type

```
data Decision = Left | Right
```

for decisions and use an association list[7] as an additional argument to the search operation to store such decisions. The adjusted depth-first search then looks as follows:

```
searchDFS :: [(ID,Decision)]  → ST a → [a]
searchDFS _ (Val x)       = [x]
searchDFS _ Fail          = []
searchDFS m (Choice i x1 x2) = case lookup i m of
  Nothing    → searchDFS ((i,Left):m) x1 ++
               searchDFS ((i,Right):m) x2
  Just Left  → searchDFS m x1
  Just Right → searchDFS m x2
```

When extracting all the values from a search tree, we initially pass an empty list to the search operation since no decisions have been made at that point:

```
stValues :: NF a => ST a  → [a]
stValues = searchDFS [] . nfST
```

Finally, we have to ensure that the choices occurring in synthesized plural functions are provided with unique identifiers. To this end, we assume a type IDSupply that represents an infinite set of such identifiers along with the following operations:

```
initSupply                ::  IDSupply
uniqueID                  ::  IDSupply  → ID
leftSupply, rightSupply   ::  IDSupply  → IDSupply
```

The operation initSupply yields an initial identifier set. The operation uniqueID yields an identifier from such a set while the operations leftSupply and rightSupply both yield disjoint subsets without the identifier obtained by uniqueID (see [9] for a discussion about implementing these operations.). When synthesizing plural functions, we add an additional argument of type IDSupply and use the aforementioned operations on it to provide unique identifiers to every choice. The synthesized set function has to pass the initial identifier supply initSupply to the plural function. In the case of double01, it looks as follows:

```
double01P :: IDSupply  → ST Int
double01P s = doubleP (leftSupply s)
                      (Choice (uniqueID s) (Val 0) (Val 1))
double01S :: Values Int
double01S = fromST (doubleP initSupply)
```

With this modified synthesis, the set function yields the expected result [0,2]. Note that this extended scheme is necessary only if some operation involved in the definition of the set function has rules with non-linear right-hand sides, i.e., might duplicate argument expressions. For the sake of readability, we omit this

---

[7] Of course, one can replace such lists by more efficient access structures.

extension in the next section where we present another extension necessary when set functions are nested.

7 Synthesis of Nested Set Functions

So far we considered the synthesis of set functions that occur only at the top-level of functional computations, i.e., which are not nested inside other set functions. The synthesis was based on the translation of functions involved in the definition of a set function into plural functions and extracting all the values represented by a search tree into a list structure. If set functions are nested, the situation becomes more complicated since one has to define the plural function of an inner set function. Moreover, choices and failures produced by different set functions, i.e., levels of encapsulations, must be distinguished according to [10]. Although nested set functions are seldom used, a complete implementation of set functions must consider them. Therefore, we discuss in this section how we can extend the scheme proposed so far to accommodate nested set functions.

The original proposal of set functions [4] emphasized the idea to distinguish non-determinism of arguments from non-determinism of the function definition. However, the influence of failing computations and the combination of nested set functions was not specified. These aspects are discussed in [10] where a denotational semantics for functional logic programs with weak encapsulation is proposed. Roughly speaking, an encapsulation level is attached to failures and choices. These levels are taken into account when value sets are extracted from a nested non-determinism structure to ensure that failures and choices are encapsulated by the function they belong to and not any other. We can model this semantics by extending the structure of search trees as follows:

    data ST a = Val a | Uneval a | Fail Int | Choice Int (ST a) (ST a)

The additional argument of the constructors `Fail` and `Choice` specifies the encapsulation level.

Consider the definition

$$\text{notf} = \text{not}_S \text{ failed} \tag{8}$$

and the expression notf_S. Although the right-hand side of `notf` fails because the argument of `not` is demanded w.r.t. the Definition (7), the source of the failure is inside its definition so that the failure is encapsulated and the result of notf_S is the empty set. However, if we define

$$\text{nots x} = \text{not}_S \text{ x} \tag{9}$$

and evaluate nots_S `failed`, the computation fails since the failure comes from outside and is not encapsulated. These issues are discussed in [10] where it has been argued that failures outside encapsulated search should lead to a failure instead of an empty set only if there are no other results. For instance, the expression anyOf_S `failed` has no value (since the demanded argument is an outside failure) whereas the value of the expression

$$\text{anyOf}_S \text{ [failed,1]} \tag{10}$$

is the set with the single element 1. This semantics can be implemented by comparing the levels of failures occurring in search trees (see [10] for details).

With the extension of search trees introduced above, we are well prepared to implement this semantics in Curry itself except for one point: outside failures always lead to a failure of the complete evaluation if their value is needed in the encapsulated search. Thus, the evaluation of (10) will always fail. In order to avoid this, we have to transform such a failure into the search tree element `Fail 0` (where 0 is the "top" encapsulation level, i.e., outside any set function). For this purpose, we modify the definitions of `applyST` and `nfST` on arguments matching the `Uneval` constructor by checking whether the evaluation of the argument to a head-normal form fails:[8]

```
applyST f (Uneval x) = if isFail x then Fail 0 else f x
nfST (Uneval x) = if isFail x then Fail 0 else x 'seq' nf x
```

Then one can synthesize plural and set functions similarly to the already presented scheme. In order to set the correct encapsulation level in `Fail` and `Choice` constructors, every function has the current encapsulation level as an additional argument. Finally, one also has to synthesize plural functions of set functions if they are used inside other set functions. For instance, the set function of `not` has type

```
notS :: Bool  →  Values Bool
```

but the plural function of this set function must represent the result set again as a search tree, i.e., it has the type

```
notSP :: Int  →  ST Bool  →  ST (STList Bool)
```

(the first argument is the encapsulation level). To evaluate the search tree structure returned by such plural set functions, we need an operation which behaves similarly to `stValues` but returns a search tree representation of the list of values, i.e., this operation has the type

```
stValuesP :: NF a => Int  →  ST a  →  ST (STList a)
```

Note that this operation also takes the encapsulation level as its first argument. For instance, failures are only encapsulated (into an empty list) if they are on the same level, i.e., there is the following defining rule for `stValuesP`:

```
stValuesP e (Fail n) = if n==e then Val Nil else Fail n
```

Choices are treated in a similar way where failures in different alternatives are merged to their maximum level according to the semantics of [10], e.g.,

```
stValuesP 1 (Choice 1 (Fail 0) (Fail 1))
```

evaluates to `Val Nil` (representing the empty set of values).

Now we can define `notSP` by evaluating the result of `notP` with `stValuesP` where the current encapsulation level is increased:

```
notSP e x = stValuesP (e+1) (notP (e+1) x)
```

The plural function of `notf` (8) is straightforward (note that the level of the generated failure is the current encapsulation level):

---

[8] This requires a specific primitive `isFail` to catch failures, which is usually supported in Curry implementations to handle exceptions.

```
notfP :: Int  →  ST (STList Bool)
notfP e = notSP e (Fail e)
```

The set function of `notf` is synthesized as presented before except that we additionally provide 1 as the initial encapsulation level (this is also the level encapsulated by `fromST`):

```
notfS :: Values (Values Bool)
notfS = fromST (notfP 1)
```

As we have seen, nested set functions can be synthesized with a scheme similar to simple set functions. In order to correctly model the semantics of [10], an encapsulation level is added to each translated operation which is used to generate the correct `Fail` and `Choice` constructors. In order integrate the synthesized set functions into standard Curry programs, arguments passed to synthesized set functions must be checked for failures when their values are demanded.

The extensions presented in the previous and this section can be combined without problems. Concrete examples for this combination and more examples for the synthesis techniques presented in this paper are available on-line.[9] In particular, there are also examples for the synthesis of higher-order functions, which we omitted in this paper due to the additional complexity of synthesizing the plural functions of higher-order arguments.

8   Related Work

The problems caused by integrating encapsulated search in functional logic programs are discussed in [8] where the concepts of strong and weak encapsulation are distinguished. Weak encapsulation fits better to declarative programming since the results do not depend on the order of evaluation. Set functions [4] make the boundaries between different sources of non-determinism clear. The semantical difficulties caused by nesting set functions are discussed in [10] where a denotational semantics for set functions is presented.

The implementation of backtracking and non-determinism in functional languages has a long tradition [24]. While earlier approaches concentrated on embedding Prolog-like constructs in functional languages (e.g., [18,23]), the implementation of demand-driven non-determinism, which is the core of contemporary functional logic languages [2], has been less explored. A monadic implementation of the call-time choice is developed in [13] which is the basis to translate a subset of Curry to Haskell [7]. Due to performance problems with this generic approach, KiCS2, another compiler from Curry to Haskell, is proposed in [9]. Currently, KiCS2 is the only system implementing encapsulated search and set functions according to [10], but the detailed implementation is complex and, thus, difficult to maintain. This fact partially motivated the development of the approach described in this paper.

---

[9] https://github.com/finnteegen/synthesizing-set-functions.

9   Conclusions

We have presented a technique to synthesize the definition of a set function of any function defined in a Curry program. This is useful to add set functions and encapsulated search to any Curry system so that an explicit handling of set functions in the run-time system is not necessary. Thanks to our method, one can add a better (i.e., less strict) implementation of set functions to the Prolog-based Curry implementation PAKCS or simplify the run-time system of the Haskell-based Curry implementation KiCS2.

A disadvantage of our approach is that it increases the size of the transformed program due to the addition of the synthesized code. Considering the fact that the majority of application code is deterministic and not involved in set functions, the increased code size is acceptable. Nevertheless, it is an interesting topic for future work to evaluate the increase of code size for application programs and try to find better synthesis principles (e.g., for specific classes of operations) which produce less additional code.

Our work has the potential of both immediate and far reaching paybacks. We offer a set-based definition of set functions simpler and more immediate than previous ones. We offer a notion of plural function that is original and natural. We show interesting relationships between the two that allow us to better understand, reason about and compute with these concepts. The immediate consequence is an implementation of set functions competitive with previous proposals.

It is well known that a non-deterministic function can be implemented by a deterministic function that enumerates its results. A direct approach [24] may sacrifice laziness. An approach that preserves laziness [13] is cumbersome for the programmer and may sacrifice efficiency. An intriguing aspect of our work is the possibility of replacing any non-deterministic function, f, in a program with its set function, which is deterministic, by enumerating all the results of f. Our long-term goal is to execute this transformation automatically at compile time without affecting the laziness of a program and without intervention of the programmer. Thus, an (often non-deterministic) functional logic program would become a deterministic program. A consequence of this change is that the techniques for the implementation of non-determinism, such as backtracking, bubbling and pull-tabbing, which are the output of a tremendous intellectual effort of the last few decades, would no longer be an explicit element of the implementation or a concern of the programmer.

References

1. Alqaddoumi, A., Antoy, S., Fischer, S., Reck, F.: The pull-tab transformation. In: Proceedings of the Third International Workshop on Graph Computation Models, Enschede, The Netherlands, pp. 127–132 (2010). http://gcm-events.org/gcm2010/pages/gcm2010-preproceedings.pdf
2. Antoy, S., Echahed, R., Hanus, M.: A needed narrowing strategy. J. ACM **47**(4), 776–822 (2000)

3. Antoy, S., Hanus, M.: Overlapping rules and logic variables in functional logic programs. In: Etalle, S., Truszczyński, M. (eds.) ICLP 2006. LNCS, vol. 4079, pp. 87–101. Springer, Heidelberg (2006). https://doi.org/10.1007/11799573_9

4. Antoy, S., Hanus, M.: Set functions for functional logic programming. In: Proceedings of the 11th ACM SIGPLAN International Conference on Principles and Practice of Declarative Programming (PPDP 2009), pp. 73–82. ACM Press (2009)

5. Antoy, S., Hanus, M.: Functional logic programming. Commun. ACM 53(4), 74–85 (2010)

6. Atkey, R., Johann, P.: Interleaving data and effects. J. Funct. Programm. 25, e20 (2015). https://doi.org/10.1017/S0956796815000209

7. Braßel, B., Fischer, S., Hanus, M., Reck, F.: Transforming functional logic programs into monadic functional programs. In: Mariño, J. (ed.) WFLP 2010. LNCS, vol. 6559, pp. 30–47. Springer, Heidelberg (2011). https://doi.org/10.1007/978-3-642-20775-4_2

8. Braßel, B., Hanus, M., Huch, F.: Encapsulating non-determinism in functional logic computations. J. Funct. Log. Program. 6, 2004 (2004)

9. Braßel, B., Hanus, M., Peemöller, B., Reck, F.: KiCS2: a new compiler from curry to Haskell. In: Kuchen, H. (ed.) WFLP 2011. LNCS, vol. 6816, pp. 1–18. Springer, Heidelberg (2011). https://doi.org/10.1007/978-3-642-22531-4_1

10. Christiansen, J., Hanus, M., Reck, F., Seidel, D.: A semantics for weakly encapsulated search in functional logic programs. In: Proceedings of the 15th International Symposium on Principle and Practice of Declarative Programming (PPDP 2013), pp. 49–60. ACM Press (2013)

11. de Dios Castro, J., López-Fraguas, F.J.: Extra variables can be eliminated from functional logic programs. Electron. Notes Theor. Comput. Sci. 188, 3–19 (2007)

12. Dijkstra, E.W.: A note on two problems in connexion with graphs. Numer. Math. 1(1), 269–271 (1959)

13. Fischer, S., Kiselyov, O., Shan, C.: Purely functional lazy nondeterministic programming. J. Funct. program. 21(4&5), 413–465 (2011)

14. González-Moreno, J.C., Hortalá-González, M.T., López-Fraguas, F.J., Rodríguez-Artalejo, M.: An approach to declarative programming based on a rewriting logic. J. Log. Program. 40, 47–87 (1999)

15. Hanus, M.: Functional logic programming: from theory to curry. In: Voronkov, A., Weidenbach, C. (eds.) Programming Logics. LNCS, vol. 7797, pp. 123–168. Springer, Heidelberg (2013). https://doi.org/10.1007/978-3-642-37651-1_6

16. Hanus, M., et al.: PAKCS: the Portland Aachen Kiel curry system (2018). http://www.informatik.uni-kiel.de/~pakcs/

17. Hanus, M. (ed.): Curry: an integrated functional logic language (vers. 0.9.0) (2016). http://www.curry-language.org

18. Hinze, R.: Prolog's control constructs in a functional setting - axioms and implementation. Int. J. Found. Comput. Sci. 12(2), 125–170 (2001)

19. Hussmann, H.: Nondeterministic algebraic specifications and nonconfluent term rewriting. J. Log. Program. 12, 237–255 (1992)

20. López-Fraguas, F.J., Rodríguez-Hortalá, J., Sánchez-Hernández, J.: A simple rewrite notion for call-time choice semantics. In: Proceedings of the 9th ACM SIGPLAN International Conference on Principles and Practice of Declarative Programming (PPDP 2007), pp. 197–208. ACM Press (2007)

21. José Moreno-Navarro, J., Kuchen, H., Loogen, R.: Lazy narrowing in a graph machine. In: Kirchner, H., Wechler, W. (eds.) ALP 1990. LNCS, vol. 463, pp. 298–317. Springer, Heidelberg (1990). https://doi.org/10.1007/3-540-53162-9_47

22. Riesco, A., Rodríguez-Hortalá, J.: Singular and plural functions for functional logic programming. Theory Pract. Log. Program. **14**(1), 65–116 (2014)
23. Seres, S., Spivey, M., Hoare, T.: Algebra of logic programming. In: Proceedings of the ICLP 1999, pp. 184–199. MIT Press (1999)
24. Wadler, P.: How to replace failure by a list of successes a method for exception handling, backtracking, and pattern matching in lazy functional languages. In: Jouannaud, J.-P. (ed.) FPCA 1985. LNCS, vol. 201, pp. 113–128. Springer, Heidelberg (1985). https://doi.org/10.1007/3-540-15975-4_33

Towards a Constraint Solver
for Proving Confluence with Invariant
and Equivalence of Realistic CHR
Programs

Henning Christiansen$^{(\boxtimes)}$ and Maja H. Kirkeby$^{(\boxtimes)}$

Computer Science, Roskilde University, Roskilde, Denmark
{henning,majaht}@ruc.dk

Abstract. Confluence of a nondeterministic program ensures a functional input-output relation, freeing the programmer from considering the actual scheduling strategy, and allowing optimized and perhaps parallel implementations. The more general property of confluence modulo equivalence ensures that equivalent inputs are related to equivalent outputs, that need not be identical. Confluence under invariants is also considered. Constraint Handling Rules (CHR) is an important example of a rewrite based logic programming language, and we aim at a mechanizable method for proving confluence modulo equivalence of terminating CHR programs. While earlier approaches to confluence for CHR programs concern an idealized logic subset, we refer to a semantics compatible with standard Prolog-based implementations. We specify a meta-level constraint language in which invariants and equivalences can be expressed and manipulated as is needed for confluence proofs, thus extending our previous theoretical results towards a practical implementation.

1 Introduction

Confluence of a program consisting of rewrite rules means that its input-output relation is functional, even if the selection of internal computation steps is nondeterministic. Thus the underlying implementation is free to choose any optimal ordering of steps, perhaps in parallel, and the programmer do not need to care about – or even know about – the internal scheduling strategy.

Constraint Handling Rules (CHR) is a rule-based rewrite language [9,10,12], whose semantics is defined in terms of transitions between states, each being a multiset of first-order atoms (referred to as constraints). Confluence of CHR programs has been studied since the introduction of CHR, e.g., [1–3,6,13]. Most results refer to a logic-based semantics reflecting only the logical subset of CHR; this choice gave elegant confluence proofs. More recent work applies a semantics [4,5] that reflects de-facto standard implementations of CHR upon Prolog,

---

This work is supported by The Danish Council for Independent Research, Natural Sciences, grant no. DFF 4181-00442.

J. Silva (Ed.): WFLP 2018, LNCS 11285, pp. 112–130, 2019.
https://doi.org/10.1007/978-3-030-16202-3_7

e.g., [14,20], including a correct treatment of Prolog's non-logical devices (e.g., var/1, is/2) and run-time errors. Here we focus on this Prolog-based semantics.

While confluence means that the input-output relation is functional, the more general property confluence modulo equivalence means that the input-output relation may be seen as a function from equivalence classes of the input to equivalence classes of the output. In this case, we again obtain the free choice of computation order. Typical examples include redundant data structures (e.g., representing a set as a list in which the order is immaterial) and algorithms searching for a single best solution among several (two solutions are considered equivalent when they have the same score), e.g., the Viterbi algorithm [4,5].

Example 1 ([4,5]). The following non-confluent CHR program is a typical example of a program using redundant data structures; it collects items into a set represented as a list. (The syntax of CHR is explained in Sect. 3.2, below.)

$$\text{set(L), item(X)} \iff \text{set([X|L])}$$

This rule will apply repeatedly, replacing constraints matched by the left hand-side with those indicated on the right. For instance, the input query

```
?- set([]), item(a), item(b).
```

may produce two different outputs: set([a,b]) and set([b,a]), both representing the same set.

Often programs are developed with a particular set of initial queries in mind. This includes the set-program of Example 1, reflecting a tacitly assumed state invariant: only one set-constraint is allowed. While confluence requires that all states, including states that were never intended to be reached, satisfy the confluence property, confluence under invariant only requires that states in the invariant satisfy the confluence property. Thus when a program is confluent under invariant, it means that a part of the input-output relation is functional, namely its restriction to invariant states. Due to the non-logical built-in constraints of the Prolog-based semantics, the empty program is not confluent, see Example 6; thus no program is confluent under this semantics. We identify a basic invariant that ensures confluence (under invariant) of the empty program.

Most confluence results of CHR, and those we present here, are based on Newman's lemma [17] and a similar lemma for confluence modulo equivalence by Huet [15] (Sect. 2), and are only relevant for terminating programs. Methods for proving termination of CHR programs have been considered by, e.g., [11,18,19]. An example of a non-terminating CHR program is shown in Example 2 below, which we can show confluent under a suitable invariant that enforces termination.

Example 2. The following program implements a version of Euclid's algorithm for computing the greatest common divisor of two (or more) positive integers.

```
r₁: gcd(N)\gcd(N) <=> true.
r₂: gcd(N)\gcd(M) <=> N<M, L is M-N | gcd(L).
```

These rules will apply repeatedly; the first rule removes duplicates and the second one considers two unequal integers and replaces the larger by their distance. For example, the input query

```
?- gcd(49), gcd(63).
```

produces the output gcd(7). In general, the program is nonterminating since inputs with a non-positive number may make the program loop, e.g., the second rule applies to gcd(0), gcd(1) producing the same state. In addition, the program may produce run-time errors, for instance by gcd(1), gcd(1/0) (since </2 in the Prolog-based implementation/semantics evaluates its arguments).

We introduce a small but useful extension to this line of work; we propose the weaker property termination under invariant[1] (i.e., not necessarily termination outside the invariant), which is sufficient when proving confluence (modulo equivalence).

Example 3 (Example 2 continued). For the gcd-program, a relevant invariant would be one restricting the states to those containing only gcd-constraints with positive integer arguments; the program is terminating and confluent under this invariant, and moreover it excludes states that may cause run-time errors.

When the invariants remove the inputs that may cause undesired program behavior such as non-termination or encountering of run-time errors, the invariant restricted input-output function is not only partial, but total.

1.1 Related Work

Most earlier approaches worked only for an idealized set of logical built-ins managed by a "magic" constraint solver that has no counterpart in standard CHR implementations, e.g., [1–3,6,7]. It was suggested by [7] to take invariants into account (under the name of observable confluence), staying within the first-order framework. Due to the lack of a more expressive meta-level, including a formal representation of invariants, this approach explodes (as also noticed by its authors) into infinitely many proof cases for simple invariants such as groundness.

Confluence modulo equivalence was introduced for CHR by [4,5], also arguing to use a Prolog-based semantics closer to current CHR implementations. An in-depth theoretical analysis of these issues is given by [5], also suggesting to use a ground meta-level representation for invariants and equivalences. An attempt to handle confluence modulo equivalence was made by [13] based on the approach of [7], inheriting the mentioned explosion problem.

---

[1] A similar property has been studied by [8] in term rewriting under the name of "local termination".

1.2 Contributions

In this work we focus on the more realistic Prolog-based CHR semantics that is compatible with Prolog-based CHR implementations. We present essential steps towards a constraint solver to be used for proving confluence modulo equivalence under invariants for CHR programs that are terminating (under invariant). We extend previous approaches, including our own, introducing a specific meta-logic constraint language in which we can refer to states as data objects and reason with invariants and equivalences. This meta-language is used for specifying abstract transitions and joinability (modulo equivalence) proofs in relation to the Prolog-based semantics; this provides a more compact representation of proof cases so that the mentioned explosion into infinitely many cases is avoided. In a "companion paper" [6] we made a similar exercise for the logic-based semantics – as to better position our overall ideas in relation previous work – whereas the present paper aim at automatic support for doing proofs of confluence.

1.3 Overview

Section 2 provides the basic definitions and properties of transitions systems, and Sect. 3 recalls the syntax and operational semantics for CHR with correct handling of non-logical built-ins such as $var/1$, $nonvar/1$ and $is/2$. Section 4 introduces the meta-level transition system for CHR, including its meta-level constraint language, and Sect. 5 shows our confluence results. Section 6 gives some concluding remark and plans for future work.

2 Preliminaries

We give the basic definitions in a compact form here; background and motivating examples may be found in [5]. A *transition system* is a pair $\langle A, \mapsto \rangle$, where A is a set of *states* and $\mapsto \subseteq A \times A$ is the *transition relation*; $\overset{*}{\mapsto}$ is the reflexive transitive closure of $\mapsto$. An element of $s \in A$ is *final* or *normal form* if $\nexists s' : s \mapsto s'$. The system is *terminating* whenever every transition sequence $s_1 \mapsto s_2 \mapsto \cdots$ is finite. An *invariant* I is a subset of A such that $s \in I \wedge s \mapsto s' \Rightarrow s' \in I$. Whenever $s \in I$, s is an *I-state*. A *state equivalence* is an equivalence relation over A, typically written as $\sim$; the set of equivalence classes given by $\sim$ is written $A/\sim$. In the context of an invariant I, $\mapsto$ and $\sim$ are tacitly assumed to be restricted to I-states.

Two states s_1, s_2 are *joinable (modulo $\sim$)* whenever there exists a state s_{12} (states s_1', s_2') such that $s_1 \overset{*}{\mapsto} s_{12} \overset{*}{\longleftarrow} s_2$ ($s_1 \overset{*}{\mapsto} s_1' \sim s_2' \overset{*}{\longleftarrow} s_2$).

A system is *confluent* whenever, for any s_0, s_1, s_2 with $s_1 \overset{*}{\longleftarrow} s_0 \overset{*}{\mapsto} s_2$, that s_1, s_2 are joinable. It is *confluent modulo $\sim$* whenever, for any s_0, s_0', s_1, s_2 with $s_1 \overset{*}{\longleftarrow} s_0 \sim s_0' \overset{*}{\mapsto} s_2$, that s_1, s_2 are joinable modulo $\sim$.

An *α-corner* is of the form $s_1 \longleftarrow s_0 \mapsto s_2$; a *$\beta$-corner* is of the form $s_1 \sim s_0 \mapsto s_2$; in both cases, the indicated relationships must hold. A system is *locally confluent (modulo $\sim$)* whenever all α- (α- and β-) corners are joinable

(joinable modulo $\sim$). The following well-known lemmas reduce proofs of confluence (modulo equivalence) for terminating systems to proofs of the simpler property of local confluence (modulo equivalence).

Lemma 1 (Newman [17]). *A terminating transition system is confluent if and only if it is locally confluent.*

Lemma 2 (Huet [15]). *A terminating transition system is confluent modulo $\sim$ if and only if it is locally confluent modulo $\sim$.*

In accordance with [7], this extends to *observable* confluence (modulo $\sim$) in the context of an invariant, i.e., when $\mapsto$ (and $\sim$) is restricted to I-states. Similarly, transitions, corners, etc. whose states are I-states are called *observable*.

We suggest the following generalization: a transition system is *terminating under I*, whenever every observable transition sequence is finite. Lemmas 1 and 2 generalize for termination under invariant as follows.

Lemma 3. *An observably terminating transition system is observably confluent (modulo $\sim$) if and only if it is locally observably confluent (modulo $\sim$).*

Proof. Follows immediately from Lemmas 1 and 2 for an I-restricted system.

3   Prolog-Based CHR

We recall the syntax and operational semantics of CHR with non-logical Prolog built-ins such as `var/1`, `nonvar/1` and `is/2`. Here built-ins are executed immediately resulting in a substitution that is applied to the current state, analogous to how a typical CHR implementation upon Prolog works, e.g., [14,20].

3.1   Constraints, Substitutions and States

Standard first-order notions of variables, terms, predicates, atoms, etc. are assumed with two disjoint sets of *user* and *built-in constraint predicates*. A *state representation (s.repr.)* is either a multiset of constraints (a *proper* s.repr.) or one of FAILURE or ERROR. A *(proper) state* is an equivalence class of (proper) s.repr.s under variable renaming; FAILURE and ERROR identify their own classes. A *substitution* is either a *proper* substitution, which as a mapping from a finite set of variables to terms, e.g., the substitution $[x/t]$ replaces variable x by term t, or one of *failure* and *error*. For a proper substitution σ and expression E, $E\sigma$ denotes the expression that arises when σ is applied to E; composition of two proper substitutions σ, τ is written $\sigma \circ \tau$. Application of proper substitutions extends to proper s.repr.s in the usual way and thus to proper states. Applying special substitution *failure* (resp. *error*) to a proper state S is defined as $S\,failure = $ FAILURE (resp. $S\,error = $ ERROR); application of special substitutions to states FAILURE or ERROR is undefined.

The meaning of built-in predicates is given by a function *Exe* that maps them into substitutions. The set of built-in predicates may vary, see [4,5], but we assume always $=/2$ with $Exe(t_1=t_2)$ being a most general unifier of t_1, t_2 if one exists, and *failure* otherwise. Exe is extended to sequences (indicated by commas) of built-ins as follows, which is not commutative.

$$Exe((b, bs)) = \begin{cases} Exe(b) & \text{when } Exe(b) \in \{failure, error\}, \\ Exe(bs\ Exe(b)) & \text{when otherwise } Exe(bs\ Exe(b)) \\ & \in \{failure, error\}, \\ Exe(b) \circ Exe(bs\ Exe(b)) & \text{otherwise} \end{cases}$$

Thus the special substitutions are absorbing in the sense that once *failure* or *error* has been detected, this cannot be changed.

Example 4. We would expect $Exe(\texttt{nonvar(a)}) = \emptyset$ and $Exe(\texttt{nonvar(X)}) = failure$. When Exe produces the *error* substitution, it indicates that the built-in cannot evaluate due to insufficient instantiation or anomalies such as division by zero. Assuming that Exe models the $\texttt{is}/2$ predicate as it is defined in Prolog, we get the following.

$$Exe((\texttt{X is Y+1, Y=2})) = error \qquad Exe((\texttt{Y=2, X is Y+1})) = [\texttt{Y}/2, \texttt{X}/3]$$

3.2 Syntax

We use the generalized simpagation form [12] to capture all rules of CHR. A *rule* is a structure of the form $H_1 \backslash H_2 \texttt{<=>} G \,|\, C$, where $H_1 \backslash H_2$ is the *head* of the rule, where H_1 and H_2 are sequences, not both empty, of user constraints, G is the *guard* which is a sequence of built-in constraints, and C is the *body* which is a sequence of constraints of either sort. When H_1 is empty, the rule is a *simplification*, which may be written $H_2 \texttt{<=>} G \,|\, C$; when H_2 is empty, it is a *propagation*, which may be written $H_1 \texttt{==>} G \,|\, C$; any other rule is a *simpagation*; when $G = true$, $(G|)$ may be left out. The *head variables* of a rule are those appearing in the head, any other variable is *local*. A *pre-application* of a rule $r = (H_1 \backslash H_2 \texttt{<=>} G \,|\, C)$ is of the form $(H_1' \backslash H_2' \texttt{<=>} G' \,|\, C')\sigma$ where $r' = (H_1' \backslash H_2' \texttt{<=>} G' \,|\, C')$ is a variant with fresh variables of r and σ is a substitution to the head variables of r', where, for no variable x, $x\sigma$ contains a local variable of r'. The notions of head variables and local variables extends naturally to pre-applications.

3.3 Operational Semantics

A *rule application* wrt. a proper s.repr. S is a pre-application $H_1 \backslash H_2 \texttt{<=>} G \,|\, C$ such that $Exe(G)$ is a proper substitution that does not instantiate the pre-application's head variables, i.e., $H_i = H_i Exe(G)$ for $i \in \{1, 2\}$.

There are two sorts of transition steps, *by rule application* and *by built-in*; $\uplus$ denotes disjoint union of multisets (e.g., $\{a, b\} \uplus \{b, c\}\{a, b, b, c\}$).

$$H_1 \uplus H_2 \uplus S \;\mapsto\; (H_1 \uplus C \uplus S)\ Exe(G)$$

when there exists a rule application $H_1 \backslash H_2 \texttt{<=>} G \,|\, C$

$$\{b\} \uplus S \;\mapsto\; S\ Exe(b) \qquad \text{for a built-in } b \text{ constraint}$$

Notice that for a built-in step, the resulting state may be FAILURE or ERROR.

3.4 Invariants and Confluence

CHR programs without invariants are often not confluent.

Example 5. We consider the CHR program consisting of the following four rules.

$$r_1:\ \texttt{p(X) <=> q(X)} \qquad r_3:\ \texttt{q(X) <=> X>0 | r(X)}$$
$$r_2:\ \texttt{p(X) <=> r(X)} \qquad r_4:\ \texttt{r(X) <=> X≤0 | q(X)}$$

It is not confluent since the corner $\{\texttt{q(X)}\} \leftarrowtail \{\texttt{p(X)}\} \mapsto \{\texttt{r(X)}\}$ is not joinable. However, adding the invariant "reachable from an initial state $\texttt{p}(n)$ where n is a number" makes the program observably confluent, as shown in Example 16 below.

In fact, depending on which built-ins that are defined in the semantics, even the empty-program may not be confluent.

Example 6. Assuming that the semantics includes built-ins `is/2` and `=/2`, even the empty program is non-confluent; e.g., the corner (ERROR $\leftarrowtail$ $\{\texttt{X is Y+1, Y=2}\} \mapsto \{\texttt{X is 2+1}\}$) is not joinable. The invariant "2nd argument of any `is` constraint is a ground arithmetic expression without division" makes this and any other corner containing ERROR non-existent, and thus the empty program becomes confluent.

These examples signify the need for considering observable confluence for Prolog-based CHR, rather than classical confluence.

4 A Meta-Level Transition System for CHR

We introduce a transition system whose individual states each cover typically infinitely many CHR states, and such that each transition (sequence) analogously covers typically infinitely many transition (sequence)s. In this system, we can formulate critical corners, which, if shown joinable, implies joinability of all covered CHR corners. Thus a proof of local confluence of a given CHR program may be reduced to a finite number of cases. The difference between this and earlier approaches is that we step up to a meta-level representation in which we can represent invariant and state equivalence statements. We assume a specific CHR program together with an *Exe* function giving meaning to its built-ins plus invariant I and state equivalence $\sim$. The *object level system* refers to the transition system thus induced by the operational semantics for CHR given above.

Any object term, formula, etc. is *named* by a ground *meta-level term*. Variables are named by special constants, say X by 'X', and any other symbol by a function symbol written the same way; e.g., the non-ground object level atom p(A) is named by the ground meta-level term p('A'). For any such ground meta-level term mt, we indicate the object it names as $[mt]^{Gr}$. For example, $[p('A')]^{Gr} = p(A)$ and $[p('A') \wedge 'A'>2]^{Gr} = (p(A) \wedge A>2)$.

To describe meta-level states, we assume a constructor, $\langle -,- \rangle$, the *state (representation) constructor*. Intuitively, when we indicate a meta-level state as $\langle S, B \rangle$, S will represent the multiset of CHR constraints in the covered states, and B is not intended to represent a component of these states, but is a sequence of built-ins to be executed and applied to S (in suitable way) to form CHR states.

For a given object entity e, we define its *lifting* to the meta-level by (1) selecting a meta-level term that names e, and (2) replacing variable names in it consistently by fresh meta-level variables. For example, p(X) $\wedge$ X>2 is lifted to p(x) $\wedge$ x>2, where X and x are object variable and, resp., meta-variable. We will refer to a lifted n-ary built-in constraint $b(x_1, \ldots, x_n)$ where $x_1, \ldots, x_n$ are (unique) meta-variables as a *built-in template*. By virtue of this overloaded syntax, we may often read such an entity e (implicitly) as its lifting.

To characterize sets of object terms, formulas, etc. with a single meta-level term, we assume a collection of logic *meta-level constraints* whose meanings are given by a first-order theory $\mathcal{M}$.

Definition 1. *The theory $\mathcal{M}$ includes at least the following constraints.*

- *=/2 with its usual meaning of syntactic identity,*
- *Type constraints* type/2. *For example* type(var,x) *is true in $\mathcal{M}$ whenever x is the name of an object level variable;* var *is an example of a type.*[2]
- *Modal constraints* $\smiley F$, $\frownie F$, *and* $\boxminus F$ *are defined to be true in $\mathcal{M}$ whenever $Exe([F]^{Gr})$ returns a proper substitution, a failure substitution and an error substitution, respectively.*
- *The extended modal constraint* $\smiley_H F$ *is true in $\mathcal{M}$ whenever* $\smiley F$ *is true and $[H]^{Gr} = [H]^{Gr} Exe([F]^{Gr})$ holds (the substitution does not bind variables in H).*
- freshVars(L,T) *is true in $\mathcal{M}$ whenever L is a list of all different variables names, none of which occur in the term T;* freshVars(L_1,L_2,T) *abbreviates* freshVars(L_{12},T) *where L_{12} is the concatenation of L_1 and L_2.*

Substitutions are defined as usual at the meta-level, and we denote the set of grounding substitutions that satisfy a meta-level constraint M as $[M] = \{\sigma \mid \mathcal{M} \models M\sigma\}$. A *constrained meta-level term* is of the form mt WHERE M where mt is a meta-level term and M a conjunction of meta-level constraints. Such constrained meta-level terms may describe infinite sets of object level entities. The *covering function* $[-]$ from constrained meta-level terms into sets of object level notions is defined as $[mt$ WHERE $M] = \{[mt]^\sigma \mid \sigma \in [M]\}$ where the notation $[-]^\sigma$ is defined as follows.

$$
\begin{aligned}
[\langle S, B \rangle]^\sigma &= [S]^\sigma Exe([B]^\sigma) \\
[mt]^\sigma &= [mt\,\sigma]^{Gr}, \quad \text{when } mt \text{ does not contain } \langle -,- \rangle \\
[f(mt_1, \ldots, mt_n)]^\sigma &= f([mt_1]^\sigma, \ldots, [mt_n]^\sigma), \quad \text{otherwise.}
\end{aligned}
$$

---

[2] We may introduce more types in the following whenever we need them.

A constrained meta-level term T is *inconsistent* whenever $[\![T]\!] = \emptyset$; otherwise, it is *consistent*.

4.1 Meta-Level States

A *meta-level state representation* is a constrained meta-level term Σ which $[\![\Sigma]\!]$ is a set of object level state representations. Two meta-level state representations Σ_1 and Σ_2 are *variants* whenever $[\![\Sigma_1]\!] = [\![\Sigma_2]\!]$. A *meta-level state* is an equivalence class of meta-level state representations under the variant relationship. Analogous to the object level, we typically indicate a given meta-level state by one of its meta-level state representations.

Example 7. Consider the following meta-level state representation.

$$SR_1 \;=\; \big(\langle\{\mathtt{p}(x)\}, x\texttt{=}c\rangle\ \text{WHERE}\ \mathtt{type(var},x)\wedge\mathtt{type(const},c)\big)$$

It covers all CHR states $\{\mathtt{p}(c)\}$ in which c is a constant. We will use below, the property that we can add consistent meta-level constraints on variables not mentioned elsewhere without changing the set of covered CHR states. For example, $[\![SR_1]\!] = [\![SR_2]\!]$. i.e., SR_1 and SR_2 are variants, where

$$SR_2 \;=\; \big(\langle\{\mathtt{p}(x)\}, x\texttt{=}c\rangle\ \text{WHERE}\ \mathtt{type(var},x)\wedge\mathtt{type(const},c)\wedge\mathtt{type(int},i)\big).$$

A consistent meta-level state Σ is called *proper* whenever every object level state in $[\![\Sigma]\!]$ is proper, a *failed* (an *error*) state whenever $[\![\Sigma]\!] = \{\text{FAILURE}\}$ $(= \{\text{ERROR}\})$, and *mixed* whenever $[\![\Sigma]\!]$ contains two or more of FAILURE, ERROR or a proper state.

A consistent s.repr. $(\langle S, B\rangle$ WHERE $M)$ is *reduced* if $B = true$, and it is *reducible to* a s.repr. $(\langle S', true\rangle$ WHERE $M)$ whenever $[\![(\langle S, B\rangle, \langle S', true\rangle)$ WHERE $M]\!]$ is the identity relation. Notice that this property is stronger than variance introduced above, as the meta-level constraints are the same in both s.repr.s and common meta-variables in the two are instantiated simultaneously.

4.2 Operational Semantics

A *meta-level rule application* wrt. a proper and reduced meta-level state $\langle H_1 \uplus H_2 \uplus S, true\rangle$ WHERE M is a lifted pre-application $H_1\backslash H_2 \texttt{<=>} G\,|\,C$ with local variables L and head variables H, such that

$$\mathcal{M} \models M \;\rightarrow\; \boxdot_H G \wedge \mathtt{freshVars}(L, H_1 \uplus H_2 \uplus S).$$

There are two sorts of transitions from proper and reduced meta-level state representations: *By rule application*

$$\Sigma \quad\Longmapsto\quad \langle H_1 \uplus C \uplus S, G\rangle\ \text{WHERE}\ M$$

whenever Σ is reducible to $\langle H_1 \uplus H_2 \uplus S, true\rangle$ WHERE M, whenever there exists a meta-level rule application $H_1\backslash H_2 \texttt{<=>} G\,|\,C$. *By built-in*

$$\Sigma \quad\Longmapsto\quad \langle S, b\rangle\ \text{WHERE}\ M$$

whenever Σ is reducible to $\langle S \uplus \{b\}, true \rangle$ WHERE M. Notice for a built-in transition, that the resulting state may be mixed.

Example 8. Consider the rule $r_3 \colon$ q(X)<=>X>0|r(X) extracted from Example 5 below. Read as a meta-level application instance, it gives rise to the following transition.

$$(\langle \{\mathtt{q}(x), \mathtt{s}(x)\}, true \rangle \Longmapsto \langle \{\mathtt{r}(x), \mathtt{s}(x)\}, x\mathtt{>}0 \rangle) \text{ WHERE } \smiley_x(x\mathtt{>}0)$$

The freshVars/2 constraint is not needed as there are no local variables.

Lemma 4. *Let Σ be a proper and reducible s.repr. If there is a meta-level transition $\Sigma \Mapsto \Sigma'$ then any element $S \mapsto S'$ in $[\![\Sigma \Mapsto \Sigma']\!]$ is a CHR transition.*

Proof. Let $(\langle A, B \rangle$ WHERE $M \Mapsto \langle A', B' \rangle$ WHERE $M)$ be a meta-level transition and σ an arbitrary substitution in $[M]$. We must show that $([\![\langle A, B \rangle]\!]^{\sigma} \mapsto [\![\langle A', B' \rangle]\!]^{\sigma}) = ([\![A\sigma]\!]^{Gr} Exe([\![B\sigma]\!]^{Gr}) \mapsto [\![(A'\sigma)]\!]^{Gr} Exe([\![B'\sigma]\!]^{Gr}))$ is a transition in the object system. There are two cases, by rule application and by built-in.

By rule application. By def. of meta-level transition, $(\langle A, B \rangle$ WHERE $M)$ is proper and reducible to a form $(\langle H_1 \uplus H_2 \uplus S, true \rangle$ WHERE $M)$, obtaining that $[\![H_1\sigma \uplus H_2\sigma \uplus S\sigma]\!]^{Gr} = [\![A\sigma]\!]^{Gr} Exe([\![B\sigma]\!]^{Gr})$ is proper and $[\![(A'\sigma)]\!]^{Gr} Exe([\![B'\sigma]\!]^{Gr}) = [\![H_1\sigma \uplus C \uplus S\sigma]\!]^{Gr} Exe([\![G\sigma]\!]^{Gr})$. There exists a meta-level rule application, i.e., a lifted pre-application $H_1 \backslash H_2$ <=> $G\,|\,C$ with local variables L and head variables H, such that $\mathcal{M} \models M \rightarrow \smiley_H G \wedge$ freshVars$(L, H_1 \uplus H_2 \uplus S)$. Thus $Exe([\![G\sigma]\!]^{Gr})$ is a proper substitution that does not instantiate head variables H, and since these conditions are a direct formalization of the requirements for object level transition, $[\![H_1\sigma \backslash H_2\sigma$ <=> $G\sigma\,|\,C\sigma]\!]^{Gr}$ is an object level application instance, which leads to the conclusion.

By built-in. By def. of meta-level transition, $(\langle A, B \rangle$ WHERE $M)$ is proper and reducible to a form $(S \uplus \{b\}, true \rangle$ WHERE $M)$ and $\langle A', B' \rangle$ is the same as $\langle S, b \rangle$. By definition of "reducible", $[\![A\sigma]\!]^{Gr} Exe([\![B\sigma]\!]^{Gr}) = [\![S\sigma \uplus \{b\sigma\}]\!]^{Gr} = [\![S\sigma]\!]^{Gr} \uplus [\![b\sigma]\!]^{Gr}$ which is then a proper state, thus, $([\![S\sigma]\!]^{Gr} \uplus [\![b\sigma]\!]^{Gr}) \mapsto [\![S\sigma]\!]^{Gr} Exe([\![b\sigma]\!]^{Gr}) = [\![A'\sigma]\!]^{Gr} Exe([\![B\sigma]\!]^{Gr})$ concludes the proof. $\qquad\square$

4.3 Invariants and Equivalences

Meta-level invariants $I\!I$ *and equivalences* $\approx$ are defined as follows.

- $I\!I(S)$ whenever $I(s)$ for all $s \in [\![S]\!]$.
- $S_1 \approx S_2$ whenever $s_1 \sim s_2$ for all $(s_1, s_2) \in [\![(S_1, S_2)]\!]$.

The following properties that $I\!I$ is in fact an invariant and $\approx$ is in fact an equivalence relation are direct consequences of the above definition and Lemma 4.

Proposition 1. *If $I\!I(\Sigma_1)$ and $\Sigma_1 \Mapsto \Sigma_2$ then $I\!I(\Sigma_2)$.*

Proposition 2. *The $\approx$ relation is an equivalence relation, i.e., reflexive, transitive and symmetric.*

To express meta-level invariants and equivalences we assume two meta-level constraints.

Definition 2. *The theory $\mathcal{M}$ includes two constraints* inv *and* equiv *such that* inv(Σ) *is true in $\mathcal{M}$ whenever $[\![\Sigma]\!]^{Gr}$ is an I state (representation) of the Prolog-based semantics, and* equiv(Σ_1, Σ_2) *whenever $[\![(\Sigma_1, \Sigma_2)]\!]^{Gr}$ is a pair of state (representation)s (s_1, s_2) such that $s_1 \sim s_2$.*

The following correspondences follow immediately from the definitions above.

Proposition 3. $I \quad = \quad \{S \;\text{WHERE}\; M \mid \mathcal{M} \models M \rightarrow \text{inv}(S)\}$
$$\approx \;=\; \{(S_1, S_2) \;\text{WHERE}\; M \mid \mathcal{M} \models M \rightarrow \text{equiv}(S_1, S_2)\}$$

Example 9 (Example 5 cont'). The invariant defined as "reachable from an initial state p(n) where n is a number" for the program in Example 5 may be formalized at the meta-level as states of the form $\langle\{pred(n)\}, B\rangle$ WHERE type$(\text{num}, n) \wedge \boxdot_n B$ where *pred* is one of p, q and r, and B is one of $n{\le}0$, $n{>}0$, and *true*.

Example 10 (Example 1 continued). Consider again the set-program. An invariant relevant for this program may be formalized as states of the form

$\langle\{\text{set}(L)\} \uplus S, true\rangle$ WHERE type$(\text{constList}, L) \wedge$ type$(\text{constItems}, S)$;

we assume types const for all constants, constList for all lists of such, and constItems for sets of constraints of the form item(c) where c is a constant.

A state equivalence relevant for this program may be formalized as follows

$\langle\{\text{set}(L_1)\} \uplus S, true\rangle$ WHERE $M^{\approx} \quad \approx \quad \langle\{\text{set}(L_2)\} \uplus S, true\rangle$ WHERE $M^{\approx}$

where $M^{\approx}$ stands for type$(\text{constList}, L_1) \wedge$ type$(\text{constList}, L_1) \wedge$ perm$(L_1, L_2) \wedge$ type$(\text{constItems}, S)$, and perm(L_1, L_2) means that L_1 is a permutation of L_2.

4.4   Meta-Level Joinability and Splitting

Joinability at the meta-level is related to joinability at the object level.

Proposition 4. *If a meta-level corner is joinable modulo $\approx$ then all corners covered by it are joinable modulo $\sim$.*

Proof. This is a direct consequence of Lemma 4 and definition of $\approx$.

However, a meta-level corner covering only joinable (mod. $\sim$) object corners may not be joinable (mod. $\approx$), as demonstrated by following example.

Example 11 (Examples 5–9 cont'). Consider the meta-level corner

$$\Lambda = (\langle\{\mathtt{q}(n)\}, \mathit{true}\rangle \Leftarrow\!\shortmid \langle\{\mathtt{p}(n)\}, \mathit{true}\rangle \shortmid\!\Rightarrow \langle\{\mathtt{r}(n)\}, \mathit{true}\rangle) \text{ WHERE } \mathtt{type}(\mathtt{num}, n).$$

No rule apply to either of the wing states and, thus, they are not joinable. However, all the covered corners are joinable, e.g., using rule r_3 for $\{\mathtt{q}(1)\} \mapsto \{\mathtt{r}(1)\}$ and rule r_4 for $\{\mathtt{q}(-1)\} \leftarrow\!\shortmid \{\mathtt{r}(-1)\}$.

To accommodate this phenomenon we introduce splitting of meta-level terms such as states, transitions, equivalences, or corners and afterwards split-joinability (mod. $\approx$).

Let $(mt \text{ WHERE } M)$ be a constrained meta-level term, and $\{M_i\}_{i \in Inx}$ a set of meta-level constraints such that $\mathcal{M} \models (\bigvee_{i \in Inx} M_i) \leftrightarrow \mathit{true}$. We can now define a *splitting* of $(mt \text{ WHERE } M)$ into the following set of constrained meta-level terms

$$\{mt \text{ WHERE } M \wedge M_i\}_{i \in Inx}.$$

The following is a direct consequence of the definitions.

Proposition 5. *If $\{mt \text{ WHERE } M \wedge M_i\}_{i \in Inx}$ is a splitting of $(mt \text{ WHERE } M)$ then $[\![mt \text{ WHERE } M]\!] = \bigcup_{i \in Inx}[\![mt \text{ WHERE } M \wedge M_i]\!]$.*

Example 12 (Examples 5, 9, 11 cont'). The meta-level corner Λ (Example 11) is a constrained meta-level term and $\{\boxdot(n>0), \boxdot(n\leq0)\}$ is a set of constraints with $\mathcal{M} \models (\boxdot(n>0) \vee \boxdot(n\leq0)) \leftrightarrow \mathit{true}$. Thus, we may split Λ into the corners

$$(\langle\{\mathtt{q}(n)\}, \mathit{true}\rangle \Leftarrow\!\shortmid \langle\{\mathtt{p}(n)\}, \mathit{true}\rangle \shortmid\!\Rightarrow \langle\{\mathtt{r}(n)\}, \mathit{true}\rangle) \text{ WHERE } \mathtt{type}(\mathtt{num}, n) \wedge \boxdot(n>0)$$

$$(\langle\{\mathtt{q}(n)\}, \mathit{true}\rangle \Leftarrow\!\shortmid \langle\{\mathtt{p}(n)\}, \mathit{true}\rangle \shortmid\!\Rightarrow \langle\{\mathtt{r}(n)\}, \mathit{true}\rangle) \text{ WHERE } \mathtt{type}(\mathtt{num}, n) \wedge \boxdot(n\leq0).$$

Definition 3 (split-joinable). *A meta-level corner Λ is split-joinable modulo $\approx$ if there is a splitting $\{\Lambda_i\}_{i \in Inx}$ such that each Λ_i is joinable modulo $\approx$.*

Example 13 (Examples 5, 9, 11 cont'). The splitted corners of Example 12 are joinable as follows; thus, the corner Λ of Example 11 is split-joinable.

$$(\langle\{\mathtt{q}(n)\}, \mathit{true}\rangle \shortmid\!\Rightarrow \langle\{\mathtt{r}(n)\}, \mathit{true}\rangle) \text{ WHERE } \mathtt{type}(\mathtt{num}, n) \wedge \boxdot(n>0)$$

$$(\langle\{\mathtt{q}(n)\}, \mathit{true}\rangle \Leftarrow\!\shortmid \langle\{\mathtt{r}(n)\}, \mathit{true}\rangle) \text{ WHERE } \mathtt{type}(\mathtt{num}, n) \wedge \boxdot(n\leq0)$$

Proposition 6. *A meta-level corner is split-joinable modulo $\approx$ if and only if all corners covered by it are joinable modulo $\sim$.*

Proof. "*If*": Index the set of object corners by Inx, and lift every object corner λ_i to a ground meta-level corner Λ_i such that $[\![\Lambda_i]\!] = \{\lambda_i\}$. Now, we choose a splitting of the meta-level corner Λ into a set $\cup_{i \in Inx} \Lambda_i$, each of which is joinable modulo $\approx$, obtaining, by Definition 3, that Λ is split-joinable modulo $\approx$.

"*Only if*": Let Λ denote a meta-level corner that is split-joinable modulo $\approx$; that is there exists an indexed set of corners $\{\Lambda_i\}_{i \in Inx}$ such that $[\![\Lambda]\!] = \cup_{i \in Inx}[\![\Lambda_i]\!]$ where each Λ_i is joinable modulo $\approx$. Thus, for any object corner λ covered by Λ, there is some Λ_i that covers λ and is joinable modulo $\approx$. By Proposition 4, λ is joinable modulo $\sim$. $\square$

5   Confluence

As noted in Sect. 2, (observable) confluence (modulo equivalence) of a terminating system can be shown by (observable) local confluence (modulo equivalence). As in the referenced, previous work, we define a smaller set of critical corners whose joinability ensures this property.

Definition 4 (critical α-corners).
critical α_1-corners. *Let $\langle A \uplus S, true \rangle$ WHERE M be a proper and reduced meta-level state where $A = (H_1 \uplus H_2) \cup (H_1' \uplus H_2')$, $M = \boxdot_H G \wedge \boxdot_{H'} G' \wedge \texttt{freshvars}(L, L', A \uplus S)$ and $(H_1 \uplus H_2) \cap H_2' \neq \emptyset$. Furthermore, let $H_1 \backslash H_2 \texttt{<=>} G \, | \, C$ and $H_1' \backslash H_2' \texttt{<=>} G' \, | \, C'$ be two meta-level rule applications with local and head variables L, H, and L', H', respectively. A critical α_1-corner is defined as*

$$\left(\langle (A \backslash H_2) \uplus C \uplus S, G \rangle \;\Leftarrow\; \langle A \uplus S, true \rangle \;\Rightarrow\; \langle (A \backslash H_2') \uplus C' \uplus S, G' \rangle \right) \text{ WHERE } M.$$

critical α_2-corners. *Let $\langle A \uplus S, true \rangle$ WHERE M be a meta-level state where $A = H_1 \uplus H_2 \uplus \{b\}$, $M = \boxdot_H G \wedge \texttt{freshvars}(L, A \uplus S)$, b is a built-in template and there is a meta-level rule application $H_1 \backslash H_2 \texttt{<=>} G \, | \, C$ with local and head variables L and H. A critical α_2-corner is defined as*

$$\left(\langle (A \backslash H_2) \uplus C \uplus \{b\} \uplus S, G \rangle \;\Leftarrow\; \langle A \uplus S, true \rangle \;\Rightarrow\; \langle A \backslash \{b\} \uplus S, b \rangle \right) \text{ WHERE } M.$$

critical α_3-corners. *Let $\langle \{b, b'\} \uplus S, true \rangle$ WHERE M be a meta-level state where b and b' are built-in templates. A critical α_3-corner is defined as*

$$\left(\langle \{b'\} \uplus S, b \rangle \;\Leftarrow\; \langle \{b, b'\} \uplus S, true \rangle \;\Rightarrow\; \langle \{b\} \uplus S, b' \rangle \right) \text{ WHERE } M.$$

Example 14 (Examples 6 cont'). Assuming built-ins is/2 and =/2, the empty program is shown non-confluent; the critical α_3-corner (ERROR $\Leftarrow$ $\{x \text{ is } y\texttt{+1}, y\texttt{=2}\} \Rightarrow \{x \text{ is } 2\texttt{+1}\}$) WHERE $\texttt{type}(\texttt{var}, x) \wedge \texttt{type}(\texttt{var}, y)$ is not split-joinable. The program is confl. under invariants excluding built-ins; the corners are inconsistent.

Example 15 (Examples 5, 9, 11–13 cont'). Consider again the non-confluent program without the invariant. There is a single non-split-joinable critical α_1-corner $q(n) \Leftarrow p(n) \Mapsto r(n)$ WHERE *true*. There is a series of joinable α_2-corners where the rule and the built-in transition commute. There are many non-joinable critical α_3-corners, see Example 14.

Definition 5. *Let* $(\Sigma_1 \Leftarrow \Sigma_0 \Mapsto \Sigma_2)$ WHERE M *be a critical α_i-corner for $i \in \{1, 2, 3\}$; a critical observable α_i-corner is defined as* $(\Sigma_1 \Leftarrow \Sigma_0 \Mapsto \Sigma_2)$ WHERE $M \wedge \text{inv}(\Sigma_0)$.

Notice that by Proposition 1, it follows that $\mathcal{M} \models M \rightarrow \text{inv}(\Sigma_1) \wedge \text{inv}(\Sigma_2)$.

Theorem 1. *An observable terminating program Π is observably confluent iff its observable critical α-corners are joinable.*

Proof. A direct consequence of the subsequent Theorem 2.

Example 16. (Examples 5, 9, 11–13, 15, cont'). Consider the program and its invariant. There is a single critical α_1-corner, namely Λ of Example 11 that was shown split-joinable. There are zero observable critical α_2-corners and α_3-corners. Thus, the program is observably confluent.

Definition 6 (critical β-corners). *critical β_1-corners. Let* $(\langle A, \textit{true} \rangle$ WHERE $M)$ *be a consistent meta-level state,* $(\langle H_1 \uplus H_2 \uplus S, \textit{true} \rangle$ WHERE $M)$ *a proper meta-level state with* $M = \boxdot_H G \wedge \text{freshvars}(L, H_1 \uplus H_2 \uplus S) \wedge \text{equiv}(\langle A, \textit{true} \rangle, \langle H_1 \uplus H_2 \uplus S, \textit{true} \rangle)$, *and* $H_1 \backslash H_2 \texttt{<=>} G \,|\, C$ *a meta-level rule application with local variables L and head variables H. A critical β_1-corner is defined as*

$$\langle A, \textit{true} \rangle \approx \langle H_1 \uplus H_2 \uplus S, \textit{true} \rangle \Mapsto \langle H_1 \uplus C \uplus S, G \rangle \qquad \text{WHERE } M.$$

critical β_2-corners. Let $(\langle A, \textit{true} \rangle$ WHERE $M)$ *and* $(\langle \{b\} \uplus S, \textit{true} \rangle$ WHERE $M)$ *be meta-level states where* $M = \text{freshvars}(L, H_1 \uplus H_2 \uplus S) \wedge \text{equiv}(\langle A, \textit{true} \rangle, \langle H_1 \uplus H_2 \uplus S, \textit{true} \rangle)$ *and b is a built-in template. A critical β_2-corner is defined as*

$$\langle A, \textit{true} \rangle \approx \langle \{b\} \uplus S, \textit{true} \rangle \Mapsto \langle S, b \rangle \qquad \text{WHERE } M.$$

Definition 7. *Let* $(\Sigma_1 \approx \Sigma_0 \Mapsto \Sigma_2)$ WHERE M *be a critical β_i-corner for $i \in \{1, 2\}$. A critical observable β_i-corner is defined as* $(\Sigma_1 \approx \Sigma_0 \Mapsto \Sigma_2)$ WHERE $M \wedge \text{inv}(\Sigma_0) \wedge \text{inv}(\Sigma_1)$.

Note that, by Proposition 1, it follows that $\text{inv}(\Sigma_2)$.

Lemma 5 (Critical Corner Lemma). *Any observable object level corner $s_1 \sim s_0 \mapsto s_2$ (resp. $s_1 \leftarrowtail s_0 \mapsto s_2$) is either joinable modulo $\sim$, or it is covered by an observable critical α-corner (resp. β-corner).*

Proof. We will go through the different sorts of observable corners and show that either they are not covered by a corner and joinable, or they are covered by some observable critical corner. In the following we let $\overset{r}{\mapsto}$ refer to a transition by a rule application being an instance of rule r, and $\overset{b}{\mapsto}$ refer to a transition by built-in.

$s_1 \overset{r}{\hookleftarrow} s_0 \overset{r'}{\mapsto} s_2$ This is possible in three ways. (1) There is no overlap between the heads of the rule applications, thus, the rule applications commute. (2) The rule applications $r = h_1 \backslash h_2 \texttt{<=>} g \,|\, c$ and $r' = h_1' \backslash h_2' \texttt{<=>} g' \,|\, c'$ have an overlap $(h_1 \uplus h_2) \cap h_2' \neq \emptyset$. Hence, we can construct an observable critical α_1-corner $\Sigma_1 \Leftarrow\!\!\mid \Sigma_0 \mapsto \Sigma_2$ WHERE M such that $(s_1 \overset{r}{\hookleftarrow} s_0 \overset{r'}{\mapsto} s_2) \in [\![\Sigma_1 \Leftarrow\!\!\mid \Sigma_0 \mapsto \Sigma_2$ WHERE $M]\!]$. (3) There is no overlap $(H_1 \uplus H_2) \cap H_2' = \emptyset$ but there is one by $(H_1' \uplus H_2') \cap H_2 \neq \emptyset$; in this case Definition 4 states that there exists an observable critical α_1-corner $\Sigma_1 \overset{r'}{\hookleftarrow} \Sigma_0 \overset{r}{\mapsto} \Sigma_2$ covering the corner $s_2 \overset{r'}{\hookleftarrow} s_0 \overset{r}{\mapsto} s_1$, thus, by symmetry it also covers this corner.

$s_1 \overset{r}{\hookleftarrow} s_0 \overset{b}{\mapsto} s_2$ Refer to the corner in question as λ, and let Λ be a the critical meta-level corner constructed from r (Definition 5) and the built-in template of the built-in predicate in b. It is straightforward to show that $\lambda \in [\![\Lambda]\!]$; thus there are no such object level α_2 corner that is not covered by some critical α_2 meta-level corner.

$(s_1 \overset{b}{\hookleftarrow} s_0 \overset{b}{\mapsto} s_2), (s_1 \sim s_0 \overset{r}{\mapsto} s_2), (s_1 \sim s_0 \overset{b}{\mapsto} s_2)$ The proofs are similar in structure to the previous and is left out. $\square$

Proposition 7. *An observable critical corner is split-joinable modulo $\approx$ if and only if every corner covered by it is joinable modulo $\sim$.*

Proof. This is a special case of Proposition 6. $\square$

Theorem 2 (Critical Corner Theorem). *A program is observable locally confluent modulo $\sim$ if and only if its observable critical α- and β-corners are split-joinable modulo $\approx$.*

Proof. $\Leftarrow$: Assume that the observable critical α- and β-corners are split-joinable modulo $\approx$; by the Critical Corner Lemma (Lemma 5) and Proposition 7 we conclude that the program is observable locally confluent. $\Rightarrow$: Assume that the program is observable locally confluent modulo $\sim$, thus all corners covered by observable critical corners are joinable modulo $\sim$, thus, by Proposition 7, the observable critical corners are also split-joinable modulo $\approx$. $\square$

Theorem 3. *An observable terminating CHR program is observably confluent modulo $\sim$ if and only if its observable critical α- and β-corners are split-joinable modulo $\approx$.*

Proof. A direct consequence of Theorem 2 and Lemma 2 generalized under invariant, i.e., an observable terminating system is observably confluent modulo $\sim$ if and only if it is observable locally confluent modulo $\sim$. $\square$

When showing joinability (modulo equivalence) of the observable critical corners we will leave out duplicates and corners with similar wing states.

Example 17 ([6]). (Example 1 cont') Consider the one-rule set-program together with the invariant and equivalence from Example 10. There are two critical α-corners, given by the two ways, the rule can overlap with itself.

$$\langle\{\mathtt{set}([x_1\,|\,L_1]),\mathtt{item}(x_2)\},\textit{true}\rangle \qquad \langle\{\mathtt{set}([x_1\,|\,L_1]),\mathtt{set}(L_2)\},\textit{true}\rangle$$
$$\Updownarrow \qquad\qquad\qquad\qquad \Updownarrow$$
$$\langle\{\mathtt{item}(x_1),\mathtt{set}(L_1),\mathtt{item}(x_2)\},\textit{true}\rangle \quad \langle\{\mathtt{set}(L_1),\mathtt{item}(x_1),\mathtt{set}(L_2)\},\textit{true}\rangle$$
$$\Downarrow \qquad\qquad\qquad\qquad \Downarrow$$
$$\langle\{\mathtt{item}(x_1),\mathtt{set}([x_2\,|\,L_1])\},\textit{true}\rangle \qquad \langle\{\mathtt{set}(L_1),\mathtt{set}([x_1\,|\,L_2])\},\textit{true}\rangle$$

Each corner is assumed encapsulated in "WHERE M" with $M =$ $\mathtt{type}(\mathtt{const},x_1) \wedge \mathtt{type}(\mathtt{const},x_2) \wedge \mathtt{type}(\mathtt{constList},L_1)\wedge\mathtt{type}(\mathtt{constList},L_2)\wedge$ $\mathtt{type}(\mathtt{constItems},S)$. The corner on the right is inconsistent due to the two set-constraints and the corner on the left is joinable modulo the equivalence as follows.

$$\langle\{\mathtt{item}(x_1),\mathtt{set}(L),\mathtt{item}(x_2)\}\uplus S,\textit{true}\rangle$$

$$\langle\{\mathtt{set}([x_1\,|\,L]),\mathtt{item}(x_2)\}\uplus S,\textit{true}\rangle \qquad \langle\{\mathtt{item}(x_1),\mathtt{set}([x_2\,|\,L]),\}\uplus S,\textit{true}\rangle$$
$$\Downarrow^{\pi} \qquad\qquad\qquad\qquad \Downarrow^{\pi}$$
$$\langle\{\mathtt{set}([x_2,x_1\,|\,L])\},\textit{true}\uplus S\rangle \approx\!\!\approx\!\!\approx \langle\{\mathtt{set}([x_1,x_2\,|\,L])\}\uplus S,\textit{true}\rangle$$

In addition, there is one β-corner (assumed encapsulated in "WHERE $M \wedge$ $\mathtt{perm}(L_1,L_2)$") which is joinable modulo $\approx$ as follows.

$$\langle\{\mathtt{item}(x),\mathtt{set}(L_1)\} \uplus S,\textit{true}\rangle$$
$$\approx\!\!\approx\qquad\qquad\longrightarrow$$
$$\langle\{\mathtt{item}(x),\mathtt{set}(L_2)\} \uplus S,\textit{true}\rangle \qquad \langle\{\mathtt{set}([x\,|\,L_1])\} \uplus S,\textit{true}\rangle$$
$$\longrightarrow\qquad\qquad \approx\!\!\approx$$
$$\langle\{\mathtt{set}([x\,|\,L_2])\} \uplus S,\textit{true}\rangle$$

Thus this proves the program observably locally confluent.

Example 18. Consider the gcd-program together with the invariant "states with gcd-constraints with positive integers"; we assume a type posGcd for sets of constraints of the form $\mathtt{gcd}(n)$ where n is a positive integer. In the following we indicate the five corners (leaving out one duplicate), with the proof of joinability hinted for the first one.

$$\langle\{\mathtt{gcd}(n),\mathtt{gcd}(n),\mathtt{gcd}(m)\}\uplus S,\textit{true}\rangle$$
$$r_1\swarrow\qquad\qquad\qquad\qquad\searrow r_2$$
$$\langle\{\mathtt{gcd}(n),\mathtt{gcd}(m)\}\uplus S,\textit{true}\rangle \quad \langle\{\mathtt{gcd}(n),\mathtt{gcd}(n),\mathtt{gcd}(l)\}\uplus S,(n\!<\!m,l\text{ is }m\!-\!n)\rangle\!\rangle$$
$$r_2\searrow\qquad\qquad\qquad\qquad\qquad\qquad\qquad\nearrow r_1$$
$$\langle\{\mathtt{gcd}(n),\mathtt{gcd}(l')\}\uplus S,(n\!<\!m,l'\text{is }m\!-\!n)\rangle\!\rangle \approx\!\!= \langle\{\mathtt{gcd}(n),\mathtt{gcd}(l)\}\uplus S,(n\!<\!m,l\text{ is }m\!-\!n)\rangle\!\rangle$$

This corner is assumed encapsulated in "WHERE $\boxdot_{[n,m]}(n\!<\!m,l\text{ is }m\!-\!n) \wedge$ $\mathtt{freshvars}(l,\{\mathtt{gcd}(n),\mathtt{gcd}(m)\}\uplus S)\wedge\mathtt{type}(\mathtt{posGcd},\{\mathtt{gcd}(n),\mathtt{gcd}(m)\} \uplus S)$". For the proof joinability, i.e., the lower part of the diagram, we need to extend the meta-level constraint with $\mathtt{freshvars}(l',\{\mathtt{gcd}(n),\mathtt{gcd}(m)\} \uplus S)$, which we can do without changing the set of covered CHR states.

For reasons of space, we indicate the four remaining corners by their common ancestor state; the corners can be determined based on their meta constraints.

$\langle\{\mathtt{gcd}(n),\mathtt{gcd}(m),\mathtt{gcd}(m)\}\uplus S, true\rangle$ WHERE M

where M is the same meta-level constraint as in the first corner above.

$\langle\{\mathtt{gcd}(n),\mathtt{gcd}(m_1),\mathtt{gcd}(m_2)\}\uplus S, true\rangle$ WHERE
$\smiley_{[n,m_1]}(n<m_1, l_1 \text{ is } m_1 - n) \wedge \smiley_{[n,m_2]}(n<m_2, l_2 \text{ is } m_2 - n)\wedge$
$\mathtt{freshvars}(l_1, l_2, \{\mathtt{gcd}(n),\mathtt{gcd}(m_1),\mathtt{gcd}(m_2)\} \uplus S)\wedge$
$\mathtt{type}(\mathtt{posGcd}, \{\mathtt{gcd}(n),\mathtt{gcd}(m_1),\mathtt{gcd}(m_2)\} \uplus S)$

$\langle\{\mathtt{gcd}(n_1),\mathtt{gcd}(n_2),\mathtt{gcd}(n_3)\}\uplus S, true\rangle$ WHERE
$\smiley_{[n_1,n_2]}(n_1<n_2, l_2 \text{ is } n_2 - n_1) \wedge \smiley_{[n_2,n_3]}(n_2<n_3, l_3 \text{ is } n_3 - n_2)\wedge$
$\mathtt{freshvars}(l_2, l_3, \{\mathtt{gcd}(n_1),\mathtt{gcd}(n_2),\mathtt{gcd}(n_3)\} \uplus S)\wedge$
$\mathtt{type}(\mathtt{posGcd}, \{\mathtt{gcd}(n_1),\mathtt{gcd}(n_2),\mathtt{gcd}(n_3)\} \uplus S)$

$\langle\{\mathtt{gcd}(n_1),\mathtt{gcd}(l_1),\mathtt{gcd}(n_2)\}\uplus S, (n_1<m, l_1 \text{ is } m - n_1)\rangle$ WHERE
$\smiley_{[n_1,m]}(n_1<m, l_1 \text{ is } m - n_1) \wedge \smiley_{[n_2,m]}(n_2<m, l_2 \text{ is } m - n_2)\wedge$
$\mathtt{freshvars}(l_1, l_2, \{\mathtt{gcd}(n_1),\mathtt{gcd}(n_2),\mathtt{gcd}(m)\} \uplus S)\wedge$
$\mathtt{type}(\mathtt{posGcd}, \{\mathtt{gcd}(n_1),\mathtt{gcd}(n_2),\mathtt{gcd}(m)\} \uplus S)$

6   Conclusion

The work presented here is part of a research project aiming to provide automatic or semi-automatic tools for proving confluence modulo equivalence of CHR programs. We described a meta-level language and used it to define a meta-level transition system, able to simulate infinitely many CHR transitions by a single meta-level transitions. Our approach is the first to obtain this in the context of invariants and modulo equivalence. Furthermore, we stepped from a theoretically interesting semantics, to one describing CHR as it is implemented and used. Instead of assuming termination, we proposed the weaker property observable termination and demonstrated it useful. Methods for proving termination of CHR programs have been studied, e.g., [11,18,19], but they still need to be adapted for observable termination.

A constraint solver for the meta-level language is under development in CHR as the obvious implementation language. Its main job is to reduce meta-level states or to identify when this is not possible, and to decide satisfiability of a conjunction of meta-level constraints. Our current experiments indicate that when splitting is not necessary, we can implement proofs of joinability similarly to existing confluence checkers for CHR, e.g., [16], referring to the mentioned constraint solver in each step. When and how to split is an open challenge, and there are cases requiring infinite splitting [5]; the necessary induction principles still need to be investigated.

References

1. Abdennadher, S.: Operational semantics and confluence of constraint propagation rules. In: Smolka, G. (ed.) CP 1997. LNCS, vol. 1330, pp. 252–266. Springer, Heidelberg (1997). https://doi.org/10.1007/BFb0017444
2. Abdennadher, S., Frühwirth, T., Meuss, H.: On confluence of Constraint Handling Rules. In: Freuder, E.C. (ed.) CP 1996. LNCS, vol. 1118, pp. 1–15. Springer, Heidelberg (1996). https://doi.org/10.1007/3-540-61551-2_62
3. Abdennadher, S., Frühwirth, T.W., Meuss, H.: Confluence and semantics of constraint simplification rules. Constraints 4(2), 133–165 (1999)
4. Christiansen, H., Kirkeby, M.H.: Confluence modulo equivalence in constraint handling rules. In: Proietti, M., Seki, H. (eds.) LOPSTR 2014. LNCS, vol. 8981, pp. 41–58. Springer, Cham (2015). https://doi.org/10.1007/978-3-319-17822-6_3
5. Christiansen, H., Kirkeby, M.H.: On proving confluence modulo equivalence for constraint handling rules. Formal Aspects Comput. 29(1), 57–95 (2017)
6. Christiansen, H., Kirkeby, M.H.: Confluence of CHR revisited: invariants and modulo equivalence. In: LOPSTR 2018, vol. 11408. LNCS, pp. 83–99. Springer, Heidelberg (2019)
7. Duck, G.J., Stuckey, P.J., Sulzmann, M.: Observable confluence for constraint handling rules. In: Dahl, V., Niemelä, I. (eds.) ICLP 2007. LNCS, vol. 4670, pp. 224–239. Springer, Heidelberg (2007). https://doi.org/10.1007/978-3-540-74610-2_16
8. Endrullis, J., de Vrijer, R.C., Waldmann, J.: Local termination: theory and practice. Logical Methods Comput. Sci. 6(3), 1–37 (2010)
9. Frühwirth, T.W.: User-defined constraint handling. In: ICLP, pp. 837–838. MIT Press (1993)
10. Frühwirth, T.W.: Theory and practice of constraint handling rules. J. Logic Program. 37(1–3), 95–138 (1998)
11. Frühwirth, T.: Proving termination of constraint solver programs. In: Apt, K.R., Monfroy, E., Kakas, A.C., Rossi, F. (eds.) WC 1999. LNCS (LNAI), vol. 1865, pp. 298–317. Springer, Heidelberg (2000). https://doi.org/10.1007/3-540-44654-0_15
12. Frühwirth, T.: Constraint Handling Rules. Cambridge University Press, Cambridge (2009)
13. Gall, D., Frühwirth, T.: Confluence modulo equivalence with invariants in constraint handling rules. In: Gallagher, J.P., Sulzmann, M. (eds.) FLOPS 2018. LNCS, vol. 10818, pp. 116–131. Springer, Cham (2018). https://doi.org/10.1007/978-3-319-90686-7_8
14. Holzbaur, C., Frühwirth, T.W.: A PROLOG constraint handling rules compiler and runtime system. Appl. Artif. Intell. 14(4), 369–388 (2000)
15. Huet, G.P.: Confluent reductions: abstract properties and applications to term rewriting systems. J. ACM 27(4), 797–821 (1980)
16. Langbein, J., Raiser, F., Frühwirth, T.W.: A state equivalence and confluence checker for CHRs. In: Proceedings International Workshop on Constraint Handling Rules, Report CW 588, pp. 1–8. Katholieke Universiteit Leuven, Belgium (2010)
17. Newman, M.: On theories with a combinatorial definition of "equivalence". Ann. Math. 43(2), 223–243 (1942)
18. Pilozzi, P., De Schreye, D.: Automating termination proofs for CHR. In: Hill, P.M., Warren, D.S. (eds.) ICLP 2009. LNCS, vol. 5649, pp. 504–508. Springer, Heidelberg (2009). https://doi.org/10.1007/978-3-642-02846-5_43

19. Pilozzi, P., De Schreye, D.: Improved termination analysis of CHR using self-sustainability analysis. In: Vidal, G. (ed.) LOPSTR 2011. LNCS, vol. 7225, pp. 189–204. Springer, Heidelberg (2012). https://doi.org/10.1007/978-3-642-32211-2_13
20. Schrijvers, T., Demoen, B.: The K.U. Leuven CHR system: implementation and application. In: Workshop on Constraint Handling Rules: Selected Contributions, pp. 1–5. Ulmer Informatik-Berichte, Nr. 2004–01 (2004)

Reference Type Logic Variables in Constraint-Logic Object-Oriented Programming

Jan C. Dageförde[✉] [iD]

ERCIS, Leonardo-Campus 3, 48149 Münster, Germany
dagefoerde@uni-muenster.de

Abstract. Constraint-logic object-oriented programming, for example using Muli, facilitates the integrated development of business software that occasionally involves finding solutions to constraint-logic problems. The availability of object-oriented features calls for the option to use objects as logic variables as well, as opposed to being limited to primitive type logic variables. The present work contributes a concept for reference type logic variables in constraint-logic object-oriented programming that takes arbitrary class hierarchies of programs written in object-oriented languages into account. The concept discusses interactions between constraint-logic object-oriented programs and reference type logic variables, particularly invocations on and access to logic variables, type operations, and equality. Furthermore, it proposes approaches as to how these interactions can be handled by a corresponding execution environment.

Keywords: Constraint-logic object-oriented programming ·
Multi-paradigm languages · Free objects · Object type constraints

1 Motivation

Constraint-logic object-oriented programming can be used to develop business software that involves finding solutions to constraint-logic problems in an integrated way, particularly for applications that add constraints dynamically during runtime. The mixed paradigm leverages benefits of well-known object-oriented programming languages as well as of constraint-logic programming. For example, the constraint-logic object-oriented programming language Muli augments Java with logic variables, symbolic execution, constraints, and encapsulated search using a customised symbolic Java virtual machine (SJVM) [2].

So far, symbolic expressions in Muli can involve logic variables of any type, but constraints can only be defined over (logic) variables of *primitive* types [3]. While those variables may be fields of objects, thus proving useful in an imperative context as well as in an object-oriented one, such constraints are not applicable to entire objects. Similarly, the semantics of further interactions (particularly invocations and field accesses) with unbound reference type logic variables is not defined yet. After all, objects in object-oriented languages usually do not just

© Springer Nature Switzerland AG 2019
J. Silva (Ed.): WFLP 2018, LNCS 11285, pp. 131–144, 2019.
https://doi.org/10.1007/978-3-030-16202-3_8

encapsulate data, but behaviour as well. As a result, such interactions lead to interesting behaviour, e.g., when methods are invoked on unbound logic variables or objects are compared for equality. In order to realise the benefits of an integrated programming language, the expected behaviour of such interactions needs to be defined and implemented.

Consider the following case that will be used as a running example. We have an object-oriented representation of shapes, namely `Rectangle` and `Square` that both implement an interface `Shape` (cf. Fig. 1), assuming integer edge lengths in millimetres. Implementations of `Shape` provide an appropriate method `getArea()` that calculates the area from field values of an object, as well as a method `toString()` that outputs the object's field values in a human-readable form.[1]

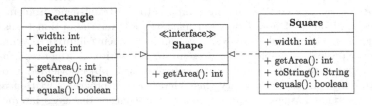

Fig. 1. Class structure assumed for the running example.

As a simple example, Listing 1 formulates a constraint to search for arbitrary shapes that have an area of $16\,mm^2$. No specific instance is provided for s; instead, s is declared as a logic variable. On invocation of either `getArea()` or `toString()` on s, the execution environment has to consider that multiple implementations of these methods are applicable, as per the definitions depicted in Fig. 1. In Muli, we expect the applicable alternatives to be evaluated non-deterministically until all alternatives are considered [2] ("don't know" non-determinism), here resulting in at least two output lines, namely one per actual type of s. Among other things, this paper will elaborate and discuss where exactly non-determinism can be introduced during the evaluation of this example and similar programs.

```
Shape s free;
if (s.getArea() == 16) {
System.out.println(s.toString()); }
else { Muli.fail(); }
```
Listing 1. A constraint-logic object-oriented program that involves a free object.

---

[1] Even though `toString()` is not declared explicitly in the given interface, the Java language specification implicitly augments interfaces with abstract methods that correspond to every method that is declared in `java.lang.Object` [5, Sect. 9.2]. Among others, this includes an implicit declaration of `toString()` that is consistent with the corresponding declaration in `Object`.

This paper contributes a concept for reference type logic variables in the context of constraint-logic object-oriented programming. To that end, all types of interactions of a program with reference type logic variables are discussed based on the example of Muli. This takes peculiarities of comparing equality of Java objects into account. For each possible interaction, this paper defines the expected behaviour and outlines approaches for handling it in the context of arbitrary object graphs. These approaches account for varying positions of objects' types in the class hierarchy that result from inheritance and implementation relations between classes.

This paper presents the contribution as follows. Section 2 provides a brief introduction to the constraint-logic object-oriented programming language Muli. Afterwards, Sect. 3 discusses interactions and explains how they can be handled. Furthermore, that section introduces constraints that are necessary to achieve these interactions. As this is a report on research in progress, Sect. 4 presents an initial implementation idea for a prototype that is going to be used for evaluation. Related research is outlined in Sect. 5. Finally, Sect. 6 summarises the contribution and provides an outlook.

2   Constraint-Logic Object-Oriented Programming with Muli

As a constraint-logic object-oriented language, Muli allows developers to use programming styles of object-oriented programming, while facilitating the specification of constraint-logic problems and finding solutions to them in the same language [2]. Muli syntax is based on Java 8. The SJVM serves as the execution environment that supports logic variables by means of symbolic execution and leverages a constraint solver to solve constraint-logic problems. Compared to Java, the syntax extension is minimal and limited to the **free** keyword. It occurs in declaration statements to indicate an unbound ("free") variable:

```
int x free;
```

At runtime, free variables of primitive types are treated as logic variables to be used as part of symbolic expressions. Similarly, free objects can be defined, but their semantics is undefined and the execution environment does not provide an implementation for treating such variables yet. Therefore, the following code compiles but invoking the method in the second line will fail:

```
Object o free;
o.toString();
```

All variables, including unbound ones, can be used in boolean or arithmetic expressions in the same way as in Java. However, if an expression contains unbound variables, they cannot evaluate to a specific value. Therefore, the execution environment treats those variables symbolically and creates a symbolic expression [3]. For instance, after executing Listing 2, y holds the constant value 5 (as expected in Java), whereas z holds the symbolic expression x + 5.

```
int x free;
int i = 2, j = 3;
int y = i + j; // y == 5.
int z = x + y; // z == x + 5.
```
Listing 2. Arithmetic expressions containing bound or unbound variables.

Ultimately, symbolic arithmetic expressions can evaluate to numeric constants (e.g., after labelling symbolic variables they contain). Therefore, an arithmetic expression that contains only **int** (logic) variables and **int** constants can be used anywhere where an **int** expression is expected.

The behaviour described so far is deterministic. However, as soon as a symbolic expression is used as part of a condition that leads to branching (e.g., in an **if** statement), it is possible that the execution environment cannot decide on a unique outcome, e.g. whether a condition evaluates to **true** or **false**. When there is more than one choice, non-determinism is introduced, so that execution may continue with any of the possible branches [3]. The execution environment makes a choice by selecting a branch, thus asserting a particular outcome (e.g., the condition shall be **false**). That assertion is maintained by imposing a corresponding constraint on the constraint store. After executing that branch, the execution environment backtracks state (constraint store, operand and frame stacks, program counter, and heap values) to the point where a choice was made, and then proceeds with the next choice. In Muli, this behaviour is referred to as search.

In order to limit the effects of non-deterministic execution, non-deterministic branching has to be encapsulated in the program. To that end, Muli offers encapsulation methods such as **getAllSolutions()** or **getOneSolution()** that take a lambda expression or a method reference as a parameter which is then executed non-deterministically. The result of non-deterministic branching is a symbolic execution tree [7]. Solutions to a constraint-logic problem correspond to the leaves of that tree, i.e. where execution ends, such as by throwing an exception or returning a value or expression. The encapsulation method collects the required solutions and returns them to the calling, deterministic program.

3   Reference Type Logic Variables (or Free Objects)

As Muli is based on Java, Muli distinguishes the same four kinds of reference types as Java [5, Sect. 4.3]: class types, interface types, array types, and type variables. Type variables are fundamentally different from the other kinds, as they are substituted by a reference type. For example, ArrayList<E> contains the type variable E that is substituted by a reference type, e.g., Object or String. In contrast, the other kinds of reference types imply that they are instantiated at runtime with values that come from the heap, i.e. they point to data structures such as objects or arrays. Since type variables are that different, they are excluded from further considerations in this work, resulting in a definition of reference types that is congruent to that of C# [10].[2] Class and interface types exhibit an identical structure [5], whereas array types are interpreted differently. Even though array types are interesting as well, this work focuses on class and interface types for now. In the following, they are subsumed as *reference types* for improved legibility.

Due to the nature of Java (and, therefore, Muli), the reference types that this work focuses on are not limited to data encapsulation. They also encapsulate behaviour (via methods) that may change along the implementation hierarchy as a consequence of overriding. Therefore, when a variable that is declared by `Object` o is of type `Object`, o may hold an instance of `Object` or of its subclasses. This affects the typecasts that can (validly) be performed on o at runtime, as well as the behaviour that is expected from invoking methods on the object. This implies that interactions with a reference type logic variable declared by `Object` o **free** need to consider that o may represent instances of subclasses of `Object` as well.

Consequently, we first need to define at which point exactly non-determinism may be introduced when interacting with reference type logic variables. Options are either during declaration/initialisation of a reference type logic variable (i.e. at `Object` o **free**), or when a feature of a variable that is not sufficiently specified is required later during runtime (e.g., on invocation of `o.toString()` or on access to a field such as `square.width`). If non-determinism were already introduced at declaration/initialisation time, this would introduce many branches that are potentially irrelevant, because the SJVM cannot determine how many choices will be required. Therefore, aiming to reduce the state space, Muli creates choices only if discriminating behaviour is expected, e.g., when control flow branches. For reference type logic variables, discriminating behaviour is not expected at the declaration of a logic variable (which can be done deterministically) but can be expected when one of its fields is accessed or its methods are invoked. Hence, we propose that non-determinism is incurred when a feature of a logic variable v is required, where v is not sufficiently specified to be handled deterministically. As a result, this allows search to focus on branches relevant to the respective access, thus effectively reducing the state space. Note that these considerations are similar to those regarding the *Label* reduction rule from [3] that is used for substituting primitive type logic variables with their potential values. Similar to the present case, *Label* is suggested to be used only as a last resort if no other rule can be applied as its application results in one branch per potential value, which usually are a lot. If this is done too early during evaluation, this increases the state space unnecessarily [3].

With this in mind, there are six different kinds of interactions between a program and a reference type logic variable that need to be examined in the following as they potentially result in non-determinism. First, accesses to fields of an object by a program, followed by invocations of methods. Moreover, the

---

[2] Note that only the standalone use of type variables is disregarded here. Consequently, the reference types that we consider in the following may still make use of type variables as part of parameterised (generic) types.

program can compare equality, which occurs in two forms in Java (and therefore in Muli), i.e. comparing reference equality or value equality, which are the third and fourth kind, respectively. Fifth, a program can perform operations on the type of a variable. Last but not least, as a novel kind of interaction, programmers may expect to be able to compare objects for structural equality, i.e. equality based on objects' field values instead of the entire object. This is similar to unification of constructor terms, which is common in logic programming but not in object-oriented programming languages.

3.1   Accessing a Field of a Free Object

In Muli and Java, fields are accessed using a dot notation, e.g., `square.width`. In contrast to methods, fields of a Java class cannot be overridden by subclasses. Although subclasses can declare fields with names identical to those in super-classes, this merely results in the original field being hidden from the overriding class, but not from the original one. Consider an artificial Java example in Listing 3. Accesses to i in both cases `a.i` and `b.i` result in the same value 2 because a and b are accessed via variables of type A. Of course, if b were stored in a variable of type B, that would not be the case. Muli shares this semantics with Java.

```
class Demo {
    public static void main(String[] args) {
        A a = new A();
        A b = new B(); } }
class A { public int i = 2; }
class B extends A { private int i = 1; }
```
Listing 3. Fields are only hidden, but not overridden.

As a result, accesses to fields of free objects do not need to consider the class hierarchy of the object's type, but only the type of the reference type logic variable through which access takes place (here, A). Since a free object is uninitialised, in its initial state all its fields are to be treated as logic variables as well. Therefore, accessing a field of a free object is a deterministic operation. Its result is the logic variable that is the field of the object. For instance, in the running example accessing `square.width` yields the logic variable of type **int** that is stored at that field.

3.2   Invoking a Method on a Free Object

For a variable `Shape s` **free**, consider the statement `s.getArea()` as seen in Listing 1. As s is declared free, this causes the execution to evaluate the method `getArea()`. Shape is merely an abstract supertype, so all the subtypes need to be taken into consideration, as they provide implementations for `getArea()`. Similarly, even in the deterministic nature of Java, the method that is actually invoked depends on the type of the referenced instance, not on that of the variable. Consequently, in order to determine which actual implementation is going to be invoked, the statement s.getArea() causes the SJVM to discover the set S of non-abstract subtypes that extend Shape.[3] If the supertype can be instantiated as well, the set of relevant types then is $S' = S \cup \{X\}$ for a non-abstract supertype X. Otherwise, the set of relevant types is just $S' = S$. For the running example, $S' = S = \{\text{Square}, \text{Rectangle}\}$, as the supertype is an interface type and is therefore abstract.

In general, the set of relevant subtypes can be restricted further, thus reducing the number of non-deterministic branches that the SJVM needs to evaluate. After all, we are only interested in those branches that potentially exhibit distinct behaviour. Therefore, the SJVM needs to discover $S'' \subseteq S'$, comprising only those classes that provide their own implementations of getArea(), thus omitting all types that merely inherit an implementation from their supertype. Afterwards, the SJVM only needs to evaluate one branch per element of S''. If S'' holds exactly one type, execution continues deterministically by invoking that type's implementation on s. Otherwise, evaluation creates a choice point in order to execute all ((t)s).getArea(), where $t \in S''$. As a result, the number of choices that this choice point provides is equal to the cardinality of S''.

Looking at the running example from Listing 1, S' cannot be reduced as all subtypes provide their own implementations, i.e. $S'' = S' = \{\text{Square}, \text{Rectangle}\}$. For this reason the System.out.println statement is expected to be executed twice, as indicated in Sect. 1; once per type in S''. To discuss a different example with a more detailed implementation hierarchy, consider the classes depicted in Fig. 2. For a logic variable A a **free**, invoking a.m() results in discovering the subtypes $S = \{\text{B}, \text{C}, \text{D}\}$ first. The supertype A is non-abstract, therefore $S' = \{\text{A}, \text{B}, \text{C}, \text{D}\}$. However, since C does not provide its own implementation of m() and relies on that of B instead, the set is reduced further to $S'' = \{\text{A}, \text{B}, \text{D}\}$. The SJVM then continues the evaluation based on S''.

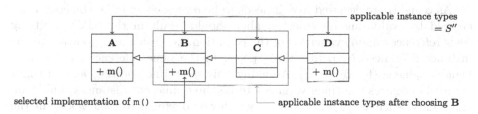

Fig. 2. Applicable instance types for a given object A a **free** before and after choosing a particular subtype.

After making a choice for a type $t \in S''$ whose method implementation is used, the actual type of the instance that the method is invoked on can be an arbitrary one from a set of types. Specifically, either the determined type

---

[3] In general, this includes parameterised (generic) types that remain in parameterised form (e.g., ArrayList<E>). Therefore, this set is finite.

or any of its subtypes. However, the set of allowed types is restricted further, as it may not contain subtypes that provide their own implementation (as *their* implementation would need to be invoked otherwise). This is illustrated in Fig. 2, where the set of types is constrained only to B and C. Even though D is a subtype, it provides an own implementation of m() and would therefore conflict with having chosen B's implementation.

As a result of choosing an implementation, the SJVM needs to add a constraint to its constraint store that restricts the type of s according to the above description. This ensures that later interactions with that object do not make conflicting assumptions regarding the type of s, i.e. to avoid assuming s to be of a type that is not in the reduced set of applicable types. Similarly, a type t cannot be assumed for s if that would violate a previously imposed constraint, so the corresponding branch must not be evaluated. Consequently, the constraint that restricts an instance's type is a set-based constraint. This type of constraint is novel to Muli, as existing constraints are only of arithmetic nature.

3.3 Comparing Reference Equality of Reference Type Logic Variables

In Muli and Java, objects are typically compared by one of two means, either reference equality or value equality. First, let us focus on the former. Based on the program in Listing 4, consider the conditional control flow statements **if** (o == p) and **if** (o == q) that compare references of reference type (logic) variables.

```
Object o free;
Object p = new Object();
Object q free;
```
Listing 4. Declaration of a set of reference type variables.

As o and q are declared free, it needs to be discussed whether the constraint created by evaluating reference equality should result in the SJVM unifying their references upon evaluation of the condition, i.e. result in o pointing to the instance referenced by p (for o == p), or to the same reference as the other logic variable q (for o == q). Arguably, this should not be the case. Listing 4 expressly declares the three variables to be three different instances, unlike an assignment, such as Object w = p, which would explicitly make w assume the same reference as p.

Therefore, the evaluation of a condition comparing reference equality is a deterministic operation even for reference type logic variables that yields **true** iff two variables reference the same free object, which is consistent with the Java semantics of comparing reference equality. No implicit unification is performed.

3.4 Comparing Value Equality of Reference Type Logic Variables

In addition to the means described in Sect. 3.3, Java (or Muli) code can also compare objects in terms of value equality, e.g., by **if** (o.equals(p)) or

if (p.equals(o)) (after an initialisation as depicted in Listing 4). This presents another opportunity for unifying objects if free objects are involved.

As equals() is a method that every class can implement individually, the interpretations of these two examples are fundamentally different. In p.equals(o), p is a concrete instance of Object, so Object's default implementation is invoked deterministically, effectively checking for reference equality. Other implementations might compare instances by accessing fields of the free object o, thus resorting to the case described in Sect. 3.1. In contrast, o.equals(p) is an invocation of equals() on the logic variable o. As a result, this case reduces to the invocation of methods (cf. Sect. 3.2), resorting to specific implementations of equals(), e.g., of Square and Rectangle. Consequently, equals() is not commutative.

As a result, Muli does not need to handle value equality comparisons specifically, as they are implicitly covered by other considerations regarding reference type logic variables.

3.5 Performing Type Operations on a Free Object

The (super-) type of a logic variable is determined by its declaration, but initially the corresponding instance may be of that type or of its subtypes (cf. the definition of S in Sect. 3.2). This affects operations that operate on the type of a free object; namely **instanceof** and typecasts. For example, the set of allowed types for the instance is reduced by (successful or failed) typecasts. Considering Listing 4 again, a program might try to cast a reference type logic variable to a subtype, e.g., (Square) o. In that case, given that this is a valid cast, the actual type of o can be Square or any of its subtypes.

Typecasts can be either valid or invalid at runtime. Invalid typecasts are those that violate the class hierarchy, such as casting an object of type Square to Rectangle. This deterministically yields a ClassCastException and therefore does not result in a choice point. The result of evaluating **instanceof** statements in a similarly invalid contexts is deterministically **false**.

In contrast, performing a valid typecast results in two choices as to how execution can continue. Either the cast is successful (unless a contradictory constraint exists in the constraint store at runtime), so a new constraint can be imposed narrowing the logic variable's type; or the cast is not successful. In regular Java, the latter case is not caught by a compiler and results in a runtime exception (ClassCastException). Similarly, Muli can handle this case by imposing a corresponding constraint and throwing that exception. Therefore, a valid typecast of a reference type logic variable results in a choice point with at most two options, depending on existing constraints in the constraint store. Similarly, using **instanceof** in a valid context results in non-deterministic execution that imposes the same constraints as successful or unsuccessful typecasts.

To support non-deterministic branching, a constraint is needed that is imposed when a choice is made for a branch that corresponds to a type operation. This constraint reduces the set of possible instance types. The set-based constraint from Sect. 3.2 can be re-used, but the sets are computed differently. Given that S describes the set of applicable types prior to imposing a constraint and U describes the set of types comprising the cast target types and all of its subtypes, on a successful cast, the set of applicable types is narrowed to the intersection $V = S \cap U$, whereas for a failed typecast all remaining types are applicable, i.e. the type is constrained to the set difference $V' = S \setminus U$. The resulting sets of types are used to impose the corresponding constraints, i.e. V for the constraint that is added to the constraint store when making the choice that the typecast is successful, and V' for the other choice.

3.6 Imposing a Constraint for Structural Equality Between Two Objects

The cases discussed so far refer to the interpretation of object-oriented concepts against the background of a constraint-logic object-oriented language. In addition to that, Muli creates a novel opportunity regarding unification of objects that cannot exist in plain object-oriented languages without symbolic execution, namely comparing (free) objects for structural equality (in combination with constraints that enforce it).

Value equality relies on the `equals()` method that a class can implement individually (cf. Sect. 3.4), for example so that equality depends only on a specific field. In contrast, we use the term structural equality to refer to a situation in which all fields of two (free) objects of the same type either share identical values (for fields of primitive types) or are structurally equal again (for reference-type fields), i.e. the following recursive definition applies: $o_1 \odot o_2 \Leftrightarrow type(o_1) = type(o_2) \wedge ((o_1.x \text{ primitive} \wedge o_1.x = o_2.x) \vee (o_1.x \text{ not primitive} \wedge o_1.x \odot o_2.x)) \forall x \in fields(o_1),$[4] where $type(o)$ is the type of an object o and $fields(o)$ is the set of its fields. For example, given two free objects `Rectangle r1` **free**, `r2` **free**, imposing structural equality $r1 \odot r2$ implies that `r1.width == r2.width` and `r1.height == r2.height` in addition to sharing their type. Similarly, if `r2` were an initialised object of type `Rectangle`, the values of `r1`'s fields are unified with those of the corresponding fields in `r2`. As a result, $r1 \odot r2 \Leftrightarrow r2 \odot r1$, i.e. structural equality is commutative.

A new operator is needed to denote the structural equality constraint $\odot$ in source code. For that purpose, I introduce the symbol `#=` to be used as a boolean, binary operator in conditions in order to add this constraint to the constraint store at runtime. It evaluates to **true** if fields of two objects are unifiable as described above, and to **false** if they are not. In both cases, a corresponding constraint is added to the constraint store that maintains this equality.

---

[4] Note that here $fields(o_1) = fields(o_2)$ since $type(o_1) = type(o_2)$, so $fields(o_2)$ could be used just as well.

4   Implementation

The considerations in Sect. 3 require modifications to the Muli SJVM in terms of additional constraints and choice point types. This results in changes that need to be made to the SJVM's solver component and its choice point generator (cf. [2]).

The *applicable type constraint* is a set-based constraint that restricts possible types for a free object. It maintains a reference to the free object that it affects, and a set of fully qualified names of types that the object may assume. This set is defined prior to instantiation of that constraint. In the solver manager, a constraint is imposed in conjunction with all other constraints in the constraint store. Therefore, the solver manager can verify consistency of a constraint store by collecting all imposed applicable type constraints involving a free object and checking that the intersection of the sets of types is non-empty for each object, i.e. there is at least one type that any object can assume; in addition to verifying consistency of the remaining constraints.

Additionally, the *structural equality constraint* translates into a conjunction of arithmetic equality and type equality constraints as specified in Sect. 3.6, hence it does not need to be represented on its own. The *type equality constraint* references two involved objects that need to be of the same type. A constraint store comprising a type equality constraint is consistent if both objects are trivially of the same type (such as for regular objects) or if there is a type that is among the applicable types of both objects.

At runtime, evaluations of bytecode instructions that incur non-determinism result in the creation of choice points. These are responsible for controlling search and, hence, for imposing constraints and removing them afterwards [2]. Therefore, the support for type operations on logic reference type variables requires a corresponding choice point. It offers choices according to the description in Sect. 3.5 and imposes an appropriate instance of the applicable type constraint for each choice. Similarly, a choice point for invoking a method according to Sect. 3.2 is required. Both choice point implementations require the implementation of new helper methods that discover sets of available types. The method `Type[] getSubtypes(Type)` discovers, for a given type, all of its subtypes from the loaded classpath. A further method `Type[] getImplementations (Type[], Method)` is required that filters a list of types such that it returns only those types that can be instantiated and that provide an own implementation of a particular method, thus supporting the case from Sect. 3.2.

Last but not least, another choice point is generated if free objects are compared for structural equality as specified in Sect. 3.6. It comprises two choices. One choice represents that equality is maintained, resulting in the corresponding constraint being imposed. The other one corresponds to imposing the negation of that constraint.

5   Related Work

Several approaches intend to integrate elements from object-oriented programming into declarative languages, mostly based on Prolog. For example, tuProlog provides a Prolog engine implemented in Java, offering access to Java features from Prolog [4]. However, referring to Java types is done rather artificially by means of string literals which cannot be checked by a compiler, and free objects and accessing their fields are not considered. As a non-Prolog-based example, Oz is a constraint language that offers OO features, but does not seem to support constraints involving logic objects [15]. Despite their integration, the mentioned programming languages follow a declarative style, which might not be as accessible for developers who are used to imperative languages.

CAPJa intends to seamlessly integrate Prolog search into Java programs, e.g. by providing a Java-based abstraction layer from Prolog [12]. The integration supports a mapping of data structures from Java to Prolog and vice-versa, but focuses on logic objects used for encapsulating data. It does not consider free (unbound) objects in terms of method invocations and field accesses, which become relevant if we consider that objects also encapsulate behaviour, which is expected in object-oriented programming. As another example, the library heya-unify facilitates unification of data structures in JavaScript [8], particularly in order to compare object contents or to perform pattern matching on them. However, it does not support defining entire objects as logic variables and is limited to comparing structural equality on weakly typed objects and arrays.

The type unification algorithm presented by [13] can be used for Java type inference. Although their work emanates from a different standpoint, the type unification could be re-used for formulating the subtype relations for the constraints in this work.

Other work demonstrates that the use of languages integrating multiple paradigms is beneficial, most notably the Java Stream API [14] and Scala [11], which integrate object-oriented programming with functional programming on the JVM. LINQ offers a similar integration, but for languages on the .NET CLR [9]. A very relevant integration of logic and functional programming is Curry [6], which incorporates logic programming into a language with Haskell syntax. Muli lends and adapts some ideas from Curry, such as encapsulated search and constraint definition via boolean equalities [1]. However, the adaptation of these concepts to constraint-logic *object-oriented* programming results in fundamentally different considerations and implementations.

6   Concluding Remarks

This work contributes a concept for reference type logic variables in constraint-logic object-oriented languages. It details interactions of programs with reference type logic variables and discusses approaches for handling such interactions, on the basis of the programming language Muli. As a result, there now is a concept for invocations on free objects and accesses to their fields, comparisons of different kinds of equality, and type operations in constraint-logic object-oriented programming.

The discussed approaches efficiently introduce non-determinism where it is specifically required and take class hierarchies into account. This requires a novel constraint that restricts types of free objects to support these approaches. Since the constraints previously supported by Muli were of a purely arithmetic nature, this work also contributes a set-based constraint to restrict the possible types of free objects.

The contribution is helpful not just for Muli but for constraint-logic object-oriented programming in general, because it allows non-deterministic search to extend beyond logic variables of primitive types. For example, a constraint-logic object-oriented language based on C# could also make use of these approaches. Furthermore, it facilitates the usage of object-oriented features in combination with free objects.

Subsequently, the implementation of this approach in the Muli SJVM will be completed in order to evaluate its benefits. The resulting virtual machine implementation will be part of the open source distribution of Muli provided via GitHub.[5] It is also planned to provide an augmented formal semantics, incorporating the aspects discussed in this paper, thus yielding an integrated semantics for a constraint-logic *object-oriented* language. Future work will tackle the extension of these considerations towards further reference types, particularly array types.

References

1. Antoy, S., Hanus, M.: From boolean equalities to constraints. In: Falaschi, M. (ed.) LOPSTR 2015. LNCS, vol. 9527, pp. 73–88. Springer, Cham (2015). https://doi.org/10.1007/978-3-319-27436-2_5
2. Dageförde, J.C., Kuchen, H.: A constraint-logic object-oriented language. In: SAC 2018, pp. 1185–1194. ACM (2018). https://doi.org/10.1145/3167132.3167260
3. Dageförde, J.C., Kuchen, H.: An operational semantics for constraint-logic imperative programming. In: Seipel, D., Hanus, M., Abreu, S. (eds.) WFLP/WLP/INAP 2017. LNCS, vol. 10997, pp. 64–80. Springer, Cham (2018). https://doi.org/10.1007/978-3-030-00801-7_5
4. Denti, E., Omicini, A., Ricci, A.: Multi-paradigm Java-Prolog integration in tuProlog. Sci. Comput. Program. **57**(2), 217–250 (2005). https://doi.org/10.1016/j.scico.2005.02.001
5. Gosling, J., Joy, B., Steele, G., Bracha, G., Buckley, A.: The Java® Language Specification - Java SE 8 Edition (2015). https://docs.oracle.com/javase/specs/jls/se8/jls8.pdf
6. Hanus, M., Kuchen, H., Moreno-Navarro, J.J., Votano, J., Parham, M., Hall, L.: Curry: a truly functional logic language. In: Workshop on Visions for the Future of Logic Programming, ILPS 1995, pp. 95–107 (1995)
7. King, J.C.: Symbolic execution and program testing. Commun. ACM **19**(7), 385–394 (1976). https://doi.org/10.1145/360248.360252

---

[5] https://github.com/wwu-pi/muli.

8. Lazutkin, E.: Unification for JS (2014). http://www.lazutkin.com/blog/2014/05/18/unification-for-js/
9. Meijer, E., Beckman, B., Bierman, G.: LINQ: reconciling objects, relations and XML in the .NET framework. In: ACM SIGMOD International Conference on Management of Data, p. 706 (2006). https://doi.org/10.1145/1142473.1142552
10. Microsoft: Reference Types (C# Reference) (2015). https://docs.microsoft.com/de-de/dotnet/csharp/language-reference/keywords/reference-types
11. Odersky, M., et al.: Scala Language Specification (2017). http://www.scala-lang.org/files/archive/spec/2.12/
12. Ostermayer, L.: Seamless cooperation of Java and Prolog for rule-based software development. In: Proceedings of RuleML 2015 (2015). http://ceur-ws.org/Vol-1417/paper2.pdf
13. Plümicke, M.: Java type unification with wildcards. In: Seipel, D., Hanus, M., Wolf, A. (eds.) INAP/WLP 2007. LNCS, vol. 5437, pp. 223–240. Springer, Heidelberg (2009). https://doi.org/10.1007/978-3-642-00675-3_15
14. Urma, R.G., Fusco, M., Mycroft, A.: Java 8 in Action: Lambdas, Streams, and Functional-Style Programming. Manning Publications Co., Greenwich (2014)
15. Van Roy, P., Brand, P., Duchier, D., Haridi, S., Schulte, C., Henz, M.: Logic programming in the context of multiparadigm programming: the Oz experience. Theory Pract. Logic Program. **3**(6), 717–763 (2003). https://doi.org/10.1017/S1471068403001741

FMS: Functional Programming as a Modelling Language

Ingmar Dasseville(✉) and Gerda Janssens

Department of Computer Science, KU Leuven, 3001 Leuven, Belgium
{ingmar.dasseville,gerda.janssens}@cs.kuleuven.be

Abstract. In this paper we introduce the Functional Modelling System (FMS). The system introduces the Functional Modelling Language (FML), which is a modelling language for NP-complete search problems based on concepts of functional programming. Internally, we translate FML specifications to an Answer Set Program to obtain models. We give a general overview of the new FML language, and how this language is handled in the system. We give a step-by-step walkthrough of the system, pointing out what features are in place, and what improvements are still possible.

1 Introduction

We have published a theoretical framework in which we explain how lambda calculus could be used to define higher order logics [4]. Based on these ideas we now present a practical Functional Modelling System (FMS), powered under the hood by an Answer Set Programming (ASP) solver. The system is focused on solving NP-complete search problems, the same class of problems its underlying engine - ASP - can solve. In this paper we give a high level overview of the system, point out which techniques and algorithms are already implemented and highlight the places where there is low-hanging fruit for improving the system. In Sect. 2 we give an overview of the language of the system, both on the external and the internal level. In Sect. 3 we explain what steps a file goes through to produce an answer. In Sect. 4 we take a deeper look into what kind of optimisation techniques are present in the system. We conclude in Sect. 5 with information on the tooling and availability of the system.

1.1 Context

Modelling Languages. In this paper we use the concept of *modelling language* to denote a language which is used to express a set of rules to which solutions should adhere. Typically, modelling languages allow for naturally expressing NP-complete problems. A solution for this set of rules is called a model. Typical examples of such languages are Minizinc [12], ASP [15] and FO(.) [2], the language of IDP3. The new Functional Modelling Language (FML) is an addition to this set of modelling languages. Most previous sytems have their roots in

© Springer Nature Switzerland AG 2019
J. Silva (Ed.): WFLP 2018, LNCS 11285, pp. 145–161, 2019.
https://doi.org/10.1007/978-3-030-16202-3_9

logic programming, and first order logic. The new FML language is based on constructs which are traditionally only found in functional programming languages. With these constructs it is still possible to use traditional first order logic specifications, but there are also new modelling possibilities.

The only other fully higher order modelling language that the authors are aware of is ProB [9]. The expressive power of ProB is very high but the solving capabilities of this language are limited. The system is mainly used to model dynamic systems and not to solve search problems.

Haskell as a Host Language. Monadiccp [16] and Ersatz are Haskell libraries, through which it is also possible to define search problems using a functional language. It allows the user to define constraint satisfaction problems using Haskell, which is then translated to respectively a constraint programming or a SAT solver. While the host language is a fully higher-order language, the problems that can be specified in monadiccp are only first order. Ersatz does have the notion of relations, but somebody writing the specification has to think about the possible range of values while declaring the relation. Oftentimes this is easy, but for example when using a Collatz sequence, it is not easy to tell the range of numbers that will occur in the chain. Ersatz also requires the relation to have a contiguous range as inputs for the relation. This is often natural for numeric problems but this makes modelling less natural when the domain elements have no natural ordering. FMS takes these issues out of the equation as the domain of the function is derived from the specification, so the user does not need to think about the input domain. Ersatz is embedded in Haskell, and this has the consequence that the user has to be conscious whether he is calling native Haskell functions (such as addition) or relations which need to be found by the solver. These have no different syntax in FMS which leads to a more streamlined experience.

1.2   Search Technologies

There are a multitude of existing technologies apt for solving search problems. SAT solvers have become very efficient and are the standard for a number of problems, but there are also a lot of other technologies: SMT (SAT modulo theories) which extends SAT with higher level concepts, constraint programming systems, mixed integer programming, ... FMS does not contribute to these search technologies, but to the modelling techniques for these.

For FMS, ASP was chosen. ASP solvers use a SAT solver with some extensions for recursive logic definitions. ASP was chosen because the language itself is already relatively high level, so it is easier to build another language on top of ASP compared to other paradigms such as SAT.

1.3   First Order or Higher Order?

FML supports higher order expressions: functions which take functions as input and return new functions. Higher order sets are also supported: it is possible to define s as the set $\{\{1,4\},\{1,6,7\},\{5,4,9\}\}$.

Listing 1. Quantification of functions (in the Full language)

```
c :: element of {3..5}.
d :: element of {3..5}.

s := {\x -> x * 2, \x -> x + c, \x -> x * c}.

! s (\f -> f d < 10).
```

We have a polynomial translation to ASP which has first order semantics, from this it follows that the semantics of our language is not higher order. The higher order aspects of the FML language are syntactical sugar for a first order encoding of higher order functionality.

Nevertheless, this approach allows for modelling techniques which were not possible before in modelling languages. For instance in Listing 1 you can see an FML specification which declares the constants c and d as numbers between 3 and 5. The next line defines the set s as the set containing the doubling function, the function which adds c to a number and the function which multiplies a number by c. The last line starts with ! which means "forall". So the line means: for every function f in the set s, f applied to d is smaller than 10. There is exactly one model for this, which maps both c and d to 3.

1.4 Advantages

There are a number of advantages when comparing FML to existing modelling languages. One driving factor for higher order language is the easy abstraction of concepts. Suppose that you want to find 2 different solutions of the N-queens problem so that no two queens occur in the same place. In traditional ASP or MiniZinc (a constraint programming language), one would need to write down the N-queens constraints twice: once for each of the two solutions. Extensions for ASP have been introduced to introduce templates [6], which circumvent this problem but make a fundamental difference between first order and higher order predicates. FML does not require the user to differentiate between first and higher order terms and allows to easily reuse the higher order predicate nqueens indicating that solution is a solution to the nqueens problem. The FMS modelling for this problem can be seen in Listing 2.

A second advantage of the FML is the propagation of the domains. In most traditional modelling languages, whenever you declare a function or predicate, you need to specify a finite domain. This would disallow a definition of prime numbers as short as "prime x := ! {2..x-1} (\y -> x % y > 0)" (x is prime if for all numbers y between 2 and x-1, x modulo y is larger than 0) because this is a function with an infinite domain (all integers). FML allows this by automatically deriving the relevant domain of the function from the constraints.

Listing 2. Find 2 N-queen solutions which have no shared queens

```
domain := {1..8}.

solution1/1 :: function to domain.
solution2/1 :: function to domain.

alldiff solution f := ! domain (\x ->
                        ! domain (\y -> x ~= y => f x ~= f y)).

nqueens solution := ! {
                        solution,
                        \x -> x - solution x,
                        \x -> x + solution x
                      } (alldiff solution).
nqueens solution1.
nqueens solution2.
! domain (\x -> solution1 x ~= solution2 x).
```

2   Language

We differentiate between the *Core* language and the *Full* language of FMS. We start by introducing the Core language in Sect. 2.1. The Core language represents the essentials of FML. The Full language extends this with syntactical sugar for ease of use and is introduced in Sect. 2.2. Internally in the system, all expressions are represented using the Core language. It makes internal transformations easier than a representation that incorporates all details of the Full language.

2.1   Core Language

FML is based on the lambda calculus. This lambda calculus is extended with some common constructs (such as let-bindings and numbers) and less common constructs (such as the built-in notion of a set). There are ten language constructs in the Core language. Nine with a semantic meaning, and one to track the values which are needed in the output. This language does not have an explicit syntax as it corresponds to the internal representation of the language. However, it can be useful to see an approximate BNF for this Core language which can be seen in Listing 3. The language constructs you can see in the BNF are:

Variable. A traditional reference to a bound identifier.
Application. This construct applies a function to an argument.
Lambda. Internally, this is the only way a function can be declared. Lambdas abstract away one single variable. If multiple arguments are required, this language construct should be nested. Note that a tuple counts as a single argument.

Listing 3. BNF for the Core language

```
e := x                            (variable)
   | e e                          (application)
   | \x -> e                      (lambda abstraction)
   | let (x := e)* in e           (let binding)
   | i                            (injection)
   | case e of (pattern -> e)*    (case expression)
   | b                            (builtin)
   | {e*}                         (set expression)
   | h(e*)                        (herbrand expression)
   | outputexp(s, e)              (output expression)

pattern := _                      (don't-care pattern)
         | h[pattern*]            (constructor match)
         | x                      (variable match)
```

Let Binding. Introduces some local definitions in a new expression. A binding binds a variable to an expression, possibly recursively. This is the only way to bind a term recursively.

Injection. This is a way to inject an arbitrary JVM object into the language. In the current system, it is only used to inject integers and strings. In the future this construct could be used to reason over arbitrary JVM objects.

Case. This language construct handles all pattern matching. This can be seen as a generalised form of an if-then-else construct. An if-then-else construct would only handle patterns: true and false.

Builtin Symbol. There is quite a list of builtin functions for the FMS. The reason for this is not always that we can't define them in the language, but that they are common functions and a dedicated method for translating them leads to a more efficient translation to ASP. Builtin functions include arithmetic operations (+,*), boolean functions (&,|) and set functions (forall: !, exists: ?).

Set Expression. Sets could be emulated through the use of constructors but for efficiency reasons we opted to have sets as an explicit built-in datatype of the language. This language construct makes a finite set containing some expressions. The type system enforces that all elements of a set are of the same type. To represent all set expressions contained in the Full language, this Core construct needs to be combined with some builtin symbols.

Herbrand Expression. This construct corresponds to the declared constructors. It is a named constructor optionally applied to some arguments. These constructors can be pattern matched using the Case construct.

Output Expression. This language construct is the only one which says nothing about the actual meaning of the expression but is a construct to annotate that the expression it contains should be outputted using a certain name. 4 + OutputExp("a",5) would denote an expression that evaluates to 9, but the subexpression 5 should be outputted under the name "a". Most languages

---

Listing 4. Minus One in Peano Arithmetic (in the Full language)

```
s/1 :: constructor.
nil/0 :: constructor.

minusOne x := case x of
              s [ a ] -> a;
              nil []    -> nil;.
```

---

use some kind of print statements for this. But as we don't have those in a modelling language like FML, we have to track the values we want to print in another way.

Types. FML is strongly typed, this means that every expression has a type which is enforced at compile time, before trying to run the program. The language is also implicitly typed, this means that these strong types are not necessary parts of the syntax and it is possible that the input file contains no type annotations.

The type system itself is a Hindley-Milner type system, which includes polymorphism through universal quantification over types. E.g. The forall quantifier has the following type: ∀ a. `Set a -> (a -> Bool) -> Bool`. In the implementation itself, the universal quantification is left implicit.

Constructors. It is possible to declare new constructors and deconstruct values which are made of these constructors using the case-construct. An example using peano arithmetic is shown in Listing 4.

2.2 Full Language

The Full language extends the Core language with a lot of syntactic sugar. The process of converting the Full language to the Core language is called desugaring. We will take the graph coloring problem as a leading example throughout this section. The formulation of a graph coloring problem in FML can be seen in Listing 5.

In the Full language, we discern three different kinds of statements: declarations, definitions and constraints. Declarations introduce new symbols for which the interpretation is not given through a definition (e.g. symbol colorof). Definitions introduce new symbols of which the interpretation is fixed (e.g. the border relation). Constraints are boolean expressions which must be true in every model (e.g. adjacent nodes have different colors).

Declarations. Declarations have the form: `name :: declarationkind..` The most important declarations are:

Listing 5. Graph Coloring (in the Full language)

```
//Definitions of given sets
borders := {("a","b"), ("b","c"), ("c","a")}.
colors := {1..3}.

//Declaration of the interpretation we are looking for
colorof/1 :: function to colors.

//Constraint: For all borders (x,y) the color of x
//           should be different than that of y
! borders (\(x,y) -> colorof x ~= colorof y).
```

- e :: **element of** set where set is an expression evaluating to a set. The interpretation of e will be a single element of the interpretation of the set.
- s :: **subset of** set where set is an expression evaluating to a set. The interpretation of s will be a subset of the interpretation of the set.
- f/arity :: **function to** set where set is an expression evaluating to a set and arity a natural number. The interpretation of f will be a function of arity arity with codomain set.
- c/arity :: **constructor** where arity is a natural number. The interpretation of c will be a new constructor function of arity arity.

There are also extra declarations like **proposition** or **predicate**. These can be rewritten in terms of other declarations such as **element of** {true,false} or **function to** {true,false}.

Example 1. A graph coloring problem needs one declaration: the coloring of the nodes, which is a function to colors.

Definitions/Constraints.   A   definition   has   the   form identifier := expression.. A constraint is just an expression by itself. Definitions can be recursive and mutually dependent (e.g. mutually dependent odd and even definitions). There is builtin support for first order logic-connectives, quantifiers, arithmetic and set-expressions. The quantifiers forall (!) and exists (?) are slightly different from the traditional notation in first order logic. They are higher order functions with two arguments: the set they are quantifying over and a boolean function explicitating the property which needs to hold.

Example 2. A graph coloring problem needs two defined relations: the borders and the colors. These can just be given as a set expression. There is one constraint, which quantifies over all borders. We can deconstruct the tuples in the border-relation in place using \(x,y) -> .... The body of the forall quantifier just states that the colors x and y should be different.

Set Expressions. Set expressions are a language feature based on the set-builder notation of mathematics. The set expressions in the Full language are much more general than those of the Core language. The syntax is heavily inspired by the notation in Haskell and Python. Set expressions can be replaced by a series of map and filter operations on sets but allow for a more readable syntax. Point-wise application of a function f over a set s looks like: {f x || x <- s}. Which can be read as: the set of evaluation of f x where x is in the set s. Or the subset of s for which the predicate p holds can be written as: {x || x <- s, p x}.

3   General Workflow

A lot of inspiration for the general workflow of FMS came from GHC [17]. FMS can be seen as a compiler to Answer Set Programming and most of the steps in the compiling process of GHC is relevant to FMS. An overview of the workflow can be seen in Fig. 1. In this section we go over these steps to investigate them in more detail, from the file containing an FML specification to the models.

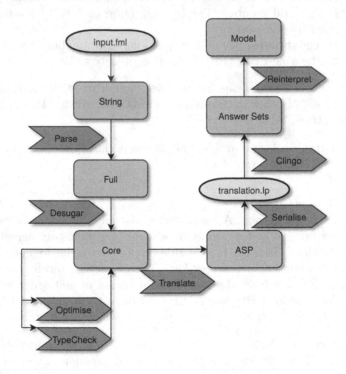

Fig. 1. The general workflow of FMS

3.1 Parse and Desugar

Parsing an FML specification is done using the ANTLR4 [13] system. Based on a BNF grammar, ANTLR4 generates an Abstract Syntax Tree (AST) of an FML specification. This syntax tree is then desugared into the Core language, as defined in Sect. 2.1. Checking whether any identifiers are used out of scope is considered the last step in the desugaring process. Once a string is fully parsed and desugared, it becomes a self-contained well-formed Core expression without free variables.

Example 3. The expression f 1 := 0. f x := 1
  is desugared to f := (\y -> case y of 1 -> 0 ; x -> 1)

Example 4. The expression (a,b) := f 5 is desugared to

```
temp := f 5.
a := case temp of (a,_) -> a.
b := case temp of (_,b) -> b.
```

The reasoning behind this desugaring is that all pattern matching needs to be done in the case-construct and definitions can internally only define a single variable, but the unsugared line defined a and b using a single assignment.

Desugaring complex set expressions results in usages of the bind builtin. The bind operation is the same as the bind for monads in Haskell [18] sometimes known as flatmap. Flatmap (specialised for sets) boils down to a pointwise application followed by a flattening. Desugaring sets could potentially be further improved by using an applicative style instead of a monadic style wherever possible [10]. An applicative style omits the flattening part and can be more efficient, but has less expressivity.

Example 5. The flattening of a set ss can be expressed by the following expression: {x || s <- ss, x <- s}
  Which is desugared to: bind ss (\s -> bind s (\x -> {x}))

Our approach directly transforms a FML specification to the Core language, which has some disadvantages. While the location information of symbols is stored inside the Core language data structures, some details about the original representation get lost. This means that every error which is detected in the file after desugaring is less clear than if the analysis would have been done on the original representation. This mainly concerns errors about out-of-scope identifiers and typing errors, these are exactly the ones which are checked on the desugared version in GHC [17].

3.2 Optimise

We could directly translate the Core language to ASP. However, there are many specification transformations which make the specification simpler. For this reason a number of optimisation techniques are applied to the expressions in the Core language. These optimisations deserve their own section and are further described in Sect. 4.

Listing 6. Translation of Listing 5 to ASP

```
1   :-not bool(X),result(X).
2   member(s0,X0):-X0=1..3.
3   out("colors",s0).
4   {lamInter(l0,X2,X1):member(s0,X1)}==1:-lamDom(l0,X2).
5   out("colorof",l0).
6   member(s1,("a","b")).
7   member(s1,("b","c")).
8   member(s1,("c","a")).
9   out("borders",s1).
10  lamDom(l0,X4):-member(s1,X3),(X4,X5)=X3.
11  lamDom(l0,X5):-member(s1,X3),(X4,X5)=X3.
12  bool((b0,X3)):-X6<>X7,lamInter(l0,X4,X6),
13              member(s1,X3),(X4,X5)=X3,lamInter(l0,X5,X7).
14  bool(b1):-not bool((b0,X3)),member(s1,X3).
15  bool(b2):-not bool(b1).
16  result(b2).
```

3.3 Type Check

Types have no semantic value in FML. This means that the evaluation of a specification can be done without taking typing information into account. Nevertheless, types are an important tool to detect mistakes in a specification, both for the end-user who writes a specification, and for a compiler writer when implementing optimisations to check that the optimised version of the specification is still well-typed. A fairly standard Hindley-Milner [14] type system is implemented on the Core language (and not on the Full language). As explained in Sect. 3.1, a second implementation on the Full language would improve the error messages produced by the type system. Note that doing type checks on the Full language does not fully eliminate the need for a type checker at the Core level, type checking on Core is still useful to detect errors in the optimisers. The error diagnosis in case of a badly typed expression is also very vague in the current state of the system. Many extensions of the standard algorithm exist which would lead to clearer error messages [19], a future version of the system would benefit from those.

3.4 Translate

The translation is arguably the most important part of the system. This part of the system does the job of translating the Core language to an Abstract Syntax Tree representation of ASP. Although the algorithm is complex, it is only a minor part of the actual code. The inner workings of the translation process is considered out of scope for this paper, but we give some intuitions using

Listing 7. An Answer Set of the program in Listing 6

```
result(b2)                          lamInter(l0,"c",2)
bool((b0,("a","b")))                member(s0,1)
bool((b0,("b","c")))                member(s0,2)
bool((b0,("c","a")))                member(s0,3)
bool(b2)                            member(s1,("a","b"))
lamDom(l0,"a")                      member(s1,("b","c"))
lamDom(l0,"b")                      member(s1,("c","a"))
lamDom(l0,"c")                      out("borders",s1)
lamInter(l0,"a",1)                  out("colorof",l0)
lamInter(l0,"b",3)                  out("colors",s0)
```

Listing 6, which is the translation of the graph coloring example of Listing 5.[1] More details about translating a functional language into ASP is given in another paper presented at WFLP 2018.

The ASP programs that FMS produces contain three kinds of statements. Declarations are translated to choice rules. Definitions and constraints are translated to definitions and there is one constraint: it enforces that the evaluation of the constraints is true. This constraint can be seen on line 1. Sets are characterised by a name such as s0, and member/2 represents the membership relation between sets and their elements. Line 2 in the translation defines the set s0 as the numbers of 1 to 3. In line 3 you can see that this set represents the set of colors of the input. The lamInter/3 relation is used to define the relation between a function (the first argument), an input (the second argument) and its output (the third argument). Line 4 defines l0 as an uninterpreted function mapping every member of lamDom (the predicate which is used to represent the relevant domain of the function) to a member of the set s0. This corresponds to the colorof function, this is explicitated in line 5. Lines 6–9 do the same thing for borders as lines 2–3 did for colors. Lines 10 and 11 define that the relevant domain are the first and second components of the elements in the set of borders. Line 12–15 make up the translation of the constraint. Just like functions, booleans are given a name like b0. The bool/1 relation is used to indicate whether the boolean is considered true. In line 16, it can be seen that the boolean b2 is considered the top constraint.

As a whole this ASP program has models which correspond to the 6 possible colorings of the graph. One example answer set can be seen in Listing 7. Once the translation is obtained, we send this ASP program further into our workflow towards Clingo.

---

[1] The translation presented is slightly simplified for readability. The only difference lies in the omission of superfluous empty tuples.

3.5   Clingo

We chose the ASP solver Clingo as a backend for our system. We communicate with Clingo via text files and use JSON output facilities of Clingo to be able to easily parse the answer sets. From the viewpoint of implementing FMS this is a very easy step. We print the ASP AST to a text file, call Clingo and reparse its output. The advantages of file-based communication are that it is easily debugged as it is human readable and it is easy to replace Clingo with another solver using the ASP Core [3] standard. It would be more efficient to directly use the internal APIs of Clingo to build the ASP program. Clingo produces answer sets, which represent models for the problem, but it is still not the end of our workflow.

3.6   Reinterpreting the Answer Sets

Answer sets map one-to-one to FML models. However, it is not obvious how the answer sets from Clingo relate to the original problem statement, as can be seen in Listing 7. The answer set possibly contains higher order functions and sets, which are relatively complicated when encoded in answer set. This step reorders the information of the answer set into a more natural format.

Example 6. The answer set in Listing 7 is transformed to the following model for the end user:

```
{borders=[(a,b), (b,c), (c,a)],
 colorof=[(a,1), (b,3), (c,2)],
 colors=[1, 2, 3]
}
```

In this step we also notice the consequences of file-based communications with Clingo. In most situations, not all information in the answer set must be presented to the end user. The current approach only lets us filter the information after the solver has finished and printed the complete answer set. A tighter integration with Clingo could overcome this problem.

4   Optimisations

FMS contains a number of optimisations which are transformations of Core expressions. Optimisations have the goal to make the expression that needs to be translated simpler. In most cases this has a direct correspondence to smaller expressions. Shorter expressions will lead to a smaller translation, which leads to a smaller, but equivalent SAT formula. This potentially results in exponential speedups. In this section we give an overview of the implemented techniques.

4.1 Stratifying Definitions

Let-bindings are potentially very large, containing definitions for a lot of different symbols. Translating mutually recursive definitions leads to extra intermediate symbols in the translation process. Smaller, but deeper nested bindings explicitate that there is no recursion between symbols and result in better translations. We can use a topological ordering of the bindings to transform the bindings. Tarjan's algorithm is used to find this ordering. This has already been done in other systems such as IDP3 [7]. As a side effect of this topological ordering, definitions which are unused can be thrown away, because the formula after the "in" provides the starting points for the stratification. If a definition is unconnected to the formula, it is not included in the topological ordering.

Example 7. let odd x := even (x-1) ; even x := if x = 0 then true
     else odd (x-1) ; c := 4 ; e := even c ; d := 8 in e.

   can be stratified into:

let odd x :=... ; even x :=... in
     (let c := 4 in (let e := even c in e)).

Benefits. Stratification potentially removes unneeded definitions. These definitions do not need to be translated and thus are prevented of taking up time or space in the actual translation or solving process.

4.2 Inlining

Let-bindings contain definitions for certain symbols. These symbols occur in the inner expression of the let-binding. Sometimes it is benificial to replace the defined symbol with its definition. It allows for other optimisations and prevents the need to always define the symbol. The process of replacing a symbol with its definition is called inlining. Inlining is done in a lot of major compilers. The GHC compiler for Haskell excels in this [8] and we copied some of their techniques into FMS. One simple observation is that if a binding only has one single usage, it is always better to optimise the binding for this usage, as we can remove the original binding because it becomes unused.

Example 8. In the expression let y := 2*x in y+5, the variable y can easily be inlined, so the new expression becomes: 2*x+5.

Example 9. In the expression let y := f x in y+y, the variable y would not be inlined, as f x would occur twice in the resulting expression, which could duplicate work in further steps.

   Another inlining rule is that bindings to constant integers or strings should always be inlined, as handling those is generally not any more complex than handling a variable, but allows for more specialised optimisations. Sometimes the end user knows that inlining a function would be beneficial but the compiler could not derive this. For this reason FML allows for compiler directives which force the compiler to inline (or not inline) certain functions.

Benefits. A let-binding can make it harder to see opportunities for optimisation such as boolean simplifications of the next section. Inlining f in let f := not in not (f p) is essential to be able to perform the boolean simplification optimisation.

4.3   Boolean Simplifications

When handling complex nested boolean formulas, applying some boolean rewrite rules can simplify them greatly. For this reason, pushing of negations is implemented just like in IDP3 [5]. This technique uses the standard rewriting rules for propositional and first order logic.

Example 10. The boolean expression not (or (not p) (not q)) is simplified to the expression and p q

Benefits. Expressions with more nested function applications will lead to more calculation steps for the evaluation of the expressions. The expression not (not q) will always have the same value as q. However, after translation the ASP solver would need two propagation steps to obtain the truth value of the former and immediately know the truth value of the latter. Note that it is possible that the value of q can potentially change a lot of times due to the backtracking in the SAT solver component of the solver. So the netto effect of this optimisation is much bigger than two propagation steps.

4.4   Constant Folding and Beta Reductions

Constant folding [1] is a common optimisation technique for compilers. Whenever the arguments of builtin functions like addition or multiplication are fully known, we can replace the expression with its evaluation. This can be extended to more complex expressions: if the "if"-part of an if-then-else expression is trivially true, the if-then-else can be replaced by just the then-part.

When the arguments of an anonymous function are known, we can specialise the function body with the given arguments. This corresponds to the concept of beta reduction in the lambda calculus. Using beta reduction prevents the overhead of translating an extra lambda and can pair up with other optimisations such as constant folding for more efficiency gains.

Example 11. In the expression (\x -> x + 4) ((\x -> 5) a), the second part ((\x -> 5) a) can be beta reduced to 5. The resulting expression (\x -> x + 4) 5 can be beta reduced to 4 + 5 which can be reduced to 9 through constant folding.

Benefits. The benefits of this technique are the same as for the boolean simplification case. This is a generalisation which works for non-boolean expressions and leads to the same prevention of propagation steps.

4.5   Combining the Optimisations

All of the above optimisations can rewrite part of the expression tree. The application of an optimisation possibly opens up possibilities for other optimisations or sometimes, even the same optimisation. To fully optimise an expression, all optimisations should be repeated until a fixpoint on the expression is reached.

4.6   Future Optimisations

All above optimisations are already present in the current system. There are also a few optimisation techniques which have not been implemented but could be interesting future expansions.

Rewrite Rules. Boolean simplifications are applications of rewrite rules which make the expressions simpler. If the user writes new complex functions, it can be beneficial that the end-user is able to write such rewrite rules for his own functions as meta-information for his definitions. This technique would be able to generalise the boolean simplifications and make it applicable to more situations. Such rules are already available in some programming languages such as Haskell.

Example 12. A rewriting rule like not (not x) => x could explain that double negations can be ignored.

Ground with Bounds. There are a lot of optimisations for grounding researched in the context of the IDP3 system. While some are subsumed by new techniques which are explained in this section, a lot of them are also applicable for the FML system. Grounding with bounds [20, 21] is such a technique that proved to be significant for the performance of IDP3. Grounding with bounds uses symbolic reasoning to limit the size of quantifications. It is our hypothesis that these techniques generalize naturally to the higher order case of FML. This would allow quantifications over implicit domains so the forall quantifier could have type (a -> Bool) -> Bool instead of type Set a -> (a -> Bool) -> Bool.

Example 13. Ground with bounds could rewrite an unbounded quantification like ! (\x -> (5 < x & x > 10) => p x) to a bounded expression ! {6..9} p which can be handled by the algorithms which are already in place.

5   Dependencies and Availability

The system is fully written in Kotlin, with a Gradle build system, in conjunction with a set of libraries. The most important ones are ANTLR4 for parsing, logback and slf4j for logging, JUnit for testing, and klaxon for JSON communication.

The software and its source can be found online at https://dtai.cs.kuleuven.be/krr/fms. There is support for testing the software online on the website itself or you can download it yourself. The only external dependency is Clingo, which can be downloaded from https://potassco.org/clingo/.

At the moment there is no IDE support for FML, but the development of an implementation for the Language Server Protocol [11] is in the early stages of development. This is a generic framework which editors can support to automate the integration with a new language.

6   Conclusion

This paper introduces FMS and its general internal workflow. As far as the authors are aware this is the first attempt for using a higher-order functional language as a modelling language. We introduced the Core language and its syntactical extensions into the Full language. We touched upon the different steps in the solving process and on the optimisation techniques which are available in the system. We also highlighted points where further work could significantly improve the system. A thorough comparison with other systems such as SMT or ASP is also an ambition for the close future. FMS is not a finished product yet, but it introduces some interesting new concepts.

References

1. Appel, A.W.: Modern Compiler Implementation in C. Cambridge University Press, Cambridge (1998)
2. Blockeel, H., et al.: Modeling machine learning and data mining problems with FO(·). In: Dovier, A., Costa, V.S. (eds.) Proceedings of the 28th International Conference on Logic Programming - Technical Communications (ICLP 2012). LIPIcs, vol. 17, pp. 14–25. Schloss Daghstuhl - Leibniz-Zentrum fuer Informatik, September 2012
3. Calimeri, F., et al.: ASP-Core-2 input language format. Technical report, ASP Standardization Working Group (2013)
4. Dasseville, I., van der Hallen, M., Bogaerts, B., Janssens, G., Denecker, M.: A compositional typed higher-order logic with definitions. In: Carro, M., King, A., De Vos, M., Saeedloei, N. (eds.) ICLP 2016. OASIcs, vol. 52, pp. 14.1–14.14. Schloss Dagstuhl, November 2016
5. De Cat, B.: Separating knowledge from computation: an FO(·) knowledge base system and its model expansion inference. Ph.D. thesis, KU Leuven, Leuven, Belgium, May 2014
6. Ianni, G., Ielpa, G., Pietramala, A., Santoro, M.C., Calimeri, F.: Enhancing answer set programming with templates. In: Delgrande, J.P., Schaub, T. (eds.) 10th International Workshop on Non-Monotonic Reasoning (NMR 2004), Whistler, Canada, 6–8 June 2004, pp. 233–239 (2004)
7. Jansen, J., Jorissen, A., Janssens, G.: Compiling input* FO(·) inductive definitions into tabled Prolog rules for IDP3. TPLP 13(4–5), 691–704 (2013)
8. Peyton Jones, S.L., Marlow, S.: Secrets of the Glasgow Haskell Compiler inliner. J. Funct. Program. 12(4&5), 393–433 (2002)
9. Leuschel, M., Butler, M.: ProB: a model checker for B. In: Araki, K., Gnesi, S., Mandrioli, D. (eds.) FME 2003. LNCS, vol. 2805, pp. 855–874. Springer, Heidelberg (2003). https://doi.org/10.1007/978-3-540-45236-2_46

10. Marlow, S., Peyton Jones, S., Kmett, E., Mokhov, A.: Desugaring Haskell's do-notation into applicative operations. In: Proceedings of the 9th International Symposium on Haskell, pp. 92–104. ACM (2016)
11. Microsoft. Language Server Protocol (2018)
12. Nethercote, N., Stuckey, P.J., Becket, R., Brand, S., Duck, G.J., Tack, G.: MiniZinc: towards a standard CP modelling language. In: Bessière, C. (ed.) CP 2007. LNCS, vol. 4741, pp. 529–543. Springer, Heidelberg (2007). https://doi.org/10.1007/978-3-540-74970-7_38
13. Parr, T.: The definitive ANTLR 4 reference. In: Pragmatic Bookshelf (2013)
14. Pierce, B.C.: Types and Programming Languages. MIT Press, Cambridge (2002)
15. Provetti, A., Son, T.C. (eds.): Answer Set Programming, Towards Efficient and Scalable Knowledge Representation and Reasoning, Proceedings of the 1st International ASP 2001 Workshop, Stanford, 26–28 March 2001
16. Schrijvers, T., Stuckey, P.J., Wadler, P.: Monadic constraint programming. J. Funct. Program. **19**(6), 663–697 (2009)
17. Peyton-Jones, S., Marlow, S.: The Glasgow Haskell Compiler (2012)
18. Wadler, P.: Comprehending monads. Math. Struct. Comput. Sci. **2**(4), 461–493 (1992)
19. Wazny, J.R.: Type inference and type error diagnosis for Hindley/Milner with extensions. Citeseer (2006)
20. Wittocx, J., Mariën, M., Denecker, M.: Grounding with bounds. In: Fox, D., Gomes, C.P. (eds.) AAAI, pp. 572–577. AAAI Press (2008)
21. Wittocx, J., Mariën, M., Denecker, M.: Grounding FO and FO(ID) with bounds. J. Artif. Intell. Res. (JAIR) **38**, 223–269 (2010)

Functional Federated Learning
in Erlang (`ffl-erl`)

Gregor Ulm[1,2]([✉]) [iD], Emil Gustavsson[1,2] [iD], and Mats Jirstrand[1,2] [iD]

[1] Fraunhofer-Chalmers Research Centre for Industrial Mathematics,
Chalmers Science Park, 412 88 Gothenburg, Sweden
{gregor.ulm,emil.gustavsson,mats.jirstrand}@fcc.chalmers.se
[2] Fraunhofer Center for Machine Learning,
Chalmers Science Park, 412 88 Gothenburg, Sweden
http://www.fcc.chalmers.se/

Abstract. The functional programming language Erlang is well-suited for concurrent and distributed applications, but numerical computing is not seen as one of its strengths. Yet, the recent introduction of Federated Learning, which leverages client devices for decentralized machine learning tasks, while a central server updates and distributes a global model, motivated us to explore how well Erlang is suited to that problem. We present the Federated Learning framework `ffl-erl` and evaluate it in two scenarios: one in which the entire system has been written in Erlang, and another in which Erlang is relegated to coordinating client processes that rely on performing numerical computations in the programming language C. There is a concurrent as well as a distributed implementation of each case. We show that Erlang incurs a performance penalty, but for certain use cases this may not be detrimental, considering the trade-off between speed of development (Erlang) versus performance (C). Thus, Erlang may be a viable alternative to C for some practical machine learning tasks.

Keywords: Machine learning · Federated Learning ·
Distributed computing · Functional programming · Erlang

1 Introduction

With the explosion of the amount of data gathered by networked devices, more efficient approaches to distributed data processing are needed. The reason is that it would be infeasible to transfer all data gathered from edge devices to a central data center, process it, and afterwards transfer results back to edge devices via the network. There are several approaches to taming the amount of data received, such as filtering on edge devices, transferring only a representative sample, or performing data processing tasks decentrally. A recently introduced example of distributed data analytics is Federated Learning [14]. Its key idea is the distribution of machine learning tasks to a subset of available devices,

© Springer Nature Switzerland AG 2019
J. Silva (Ed.): WFLP 2018, LNCS 11285, pp. 162–178, 2019.
https://doi.org/10.1007/978-3-030-16202-3_10

followed by performing machine learning tasks locally on data that is available on edge devices, and iteratively updating a global model.

In this paper, we present `ffl-erl`, a Federated Learning framework implemented in the functional programming language Erlang.[1] This work was produced in the context of an industrial research project with the goal of exploring and evaluating various approaches to distributed data analytics in the automotive domain. Our contribution consists of the following:

- Creating `ffl-erl`, the first open-source implementation of a framework for Federated Learning in Erlang
- Highlighting the feasibility of functional programming for the aforementioned framework
- Creating a purely functional implementation of an artificial neural network in Erlang
- Comparing the performance of a Federated Learning implementation fully in Erlang with one in which client processes are implemented in C
- Exploring two approaches of integrating C with Erlang: NIFs and C nodes.

The remainder of our paper is organized as follows: Sect. 2 contains background information and describes the motivating use case. Section 3 covers our implementation in detail and presents experimental results. Section 4 gives a brief overview of related work, while Sect. 5 describes future work. Appendix A contains a mathematical derivation of Federated Stochastic Gradient Descent.

2   Background

This section gives an overview of Federated Learning (Sect. 2.1) and presents the mathematical foundation of Federated Stochastic Gradient Descent (Sect. 2.2). It furthermore describes our motivating use case (Sect. 2.3).

2.1   Federated Learning

Federated Learning is a decentralized approach to machine learning. The general idea is to perform machine learning tasks on a potentially very large number of edge devices, which process data that is only accessible locally. A central server is relegated to assigning tasks and updating the global model based on the local models it receives from edge devices. One iteration of Federated Learning consists of the following steps, following McMahan et al. [14]:

1. Select a subset c of the set of clients C
2. Send the current model from the server to each client $x \in c$
3. For each x, update the provided model based on local data by performing iterations of a machine learning algorithm

---

[1] Source code artifacts accompanying this paper are available at https://gitlab.com/fraunhofer_chalmers_centre/functional_federated_learning.

4. For each x, send the updated model to the server
5. Aggregate all received local models and construct a new global model.

There are several motivations behind Federated Learning. First, there is the bandwidth problem in a big data setting. The amount of data generated by local devices is too large to be transferred via the network to a central server for processing. Second, edge devices are getting more and more powerful. Modern smartphones, for instance, have been compared to (old-generation) supercomputers in our pockets in terms of raw computational power [2]. Therefore, it seems prudent to more efficiently use these resources. Third, there are data privacy issues, as some jurisdictions have strict privacy laws. Thus, transmitting data via the network in order to perform central machine learning tasks is frayed with data privacy issues. This is summarized by Chen et al. [3], while Tene et al. point out legal issues [20]. Federated Learning sidesteps potential legal quagmires surrounding data privacy laws and regulations as data is not centrally collected.

2.2 Federated Stochastic Gradient Descent

Federated Stochastic Gradient Descent (Federated SGD) is based on Stochastic Gradient Descent (SGD), which is a well-established method in the field of statistical optimization. We first describe SGD, followed by a presentation of Federated SGD. The latter is based on McMahan et al. [14].

Stochastic Gradient Descent. The aim of SGD is to minimize an objective function F that is defined as the following sum:

$$F(w) = \frac{1}{n} \sum_{i=1}^{n} F_i(w). \tag{1}$$

The goal is to find a value for the parameter vector w that minimizes F. The value F_i represents the contribution of element i of the input data to the objective function. In order to minimize F, the gradient ∇ is computed. The learning rate η is a factor that adjusts how far along the gradient the parameter update step is taken. It modifies the magnitude of change of w between iterations. The parameter w is updated in the following way:

$$w := w - \eta \nabla F(w). \tag{2}$$

This means that the parameter w is updated by computing the gradient of the objective function, evaluated for the previous parameter value, which is subtracted from the previous parameter value w. Since F is a separable function, Eq. 2 can be reformulated as

$$w := w - \frac{\eta}{n} \sum_{i=1}^{n} \nabla F_i(w). \tag{3}$$

As indicated before, the learning rate η is a modifier for slowing down or speeding up the training process. In practice, small positive values in the half-closed interval $(0, 1]$ are used. A common starting value is 0.01. A learning rate that is too high may overshoot a global optimum. A learning rate that is too low, on the other hand, may severely impact the performance of the algorithm.

Federated Stochastic Gradient Descent. Federated SGD is an extension of SGD. It takes into account that there are k partitions P_j of the training data, with j ranging from 1 to k, i.e. there is a bijection between partitions and clients. Consequently, Eq. 3 has to be modified as we need to consider the work performed on each client $\in c$, where c is the chosen subset of all clients C. The objective function is attempted to be minimized for each of the k clients. However, the goal is to optimize the global model, not any of the local models. For Eq. 4, keep in mind that there are n elements in the input data, thus $n = \sum_j |P_j|$.

$$F^j(w) = \frac{1}{|P_j|} \sum_{i \in P_j} F_i(w) \ for \ j = 1, \ldots, k \tag{4}$$

The global objective function is shown in Eq. 5. Its full derivation is provided in Appendix A.

$$F(w) = \frac{1}{n} \sum_{j=1}^{k} |P_j| F^j(w) \tag{5}$$

2.3 Motivating Use Case

Intelligent vehicles generate vast amounts of data. According to recent industry figures, they can generate dozens of gigabytes of data per hour [4]. Considering even a moderately sized fleet of just a few hundred cars, collecting data, transferring data to a central server, processing data on a central server and afterwards sending results to each car is infeasible as we are already in the region of terabytes of data per hour. Yet, even simple tasks like filtering on the client can provide valuable insights. This is an example of a relatively straightforward way of reducing input data to a small fraction of its original volume, which highlights the importance of decentralized data processing.

However, our focus is on a more complex use case in the context of distributed data analytics. We explore training a machine learning model on client devices with local data, while a central server performs supplementary tasks. This relates to a real-world setting in which connected cars [6] are equipped with on-board units that continuously gather data. These on-board units are general-purpose computers with performance metrics comparable to smartphones. For instance, our hardware uses an ARM-based multi-core CPU, similar to those found in a typical mid-range smartphone. On-board units are connected via wireless or 4G broadband networking to a central server, possibly via intermediaries, so-called road-side units. This is by no means a merely theoretical scenario. For instance, a recent large-scale experiment with road-side units was carried out by Lee and Kim [12] in South Korea in 2010.

3 Solution

Our research prototype simulates a distributed system in which a central server interacts with a large number of clients. We first describe the main components of the framework itself (Sect. 3.1). This is followed by a discussion of a purely functional implementation of an artificial neural network (ANN) in Erlang (Sect. 3.2). Subsequently, we describe how the skeleton and the ANN can be combined (Sect. 3.3). Finally, we discuss experimental results (Sect. 3.4).

3.1 The Skeleton of the Framework

This section illustrates the main ideas behind implementing a distributed machine learning framework. Consequently, we present the main parts of our skeleton, i.e. the client and server processes. The source code in this section leaves some details unspecified, but these can be filled in easily or referenced in the accompanying code repository. It seems appropriate to preface the discussion of our source code by briefly explaining the communication model of Erlang. In Erlang, processes communicate asynchronously by sending messages to each other. Each process has its own mailbox for incoming messages, which are processed in the order they arrive. However, the order in which they arrive is non-deterministic. If process C receives one message each from processes A and B, in this order, there is no guarantee that they were also sent in this order.

The skeleton consists of a client process, which may be instantiated an arbitrary number of times, and a server process. Both are shown in Code Listing 1.1. In the client process, the `receive` clause awaits a tuple tagged with the atom `assignment`. The received model is trained with local data via the function `train`. Examples of such a model are the weights of an ANN or parameters of a linear regression equation. After training has concluded, the updated model is sent to the server process. A tuple that is tagged with the atom `update` is sent to the server, using the operator '`!`', which is pronounced as *send*. The server is addressed via the process identifier `Server_Pid`. Thus, line 5 has to be read from right to left to trace the execution, i.e. we take a tuple tagged as `update`, containing the process identifier of the current process that is returned when calling the function `self` as well as the new local model, and send it to the server identified by `Server_Pid`. Afterwards, the client function is called recursively, awaiting an updated model.

The server process shown in Code Listing 1.1 does not perform computationally intensive tasks. Instead, its role is to maintain a global model, based on updates received from client processes. Our system selects a random subset of all available devices. Sending the current model to the selected subset of client processes can be concisely expressed via mapping over a list or a list comprehension. It is assumed that all devices complete their assignments. This is reflected in the list comprehension in line 14, which blocks until the results of all assignments have been received. The resulting list of values `Vals` contains the updated local models of all client processes, with which a new global model will be constructed.

```
1 client () ->
2   receive
3   { assignment , Model , Server_Pid } ->
4     Val = train (Model) , % computes 'w_j'
5     Server_Pid ! { update , self () , Val },
6     client ()
7   end .
8
9 server (Client_Pids , Model) ->
10   Subset = select_subset (Client_Pids) ,
11   % Send assignment :
12   [ X ! { assignment , Model , self () } || X <- Subset ] ,
13   % Receive values :
14   Vals = [ receive { update , Pid , Val } -> Val end || Pid <- Subset ] ,
15   % Update model , i.e. compute global 'w':
16   Model_ = update_model (Model , Vals , length (Client_Pids)) ,
17   % Note: it is a simplification to use the number of clients ; in this
18   % case , each client has the same number of data points to work with
19   server (Client_Pids , Model_) .
```

Listing 1.1. Client and server processes

The corresponding function **update_model** is unspecified, however. After updating the model, the server process calls itself recursively. Overall, the preceding code is a textbook case of message passing in Erlang.

3.2   A Neural Network with Backpropagation in Erlang

Artificial Neural Networks. Artificial Neural Networks (ANNs) are a standard method in machine learning for a variety of learning tasks. A prime example is classification based on pattern recognition, for instance tagging images with keywords. The general principle is to minimize an objective function that computes the magnitude of an error. There are normally three steps to deploying an ANN: training, validation, and use in production. First, a labeled data set is used to train an ANN, which has the goal of minimizing the objective function. There is the risk that the ANN has been over-trained, i.e. it has memorized its input. Therefore, a labeled validation set is used to ensure that a data set that is similar to the test set is also correctly classified. If those two steps have been performed satisfactorily, the ANN is ready to be used for real-world data classification tasks.

Figure 1 shows a typical ANN. It consists of two input neurons, three hidden neurons, and two output neurons. The two input neurons on the left are shaded in order to indicate that an ANN is normally not applied to fixed input values but instead applied sequentially to each element of a larger data set. The layer of neurons in the middle is the hidden layer; the layer on the right is the output layer. The edges labeled with their weights represent connections between neurons. The edges leaving the output layer transmit the final output. There are two sets of labeled edges, one set connecting the input layer to the hidden layer and the other connecting the hidden layer to the output layer. Edge weights are initialized to a small random value and updated via training. The goal is to minimize the output error, which is based on the difference between the target values and the values the output layer neurons emit. After a forward pass we can determine how close the values emitted by the output neurons are to the target values. This is followed by adjusting the weights of the ANN with the backpropagation algorithm. Together, these two steps amount to one *epoch*. In the end, the output error is minimized via iterative adjustments of the weights of the ANN.

Using the ANN in Fig. 1 as an example, we first perform a forward pass, which consists of computing the input of each hidden layer neuron by calculating the dot product of the input weights and all edges connecting the input nodes with that hidden layer neuron. For instance, the input of the

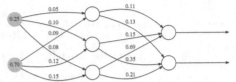

Fig. 1. Artificial neural network

topmost hidden layer neuron is $0.25 \times 0.05 + 0.70 \times 0.09 = 0.0755$. After applying the *activation function* to that value, the input and output values of the output layer neurons are computed similarly. The activation function computes the output of a node, taking its input as the argument. Afterwards, the difference between target and actual output values can be calculated. This is followed by a backpropagation pass, in which the weights of the ANN are updated: first the weights of the edges from the output layer to the hidden layer, then the weights of the edges from the hidden layer to the input layer. These calculations are similar to the forward pass, except that the gradient, i.e. the derivative of the objective function we want to minimize, is used when calculating the respective dot products. Training an ANN with a batch of input data is done by processing all elements of the provided data, using them one by one as input for the input layer and performing one epoch. After each iteration, the weights are retained as the goal is to train on the entire set of input data.

For the sake of brevity, our description of an ANN does not consider common modifications such as setting a specific learning rate or using adaptive behavior based on previous results. We furthermore use a standard activation function, the *sigmoid function*. Practitioners may use different activation functions or resort to various engineering techniques for improving the performance of ANNs as described, for instance, by Orr et al. [16]. As a final note, we would like to highlight that ANNs can approximate any function [8,9], which is commonly referred to as the universal approximation theorem. Consequently, ANNs are widely used in practice. The example described above, consisting of three layers, is a shallow ANN. Those are versatile, but they are not efficient for large and very complex problems. A particularly noteworthy early breakthrough of shallow ANNs was the successful classification of handwritten digits, which is used by postal services [19]. More recent developments include deep neural networks, often referred to as deep learning. Those are ANNs with multiple hidden neuron layers, consisting of large numbers of neurons.

Implementation. In the following, we cover some aspects of an exemplary implementation of a basic ANN in Erlang. We will again leave out some implementation details, and instead focus on the big picture.[2] Code Listing 1.2 shows the function **ann**, which models an artificial neural network. The various helper functions it calls are shown in Code Listing 1.3. The input of the function **ann** consists of the values of the input neurons **Input**, the weights of both layers **Weights**, and the target values of the output layer **Targets**.

```erlang
 1  ann(Input, Weights, Targets) ->
 2    { W_Input, W_Hidden } = Weights,
 3    % Forward Pass:
 4    Hidden_In  = forward(Input, W_Input, []),
 5    Hidden_Out = [ activation_fun(X) || X <- Hidden_In ],
 6    Output_In  = forward(Hidden_Out, W_Hidden, []),
 7    Output_Out = [ activation_fun(X) || X <- Output_In ],
 8    % Target vs. output:
 9    Delta = lists:zipwith(fun(X, Y) -> X - Y end, Targets, Output_Out),
10    % Reverse pass:
11    Output_Errors = output_error(Output_Out, Targets),
12    % Update weights for output layer:
13    W_Hidden_  = backpropagate(Hidden_Out, Output_Errors, W_Hidden,  []),
14    Hidden_Err = errors_hidden(Hidden_Out, Output_Errors, W_Hidden_, []),
15    W_Input_   = backpropagate(Input, Hidden_Err, W_Input, []),
16    { Output_Errors, { Input, { W_Input_, W_Hidden_ }, Targets } }.
```

Listing 1.2. The core ANN function

As described earlier, as a first step the ANN computes the input of the hidden layer. The output of the hidden layer is the result of mapping the activation function over the list **Hidden_In**; the corresponding values of the output layer are computed in the exact same way. The list **Delta** contains the differences between the target values and the actual values.[3] The function **forward** computes the dot product of the input values and the weights of the outgoing edges. It is called twice by the function **ann** because there are two transitions between layers, first from the input layer to the hidden layer, and afterwards from the hidden layer to the output layer. Computing the dot product maps nicely to a functional programming style, as the required computation is the element-wise multiplication of two lists, followed by the summation of the results of that computation. The backpropagation pass starts with computing the output error, zipped with a *squashing factor*. In our case, the activation function used for that purpose is a standard sigmoid function, the logistic function $f(x) = \frac{1}{1+e^{-x}}$. The derivative of the logistic function is $f'(x) = f(x)(1 - f(x))$. This makes it possible to efficiently compute gradients as we can use the activations of the hidden layer for computing the total error in the output layer. Computationally, the operations

---

[2] For illustrative purposes, we chose clear code over computationally more efficient code at some points. For instance, the function **forward** in Code Listing 1.3 constructs a temporary list, which could be avoided by computing the dot product with an accumulator. However, for benchmarking purposes we used more efficient code.

[3] Training normally ends after a given number of iterations or once a predefined error threshold has been met. The latter would make use of the computed error, based on the list **Delta**, but the corresponding code is omitted as it is not conceptually interesting.

involved, multiplication and subtraction, are less costly than re-evaluating the activation function, which is an exponential function.

```
 1  forward(_      , []        , Acc) -> lists:reverse(Acc);
 2  forward(Input, [W | Ws], Acc) ->
 3    Val = lists:sum(lists:zipwith(fun(X, Y) -> X * Y end, Input, W)),
 4    forward(Input, Ws, [Val | Acc]).
 5
 6  output_error(Vals, Target) ->
 7    lists:zipwith(fun(X, Y) -> X * (1.0 - X) * (X - Y) end, Vals, Target).
 8
 9  backpropagate(_ , []      , []         , Acc) -> lists:reverse(Acc);
10  backpropagate(In, [E|Es], [Ws|Wss], Acc) ->
11    A - lists:zipwith(fun(W, I) -> W - (E * I) end, Ws, In),
12    backpropagate(In, Es, Wss, [A|Acc]).
13
14  errors_hidden([]        , _        , _         , Acc) -> lists:reverse(Acc);
15  errors_hidden([H|Hs], Output_Err, Weights, Acc) ->
16    Outgoing = [ hd(X) || X <- Weights ],
17    % Remaining weights for next iteration:
18    Rest = [ tl(X) || X <- Weights ],
19    % Error of current hidden layer neuron:
20    TMP  = lists:zipwith(fun(X, E) -> E * X end, Outgoing, Output_Err),
21    A    = lists:sum(TMP) * H * (1.0 - H),
22    errors_hidden(Hs, Output_Err, Rest, [A|Acc]).
23
24  wrap_ann([]        , Weights, []      , Errors) ->
25    {lists:reverse(Errors), Weights};
26  wrap_ann([I|Is], Weights, [T|Ts], Errors) ->
27    { Error, Weights_ } = ann(I, Weights, T),
28    wrap_ann(Is, Weights_, Ts, [Error | Errors]).
```

Listing 1.3. ANN helper functions

The function **backpropagate** performs backpropagation, which computes the adjusted weights of the edges connecting the output layer to the hidden layer, and the adjusted weights of the edges connecting the hidden layer to the input layer. The new weights are computed by adding the product of the error and the input to each weight. The computation of the errors of the hidden layer is slightly trickier, due to using the list data structure. The weights assigned to the edges connecting the hidden layer with the output layer are specified as a list of lists in which each list contains the incoming weights of one of the output neurons. In the backpropagation pass, however, we need to traverse the ANN the opposite way, so the edges connecting the hidden layer to the output layer need a representation that considers all edges that point from the output layer to each node in the hidden layer. This is achieved by recursively taking the heads of the list of lists of the weights before performing the error calculation. Lastly, performing training on the entire input, so-called batch training, can be elegantly expressed in a functional style, shown by the function **wrap_ann**. Its arguments are, in order, the list of inputs that constitute the training set, the weights, the target values associated with the input data, and an accumulator **Errors** that collects the output error for each element of the input set. The weights are continually updated so that every invocation of the function **ann** uses the weights of the preceding invocation.

3.3   The Combined Framework

The parts introduced earlier can be combined to build a distributed system for Federated Learning. It boils down to using the skeleton introduced in Sect. 3.1 and adding code for an artificial network to the client process, similar to what we have shown in Sect. 3.2, as well as further program logic. What has not been covered is, for instance, code for input/output handling. Our assumption is that each client process operates on data that is only locally available. The client process needs to be adjusted correspondingly, so that the available data is processed for batch-training with the ANN. Likewise, the server process needs to process the incoming models from the clients to update the centrally maintained global model, for instance via averaging.

While the description of our implementation is exclusively in Erlang, an alternative approach consists of a C implementation of the ANN. From a user perspective, there is no difference with regards to the output. Of course, internally the client trains an ANN in C instead of Erlang. However, in order to fairly compare how well an implementation solely in Erlang compares against one in which the computationally heavy lifting is performed by C, it is necessary to take the respective idiosyncrasies of two common approaches to interoperability with C into account. The older and more established way of calling C from Erlang is via so-called Natively Implemented Functions (NIFs), which are an improvement over using ports to communicate with C. A more recent addition to Erlang are C nodes, which have the advantage that they can be interfaced with the same way as regular Erlang nodes. Overall, for the purposes of simulating the framework, concurrent execution is adequate. However, distributed execution, in which messages are sent back and forth between nodes, more closely relates to real-world use cases (cf. Sect. 2.3).

3.4   Evaluation

Setup. We created four versions of our combined Federated Learning framework: (1) a concurrent implementation, fully in Erlang, as well as (2) one in which the clients are implemented in C as NIFs. Furthermore, we implemented (3) a distributed version fully in Erlang as well as (4) a variant of it in which the clients are C nodes. By default, all Erlang nodes in a distributed system are fully connected. As this is neither practical nor desirable for our use case, this behavior was disabled with the flag -hidden. Erlang source code has also been compiled to native code, which has been made possible due to the HiPE project [10,17].

The motivation behind benchmarking a distributed system, as opposed to the simpler case of a concurrent system, is that this mirrors the real-world scenario of performing distributed data analytics tasks on a network with many edge devices and a central server. On the other hand, a concurrent system is more straightforward to design and execute. In both the distributed and the concurrent use case, we did not create our own implementation of a neural network in C. Instead, we chose Nissen's widely used Fast Artificial Neural Network (FANN) library [15] with the option FANN_TRAIN_BATCH, which uses gradient descent with backpropagation. This corresponds to our Erlang code. Our ANN implementation in Erlang mirrors the chosen architecture of the ANN in FANN, i.e. there are two input nodes, three hidden nodes, and two output nodes. Furthermore, there is one bias node each, connecting to the hidden and the output layer, respectively. Error computation is done via computing the mean squared error (MSE) in both implementations. The Erlang code does not use a learning rate η, which implies that $\eta = 1$. In FANN, η was explicitly set to 1 in order to override the default value of 0.7. Both implementations use the sigmoid activation function (cf. Sect. 3.2). The corresponding setting in FANN is FANN_SIGMOID.

Hardware and Software. We used a PC with an Intel Core i7-7700K CPU clocked at 4.2 GHz. This is a quad-core CPU that supports hyper-threading with 8 threads. Our code was executed in Ubuntu Linux 16.04 LTS on a VirtualBox 5.1.22 virtual machine hosted by Windows 10 Pro (build 1703). The total amount of RAM available on the host machine was 32 GB, of which 12 GB were dedicated to VirtualBox. We used Erlang/OTP 20.2.2 and, for C, GCC 5.4.0.

Experiment. For benchmarking novel machine learning methods, standard data sets are often used. These include the Iris data set [7], which contains observational data of the petal length of various iris species. A more ambitious data set is the MNIST handwritten digits database [11]. However, our goal was to directly compare the performance of two pairs of systems, so it seemed more appropriate to generate an artificial data set. Our data set is based on the mathematical function $f(x,y) = (\sqrt{xy}, \sqrt[4]{xy})$, where $\{x, y \in \mathbb{R} \mid x, y \in [0, 1)\}$. The ANN consists of two input nodes, three hidden nodes, and two output nodes. The training data consists of tuples (x, y). Each client randomly generated 250 such tuples prior to each round of training. As the relationship between input and output is known, it is trivial to generate an arbitrary amount of data. We performed five 500-s test runs with each of the four combined frameworks, recording time, number of executed iterations of the ANN on each client node, and total error. We used 10 client processes and hard-coded the initial weights for the sake of easy reproducibility. An alternative approach would have been to create the initial weights with the same random seed. In practice, the difference is insignificant.

The number of clients may seem small. However, the client part of our system will eventually be executed on separate hardware, such as the aforementioned on-board units in connected vehicles, which would each represent one single client node. Consequently, the focus is not on how the performance of ffl-erl scales when adding increasing numbers of client nodes to one machine. Given the recent interest in deep learning, one may also question the choice of using a shallow ANN. Shallow ANNs are still viable, however. In our case, the specified function is approximated successfully. On a related note, an interesting recent example of using a shallow ANN for computationally challenging work was presented by

Cuccu et al [5]. They show that a shallow ANN can, in some tasks, compete with deep neural networks.

Results. Experimental results are shown in Fig. 2 below. The x-axis indicates the running time in seconds, while the y-axis shows the number of epochs, i.e. the number of iterations of the server-side ANN. Clients perform batch training on 250 data points per epoch. Each training pass consists of a constant amount of work, so the expectation was that the final result would be linear. The plotted data is the average of five test runs, which yielded virtually identical results.

In the concurrent use case, the Erlang-only implementation, compiled to the BEAM virtual machine, executes ∼192,000 epochs in 500 s. This value increases to ∼286,000 epochs when compiling Erlang to native code. In comparison, the result with NIFs is ∼386,000 epochs. NIFs cannot be used together with natively compiled Erlang code, which is why a corresponding plot is missing. The performance difference between using NIFs and Erlang code compiled to BEAM amounts to a constant factor of 2.01. With native execution, the speedup compared to execution on the BEAM virtual machine amounts to 49.0%. Comparing that performance to NIFs, the resulting difference shrinks to a factor of 1.35.

An Erlang-only distributed implementation running on the BEAM virtual machine is able to compute ∼128,000 epochs in 500 s, which increases to ∼250,000 epochs (+95.3%) with native code. On the other hand, with C nodes, the resulting performance is ∼522,000 epochs on the BEAM virtual machine as opposed to ∼643,000 epochs (+23.4%) per client when compiling Erlang to native code. The performance difference between a pure Erlang implementation and one that uses C nodes amounts to a constant factor of 4.1 on the BEAM virtual machine, which shrinks to 2.6 with HiPE.

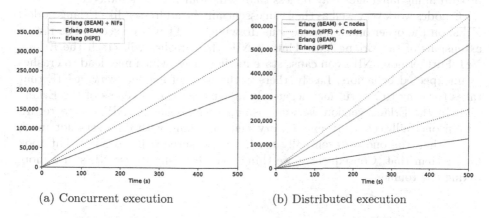

(a) Concurrent execution   (b) Distributed execution

Fig. 2. In (a), Erlang (HiPE) reaches 74.1% of the performance of Erlang code that uses NIFs. In (b), Erlang (BEAM) reaches 24.5% of the performance of Erlang with C nodes; Erlang (HiPE) reaches 38.9% of the corresponding performance.

Discussion. It is perhaps surprising that an implementation that relies on Erlang for numerical computations is fairly competitive with C, with the observed difference amounting to a modest constant factor. In particular, the performance of natively compiled Erlang code is commendable. In the concurrent use case in particular, HiPE performs remarkably well. These are significant results for a number of reasons. From the perspective of programmer productivity, the relative conciseness of Erlang code, compared to C, is worth pointing out. For instance, the line count of our C code that merely interfaces with the FANN library slightly exceeds the line count of the Erlang implementation of our entire ANN. Writing the former was more time-consuming than the latter. That being said, the tool Nifty [13], which automates the generation of NIF libraries based on C header files, may have simplified this task. However, as we wanted to limit external dependencies, this was not a viable option.

The main argument for using C is its high performance. Yet, a downside is that it is a low-level programming language. In particular, manual memory allocation and garbage collection are an abundant source of programming errors. In terms of programmer productivity, C therefore does not compare favorably with Erlang. As there are use cases where performance is not of the topmost priority, Erlang may be a viable alternative as it leads to a much shorter turnaround time between design, implementation, and execution.

The performance comparison between Erlang and C is arguably lopsided, due to using the open-source C library FANN. It originally appeared in 2003 and has been actively maintained for over a decade, even though development activity seems to have slowed down recently. On the other hand, we developed our Erlang implementation of an ANN relatively quickly and without the benefit of extensively using it in real-world situations. Because FANN has been much more optimized than our code, the true performance difference between the competing programming languages may be less than what our numbers indicate.

C nodes work very well as they can essentially be addressed like Erlang nodes. NIFs, on the other hand, have serious drawbacks.[4] They are executed as native extensions of the Erlang VM. Thus, a NIF that crashes will crash the Erlang VM. Furthermore, NIFs can cause state inefficiencies, which may lead to crashes or unexpected behaviors. Lastly, there is the issue of *lengthy work*: a NIF that takes too long to return may negatively affect the responsiveness of the Erlang VM. In the Erlang version we were using, a well-behaving NIF has to return within one millisecond. In exploratory benchmarking with data sets not much larger than the one we eventually used, we measured calls to NIFs that took longer than that. Consequently, we think it is too risky to use NIFs in a more taxing environment.

---

[4] Refer to the section on Natively Implemented Functions (NIFs) in the official Erlang documentation for further details: http://erlang.org/doc/man/erl_nif.html (accessed on June 28, 2018).

4   Related Work

There has been some preceding work in academia related to using functional programming languages for tackling machine learning tasks. About a decade ago, Allison explored using Haskell for defining various machine learning and statistical learning models [1]. Yet, that work was of a theoretical nature. Going back even further, Yu and Clack presented a system for polymorphic genetic programming in Haskell [22]. Likewise, this was from a theoretical perspective. More recently, Sher [18] did extensive work on modeling evolutionary computations. A central part of his contribution is an ANN implemented in Erlang. However, his fairly complex system could only have been used as the starting point of our work with substantial modifications. One key difference is that individual nodes of the ANN are modeled as independent processes, and so are sensors and actuators. A related ANN implementation in Erlang is yanni,[5] which follows Sher's approach of using message passing, albeit only between layers.

5   Future Work

The ffl-erl project has influenced ongoing work in our research lab on a real-world system for distributed data analytics for the automotive industry [21]. In that system, Erlang is used for distributing assignments to clients, which operate on local data. Those clients can execute code written in an arbitrary programming language. Federated Learning is one of its use cases.

Acknowledgements. Our research was financially supported by the project On-board/Off-board Distributed Data Analytics (OODIDA) in the funding program FFI: Strategic Vehicle Research and Innovation (DNR 2016-04260), which is administered by VINNOVA, the Swedish Government Agency for Innovation Systems. It was carried out in the Fraunhofer Cluster of Excellence "Cognitive Internet Technologies." Adrian Nilsson and Simon Smith assisted with the implementation. Melinda Tóth pointed us to Sher's work. We also thank our anonymous reviewers for their helpful feedback.

A   Mathematical Derivation of Federated Stochastic Gradient Descent

In Sect. 2.2 we briefly describe Federated Stochastic Gradient Descent. In the current section, we present the complete derivation. As a reminder, we stated that in Stochastic Gradient Descent, weights are updated this way:

$$w := w - \frac{\eta}{n} \sum_{i=1}^{n} \nabla F_i(w). \tag{6}$$

---

[5] The corresponding code repository is located at https://bitbucket.org/nato/yanni (accessed on August 6, 2018).

Furthermore, we started with the following equation, which is the objective function we would like to minimize:

$$F(w) = \frac{1}{n} \sum_{j=1}^{k} |P_j| F^j(w). \tag{7}$$

The gradient of F^j is expressed in the following formula:

$$\nabla F^j(w) = \frac{1}{|P_j|} \sum_{i \in P_j} \nabla F_i(w), j = 1, \ldots, k. \tag{8}$$

To continue from here, each client updates the weights of the machine learning model the following way:

$$w_j = w - \frac{\eta}{|P_j|} \sum_{i \in P_j} \nabla F_i(w). \tag{9}$$

On the server, the weights of the global model are updated. The original equation can be reformulated in a few steps:

$$w := \frac{1}{n} \left(\sum_{j=1}^{k} w_j |P_j| \right) \tag{10}$$

$$= \frac{1}{n} \sum_{j=1}^{k} \left(w - \frac{\eta}{|P_j|} \sum_{i \in P_j} \nabla F_i(w) \right) |P_j| \tag{11}$$

$$= \frac{1}{n} \sum_{j=1}^{k} |P_j| w - \frac{1}{n} \eta \sum_{j=1}^{k} \sum_{i \in P_j} \nabla F_i(w) \tag{12}$$

$$= w - \frac{\eta}{n} \sum_{i=1}^{n} \nabla F_i(w). \tag{13}$$

The reformulation in the last line is equivalent to Eq. 6 above. In case the transformation between Eqs. 12 and 13 is unclear, consider that the summand simplifies to

$$\frac{1}{n} \sum_{j=1}^{k} |P_j| w = \frac{1}{n} n w = w. \tag{14}$$

The second summand in Eq. 12 can be simplified as follows:

$$\frac{1}{n} \eta \sum_{j=1}^{k} \sum_{i \in P_j} \nabla F_i(w) = \frac{1}{n} \eta \sum_{i=1}^{n} \nabla F_i(w) = \frac{\eta}{n} \sum_{i=1}^{n} \nabla F_i(w). \tag{15}$$

References

1. Allison, L.: Models for machine learning and data mining in functional programming. J. Funct. Program. **15**(1), 15–32 (2005)
2. Bauer, H., Goh, Y., Schlink, S., Thomas, C.: The supercomputer in your pocket. McKinsey on Semiconductors, pp. 14–27 (2012)
3. Chen, D., Zhao, H.: Data security and privacy protection issues in cloud computing. In: Proceedings of the 2012 International Conference on Computer Science and Electronics Engineering (ICCSEE), vol. 1, pp. 647–651. IEEE (2012)
4. Coppola, R., Morisio, M.: Connected car: technologies, issues, future trends. ACM Comput. Surv. (CSUR) **49**(3), 1–36 (2016)
5. Cuccu, G., Togelius, J., Cudre-Mauroux, P.: Playing atari with six neurons. arXiv preprint arXiv:1806.01363 (2018)
6. Evans-Pughe, C.: The connected car. IEE Rev. **51**(1), 42–46 (2005)
7. Fisher, R., Marshall, M.: Iris Data Set. UC Irvine Machine Learning Repository (1936)
8. Gybenko, G.: Approximation by superposition of sigmoidal functions. Math. Control Signals Syst. **2**(4), 303–314 (1989)
9. Hornik, K.: Approximation capabilities of multilayer feedforward networks. Neural Netw. **4**(2), 251–257 (1991)
10. Johansson, E., Pettersson, M., Sagonas, K.: A high performance Erlang system. In: Proceedings of the 2nd ACM SIGPLAN International Conference on Principles and Practice Of Declarative Programming, pp. 32–43. ACM (2000)
11. LeCun, Y., Cortes, C., Burges, C.J.: MNIST handwritten digit database. AT&T Labs (2010). http://yann.lecun.com/exdb/mnist
12. Lee, J., Kim, C.M.: A roadside unit placement scheme for vehicular telematics networks. In: Kim, T., Adeli, H. (eds.) ACN/AST/ISA/UCMA -2010. LNCS, vol. 6059, pp. 196–202. Springer, Heidelberg (2010). https://doi.org/10.1007/978-3-642-13577-4_17
13. Löscher, A., Sagonas, K.: The Nifty way to call hell from heaven. In: Proceedings of the 15th International Workshop on Erlang, pp. 1–11. ACM (2016)
14. McMahan, H.B., Moore, E., Ramage, D., Hampson, S., et al.: Communication-efficient learning of deep networks from decentralized data. arXiv preprint arXiv:1602.05629 (2016)
15. Nissen, S.: Implementation of a fast artificial neural network library (FANN). Report, Department of Computer Science University of Copenhagen (DIKU) 31, 29 (2003)
16. Orr, G.B., Müller, K.R.: Neural Networks: Tricks of the Trade. Springer, Heidelberg (2003). https://doi.org/10.1007/978-3-642-35289-8
17. Sagonas, K., Pettersson, M., Carlsson, R., Gustafsson, P., Lindahl, T.: All you wanted to know about the HiPE compiler (but might have been afraid to ask). In: Proceedings of the 2003 ACM SIGPLAN Workshop on Erlang, pp. 36–42. ACM (2003)
18. Sher, G.I.: Handbook of Neuroevolution Through Erlang. Springer, Heidelberg (2013). https://doi.org/10.1007/978-1-4614-4463-3
19. Srihari, S.N., Kuebert, E.J.: Integration of hand-written address interpretation technology into the United States postal service remote computer reader system. In: Proceedings of the Fourth International Conference on Document Analysis and Recognition, vol. 2, pp. 892–896. IEEE (1997)

20. Tene, O., Polonetsky, J.: Privacy in the age of big data: a time for big decisions. Stan. L. Rev. Online **64**, 63–69 (2011)
21. Ulm, G., Gustavsson, E., Jirstrand, M.: OODIDA: On-board/Off-board distributed data analytics for connected vehicles. arXiv preprint arXiv:1902.00319 (2019)
22. Yu, T., Clack, C.: PolyGP: a polymorphic genetic programming system in Haskell. In: Genetic Programming, vol. **98** (1998)

Author Index

Printed in the United States
By Bookmasters